NATURAL LAW

NATURAL LAW

A Theological Investigation

JOSEF FUCHS S.J.

Translated by
HELMUT RECKTER S.J.
and
JOHN A. DOWLING

SHEED AND WARD — NEW YORK

Originally published as L E X N A T U R A E—Zur Theologie des Naturrechts
by Patmos Verlag, Dusseldorf

Nihil obstat: Eduardus Gallen,
            Censor. Theol. Deput.

Imprimi potest: + Ioannes Carolus,
                  Archiep. Dublinen.
                  Hiberniæ Primas

Dublini die 20ᵃ Aprilis, anno 1965

Library of Congress Catalog Card Number 65-20867

Manufactured in the United States of America

CONTENTS

v

ABBREVIATIONS

AAS	*Acta Apostolicae Sedis*
ASS	*Acta Sanctae Sedis*
BET	*Beiträge zur Evangelischen Theologie*
BZ	*Biblische Zeitfragen*
CIC	*Codex Juris Canonici*
DDC	*Dictionnaire du Droit Canonique*
FTS	*Freiburger theologische Studien*
MTZ	*Münchener theologische Zeitschrift*
NRT	*Nouvelle Revue Théologique*
RSR	*Recherches de Science Religieuse*
RSPT	*Recherches des Sciences Philosophiques et Théologiques*
STS	*Strassburger theologische Studien*
SZ	*Stimmen der Zeit*
TLZ	*Theologische Literaturzeitung*
TPQ	*Theologisch-praktische Quartalschrift*
TS	*Theological Studies*
TZ	*Theologische Zeitschrift*
WW	*Wissenschaft und Weisheit*
ZKT	*Zeitschrift für katholische Theologie*
Denz.	Denzinger-Rahner, *Enchiridion Symbolorum* (1953)

PREFACE

From the days of the Fathers and the mediaeval scholastics Christian teaching on natural law has been associated with a certain anthropology. This in turn was based on a theology of Revelation. Such bases were seldom indicated expressly; they were too obvious. Consequently the natural law tended to re-appear continually in philosophic dress.

A more decidedly theological cast is now being given to natural law teaching. The firm emphasis placed by Church authorities on natural law in their more recent pronouncements together with theological reflection on the reality of the supernatural have contributed to this work of reconstruction. So indeed has the encounter with Protestant theology.

Two further tasks now present themselves. It must again be made plain that natural law is an abstraction from the total reality which is Christian man and thus replace this law within a 'natural—supernatural' moral order. Precisely through the completion of its first task theology must then endeavour to protect natural law concepts against an inadmissible relativism.

Both these undertakings will be examined in this work but the second will get decidedly greater attention.

Similar considerations have determined the formulation of questions and methods of presentation. It is not presumptuous to think that the subject is of interest outside Catholic theological circles. Indeed the expert may well detect a dialogue in progress with Protestant theology through certain parts of our explanation. Evidence of this will be clearest in the footnotes. Our purpose is partly to promote further investigation and partly to help in the clarification of positions.

A modern distinction is made between natural *rights* in the strict sense and natural *law* in the sense of a natural moral order. This dichotomy has decided advantages. Outside the Catholic traditions 'rights' are not usually regarded as belonging to morals. A natural moral *order* is a generally acceptable notion but a natural moral *right* is not a concept universally considered valid. A distinction of this kind was never made by the mediaeval scholastics nor has the Church's teaching nomenclature accommodated itself to it in any marked degree. This is perfectly understandable. 'Law' and 'right' are related concepts in the language of law. They are equally at home there. The modern distinction between natural law and natural right is not used in this book because our explanations cover both. Employment of such a distinction would only serve to complicate the exposition. We prefer to use the term 'natural law' simply and shall indicate its use in the narrower sense of 'right' as often as intelligibility requires it.

A French translation of the German original of this study was published in 1960. Complete revision of the text was not then possible but some passages were re-cast more accurately and completely. An article which had appeared in *Stimmen der Zeit* was added as a supplementary chapter. This was a treatment of the relations between natural law and Christian sociology. As we have said, it was not our intention to deal explicitly with the relations of natural law and Christian morals. The supplementary chapter, therefore, did service in that regard. Similarly this English edition, following as it does on the French, contains matter additional to both its predecessors.

JOSEF FUCHS S.J.

PART ONE

THE NATURAL LAW IN REVELATION

CHAPTER ONE

THE NATURAL LAW IN
THE TESTIMONY OF THE CHURCH

Not only philosophy but the theology of revelation itself testifies to the reality of natural right or natural law. This is not the case merely because natural law is related to supernatural and revealed realities. It is especially true because God has chosen to instruct us directly about it by supernatural Revelation. Under the influence of the Holy Spirit the Church upholds and proclaims Revelation and authentically teaches everything internally related to it. Logically then she should be heard first when this subject is discussed in a theological context. Her doctrine is the source of the *reality* which philosophical reflection recognises as natural law. It follows for the theologian that this is not just a question of raising problems. It is primarily a task of simply listening.

Declarations of the Church

A survey of the documents of our teaching authorities in the early centuries compared with those of the last decades points to the interesting fact that the early Church rarely referred to the natural law. Nonetheless she does so frequently today. Of course the primitive documents were less concerned with questions of moral theology than we are now. It is understandable that our secularized culture which calls fundamental natural institutions in question, but is insensible to Church doctrine or God's revelation,

3

might yet be open to consideration of the natural existence of things. The main reason, however, for the differences between the ancient and more recent treatments of natural law concepts is our modern reaction to positivism.

The Church documents of the early centuries did occasionally speak of natural law and natural rights. They spoke in a manner quite in harmony with the theology and Christian philosophy of their times. We pointed out in the Preface that they did not always distinguish between the two concepts in their terminology. It may be of interest if we trace the progress of this reflection of natural law in the Church's documents without making any claim to completeness in the survey.

The text of the Synod of Arles (A.D. 475)[1] which we shall consider again later, did not deal with moral theology. It was concerned with the efficacy of Christ's salvific role in the times before his coming. When treating of the era of the Mosaic Law and earlier the text speaks of the time of the natural law 'which God has written into the hearts of all men' and through which salvation was possible in the hope of Christ's advent.[2]

Documents like this are rare. The use of natural law perspectives by Pius II (1359)[3], Innocent XI (1679)[4] and Alexander VIII (1690)[5] in their treatment of particular moral questions is quite evident. The fact is clear either from the actual use of the term 'natural law' or because an alternative was chosen which expressed antithesis to the 'divine or ecclesiastical' positive law.

It was only in the middle of the last century that references to the natural law became frequent. Pius IX turned to the natural law on the questions of neo-malthusianism,[6] the foundations of civil law [7] and the indissolubility of marriage.[8] Like the Synod of

---

[1] 475 A.D. circa; the year is uncertain.
[2] *Denz* 160 a and b
[3] *Denz* 717 g; Extra-marital intercourse is morally evil; this is quite evident not because of ecclesiastical prohibition only.
[4] *Denz* 1198: Extra-marital intercourse is morally evil, not only because of positive Divine Law; and *Denz* 1199; Masturbation (mollietas) contradicts the natural law.
[5] *Denz* 1292: Condemnation of the rigorist proposition that the violation of the natural law is formally sinful, even in the case of ignorance.
[6] H. Batzill o.s.b., *Decisiones S. Sedis de usu et abusu matrimonii*, Taurini 1937, 15.
[7] *Denz* 1756.
[8] *Denz* 1767.

Arles he spoke about pagans who are able to attain salvation if they fulfil 'the natural law and its commandments which are written in the hearts of all men.' [9]

Leo XIII, even more than Pius IX, based his teaching on the laws given by nature, meaning the Creator of nature. In this way also he treated the great questions of the rights of private property, the just wage and the right to form societies and associations. He considered the problems of patriotism, the right to live, to marry etc. from the same point of view.[10]

In the period following Leo XIII it was especially Pius XI and Pius XII who appealed to natural law in their comments on the essential questions of their times. We may indicate as an example the Encyclical of Pius XI on national-socialism [11] in which he attempted to protect the rights of man given by the Creator of nature, such as the right of parents in the education of their children or the right of free profession of faith. In *Quadragesimo Anno* [12] like Leo XIII he based his social teaching on natural law. In the Encyclical on Christian marriage he referred repeatedly to the institution itself, its values and moral orientations as having their foundations in the natural law.[13]

In times of international difficulty greater perhaps than had been experienced by any previous Pope, Pius XII [14] strove more evidently even than his predecessor to counter a positivist conception of law. His emphasis on natural law in his great public treatises is evidence of this. He explicitly grounded questions of political, social and international life as well as those of private life upon a natural moral order.

The notions and even the terms of natural law are also used in the Code of Canon Law (1918). Even more frequently, valid

---

[9] *Denz* 1677.
[10] Cf. the Encyclicals of Leo XIII in ASS, especially the Encyclical *Rerum novarum*, ASS 23 (1891), 641-70. In the following pages we shall quote the Pontifical texts as given in ASS and AAS.
[11] AAS 29 (1937), 145-67.
[12] AAS 23 (1931), 177-228.
[13] AAS 22 (1930), 539-90.
[14] Already his first Encyclical *Summi Pontificatus* had *emphasized* the natural law, AAS 31 (1939), 423. This point of view is repeated most significantly in Pius XII's numerous allocutions on contemporary problems.

natural law references are recognizable in it where they are not expressly formulated.[15]

These testimonies to natural law and valid natural rights which are given by the teaching authorities of the Church put it beyond all doubt that this is a question of a truth of faith.

The essence of natural law

Bearing in mind the continual progress of reflection on natural law in matters of moral theology, pre-occupations with particular problems become evident. It remains of primary importance to discover from all these numerous declarations of the Church which seldom deal purely with natural law as such, what she means explicitly by it and what precise value she attributes to it.[16]

A first series of Church texts on the essence of natural law refers to its ontological foundations. In these the being, the very essence or nature of man as composed of body and spirit appears as a norm of moral behaviour and of law. There is an objective order defined

[15] The facts in detail are these: by natural law we understand a law that cannot be changed or contradicted by positive ecclesiastical law (CIC can. 6, 6°): ' From this it follows that all these dispositions do not need further positive determination by the legislative authority and are capable of being sanctioned even legally, without special intervention of the authority (cf. can. 1667, 2222 § 1)' (Ch. Lefèbvre, in DDC, vol. 4, 989). The natural law appears to limit the possible extent of legitimate customs (can. 27) much *in the same manner that loans in the ecclesiastical law* limit those of the civil law (can. 1509 and 1529). Canon law speaks in a manner similar to natural law in the realm of acquiring ownership (can. 1499, § 1). It speaks also of the natural prohibitions in reading certain books (can. 1405, § 1); of the natural obligation to denunciation (can. 1935, § 2), of the natural obligations to be observed in charitable foundations (can. 1513 § 1). It is aware likewise of the various precepts of the natural law regarding marriage and in relation to attributes derived from natural law, especially those of unity and indissolubility (can. 1110) and the impediments of natural law regarding marriage (can. 1139, § 2 and can. 1068, § 1). Cf. A. Landolf, *Das Naturrecht im CIC*, Basle 1951; G. Oliviero, 'Diritto naturale e diritto della chiesa,' *Il diritto eccl.*, 61 (1950), 1–41.

[16] In the following pages we refer principally to the Papal encyclicals but we shall also take into account the numerous allocutions of Pius XII. Insofar as these allocutions are addressed either directly to the whole Church or to a limited audience only, the latter often express the official opinion on important questions and are therefore relatively close to the encyclicals. Yet even where a lesser authority is employed, the repeated testimony, which is in accord with the teaching of the past, is of great value. This does not mean that every single statement on natural law is an article of faith, *in the same way as is the statement of the fact and value of the natural law in general. Is it, perhaps, hardly necessary to remark* that in the following pages only a *selection* of Papal documents will be quoted.

by natural law and this in the final issue is based upon 'being.' [17] Numerous paragraphs in the texts show this clearly. Marriage is ' by its nature ' [18] monogamous. The attributes of the institution are 'something that results from the nature of man.' [19] The right to hold property is given 'to us by nature itself.' [20] The moral limits of medical activity result from 'the teleology given by nature and existence in all things and from the order of values which results from the nature of all things.' [21] The natural law is determined by the destination and nature of man; [22] it exists because of 'laws written into the nature of beings' [23] which are ontologically rooted in human nature.[24] The clear meaning of all this is even more evident in such anthropomorphic phrases as: nature admonishes [25] and commands;[26] that natural law is the voice of nature [27] or that the rights of nations are dictated by nature.[28]

Another series of texts in connection with the second chapter of the Epistle to the Romans declares that natural law is found within man himself;[29] it is written in his heart.[30] By his reason man is able to read this law written in his heart,[31] at least insofar as he is not blinded by sin or passion.[32] In a sense reason itself is called natural law [33] in that it ordains that good be done and evil avoided. Reason is the voice [34] that speaks to us distinguishing between good and evil. Another term employed is the 'good moral sense.' [35]

[17] Instruction of the Holy Office, 2 February 1956 on ' Situation-ethics,' AAS 48 (1956), 144.
[18] Leo XIII, Arcanum, AAS 12 (1879 ff.), 388.
[19] Pius XI, Casti connubii, AAS 22 (1930), 542, cf. CIC, can. 1110.
[20] Leo XIII, Quod apost. mun., ASS 11 (1878), 374.
[21] Pius XII, Allocution, 13 September 1952, AAS 44 (1952) 784.
[22] Leo XIII, Libertas, ASS 20 (1887) 597.
[23] Pius XII, Allocution, 19 May 1956, AAS 48 (1956) 471.
[24] Pius XII, Allocution, 3 October 1953, AAS 45 (1953), 739.
[25] Leo XIII, Rerum novarum, ASS 23 (1890 ff.), 662.
[26] Leo XIII, ibid.
[27] Pius XII, Summi Pontificatus, AAS 31 (1939), 423.
[28] Pius XII, Allocution, 6 December 1953 AAS 45 (1953), 795.
[29] Ibid. 437. Leo XIII, Libertas, ASS 20 (1887 ff.), 597.
[30] A frequently repeated affirmation. Cf. Pius XI, Divini Redemptoris, AAS 29 (1937), 76; Pius XII, Allocution, 24 December 1941, AAS 34 (1942), 16.
[31] Pius XI, Mit brennender Sorge, AAS 29 (1937) 159.
[32] Ibid.
[33] Leo XIII, Libertas, ASS 20 (1887 ff.), 597.   [34] Ibid.
[35] Pius XII, Allocution, 7 September 1953, AAS 45 (1953), 606.

These two series of texts are related. The middle term of the argument is evidently the rational cognition of man. The reality of being implies an objective assertion of the moral and juridical order. Subjectively this consists in the affirmation that rational knowledge is determined by real being. Reason reads the natural law in the nature of all things and particularly in the nature of man.[36] To say that reason is able to read the law written in the heart of man [37] means simply that reason is able to grasp the law of nature from the ontological reality of man and of all things.

This ontological aspect of natural law corresponds to its absolute value. It must not be assumed that this applies only in the case of a few of its more general norms.[38] Interpretations in a relativist sense are not to be tolerated.[39] Natural law is the superior court, so to speak, for all humanity [40] and is independent of the changing legislation of today and tomorrow.[41] It is the criterion of every law [42] and of every juridical order.[43] It follows that the State has a duty to protect natural law.[44] It must determine it more clearly by positive enactment and adapt it to concrete circumstances.[45] We have already said that the Church in her own Code emphatically refuses to recognize any legislation that contradicts the natural law. This is of special importance in any question of natural rights in the strict sense. They are understood by the Church not merely as idealistic norms but as true, valid [46] and inviolable [47] rights. Consequently they remain valid against any contrary but merely positive right.[48]

The common nucleus of all positive legislation must be similar

---

[36] Pius XII, Allocution, 13 November 1949, AAS 41 (1949), 607; Allocution, 13 October 1955, AAS 47 (1955), 770.
[37] Ibid.
[38] Instruction of the Holy Office, 2 February 1956, AAS 48 (1956), 144 ff.
[39] Ibid.
[40] Pius XII, Allocution, 13 October 1955, AAS 47 (1955), 769.
[41] Pius XII, Allocution, 19 October 1953, AAS 45 (1953), 749; Allocution, 3 October 1953, AAS 45 (1953), 739.
[42] Pius XII, Allocution, 13 October 1955, AAS 47 (1955), 769.
[43] Pius XII, Allocution, 13 November 1949, ASS 41 (1949), 607.
[44] Leo XIII, Rerum novarum, ASS 23 (1890 ff.), 665.
[45] Pius XII, Allocution, 6 December 1953, AAS 45 (1953), 795.
[46] Pius XI, Mit brennender Sorge, AAS 29 (1937), 159.
[47] Pius XII, Allocution, 25 September 1949, AAS 41 (1949), 556.
[48] Pius XI, Mit brennender Sorge, AAS 29 (1937), 159.

at all times and places. This is so because it is dealing with 'the exigencies derived from this nature' which are substantially the same at all times and everywhere.[49]

The noetic aspect of natural law, the fact that it is written in the heart of man and therefore naturally evident to him, ensures that the most primitive peoples are capable of a moral order and a sufficient cultural development.[50] This only serves to emphasize the necessity of fulfilling certain conditions in order that this law written in the heart (that is, the confrontation of reason and human being) can be subjectively internalized as knowledge.

It should also be obvious that the Church does not understand the natural law as a naturalistic or rationalistic creation by man in a self-sufficient world. The nature in which reason recognizes a natural order is the work of God the Creator.[51] Reason engaged upon the intelligibilities of nature must be seen as God's work. Only he has written the law of nature into man's heart when creating him.[52] The voice of nature that admonishes, orders and teaches, together with the reason that scans nature and our own hearts, are the true voices of divine reason.[53] This natural law is as certainly a manifestation of God's intellect and will as his positively revealed commandment.[54] The Code of Canon Law understands the revealed positive law, with the natural law, as being divine law.[55] Pius XII therefore said that whenever God the Creator is denied the voice of nature, too, is silenced.[56] His intention was not merely to emphasize the fact that reason, in recognizing a law in nature, needs God the Creator to support it so that it may be decisively obligatory. Rather he meant to emphasize the subjective fact that a denial of God the Creator will result in a refusal to listen to nature. It will issue ultimately in the loss of the very ability to do so.

[49] Pius XII, Allocution, 3 October 1953, AAS 45 (1953), 739.
[50] Pius XI, *Divini Redemptoris*, AAS 29 (1937), 76; Pius XII, *Summi Pontificatus*, AAS 31 (1939), 423.
[51] A frequently emphasized idea. Cf. Pius XI, *Casti connubii*, AAS 22 (1930), 539; Pius XI, *Quadragesimo anno*, AAS 23 (1931), 191; Pius XII, Allocution, 19 October 1953, AAS 45 (1953), 749.
[52] Pius XII, Allocution, 24 December 1941, AAS 34 (1942), 16. Allocution, 7 September 1953, AAS 45 (1953), 607.
[53] Leo XIII, *Libertas*, ASS 20 (1887 ff.) 597.
[54] Pius XII, Allocution, 1 May 1941, AAS 33 (1941), 196.
[55] CIC, can. 6, 6° and can. 27; Cf. can. 1038 § 1; can. 1529; can. 1926.
[56] Pius XII, *Summi Pontificatus*, AAS 31 (1939), 423.

The natural law and the order of redemption

The essence of natural law and especially the basic concept of nature as understood by the Church, becomes clearer through contrast with another divine law. The texts make a distinction between 'natural' and 'divine' law.[57] There is a law of nature and The Law contained in Holy Scripture [58]—and there is a law of Revelation.[59] Also there are principles of nature and the principles of Christianity.[60] Distinctions are made between natural law deriving from the Creator and the precepts of Christ [61] deriving from the Redeemer.[62] All these connote the same reality. Although the distinctions are necessary and valid it must not be forgotten that the natural law itself is divine. This is made plain in Canon 27 of the Code of Canon Law. In articulating these differences, divine law is to be understood as positive divine law whereas the law of nature exists independently of any positive historical intervention by God. Nothing else is meant by the distinction between the law of nature and the law found in Holy Scripture than this: the natural law exists without the Bible.

Fundamentally it is in this way that one should consider the contra-positions of the natural and of the revealed law. The latter includes the Old and New Testaments. Revelation is a somewhat wider concept than that of Holy Scripture. Similarly the distinctions which can be made between the principles of nature and those of Christianity and between the natural law and the teaching of Christ, differ from the preceding only in nuance. Christianity includes Scripture and the Revelations of the Old and the New Covenants. In considering Christ's teaching, of course, the Scripture and the

---

[57] One frequently meets these medieval expressions. Cf. Leo XIII, *Quod apost. mun.*, ASS 11 (1878), 374; *Rerum novarum*, ASS 13 (1890 ff.), 645; Pius X, *Singulari quadam*, AAS 4 (1912), 658; Pius XI, *Casti connubii*, AAS 22 (1930), 560; *Quadragesimo anno*, AAS 23 (1931), 193.
[58] Leo XII, *Pastoralis officii* (letter to the German bishops), AAS 24 (1891 ff.), 204.
[59] Leo XIII, *Rerum novarum*, ASS 23 (1890 ff.), 645; Pius XII, Allocution, 1 May 1941, AAS 33 (1941), 196; Allocution, 24 December 1944, AAS 37 (1945), 17 ff.
[60] Pius XII, Allocution, 23 December 1949, AAS 42 (1950), 127; Allocution, 7 September 1953, AAS 45 (1953), 607.
[61] Pius XII, Allocution, 13 October 1955, AAS 47 (1955), 768.
[62] Pius XI, *Casti connubii*, AAS 22 (1930), 541; Pius XII, Allocution, 1 May 1941, AAS 33 (1941), 196 ff.

Revelation of the New Testament come especially into the foreground. Taking all this into account there is one decisive fact found in all our texts: besides the positive divine law found in Holy Scripture, Revelation and Christianity, there is a natural law independent of these. In the contradistinction between law deriving from the Creator and that deriving from the Redeemer it must be noted that the Creator is related to the natural law and the Redeemer to Revelation.[63] A contrast of the Creator and the natural law with the Redeemer and Revelation corresponds to the distinction between nature and the supernatural.[64] Analogously the State and the family are considered as belonging to the natural order and the Church to the supernatural [65] order. It follows that these laws and rights which come from the Creator are not to be taken in the Protestant sense of the order of creation. This is understood as the order of man in his original state. They should rather be understood in the metaphysical sense as 'orders' of human nature distinct from the 'supernatural.' Natural law is the law corresponding to this nature which is valid independently of the supernatural, of Redemption, Christianity, Revelation and Holy Scripture. At least basically it can be known without these. It is a law that truly emanates from creation *insofar* as creation is nature and not supernatural.

The natural law is thus one of two parallel streams that flow from the same source: the eternal God who is at the same Creator and Redeemer.[66] It represents an order that is valid for the state of *fallen man* and likewise for the state of *redeemed man*. Nature (the term refers to the existential essence of man and not to his state at the beginning) is not destroyed but weakened.[67] This is the Church's teaching and its sense will be precisely determined later. Man as we now know him holds the integrity of the natural faculties of intellect and will in his natural humanity. The Church knows that natural law has been confirmed by Revelation.[68] The

[63] Pius XII, *ibid.*   [64] *Ibid.*
[65] Pius XI, *Divini illius magistri*, AAS 22 (1930), 52.
[66] Pius XII, Allocution, 1 May 1941, AAS 33 (1941), 197.
[67] Pius XII, Allocution, 25 September 1949, AAS 41 (1949), 555 ff.
[68] Pius XII, Allocution, 7 September 1953, AAS 45 (1953), 607. Cf. also Leo XIII, *Rerum novarum*, ASS 23 (1891), 645; Pius XI, *Casti connubii*, AAS 22 (1930), 541.

Christian order of salvation challenges man to a permanent and ever valid natural order and not merely to a supernatural one. The Church simply does not recognize any one-sided supernaturalism which disregards the real 'humanity' of man.[69] Consequently the natural law has no independent existence but belongs to the one 'Christian order of salvation in which nature and grace are united.'[70] Natural law achieves its fulfilment or completion in this order as Pius XI said explicitly when referring to marriage.[71] He was thinking no doubt of its evolution to the status of a sacrament and of that special stability given it by its indissolubility. He gave his Encyclical *Quadragesimo Anno* the title: 'Social order, its restoration and completion according to the plan of salvation of the Gospel.' In the Latin text the phrase 'according to the plan of salvation of the Gospel' refers only to 'completion' and not to 'restoration.' This clearly indicates that it is only in the spirit of the gospel that the social order achieves its completion. The particular point is not given any further precision.[72] The Church teaches that the natural law has been elevated [73] in the actual order of salvation. Now it serves not only the natural but the supernatural development of man.[74] Because of this status of the natural law within the Christian order of salvation it follows that it is not only the revealed law but also the natural norms of rights and morals which are subject to the teaching authority of the Church.[75] It is her duty within the actual order of salvation to form the consciences of all men, primarily those who are in charge of public life. She is the guardian of the Christian order of salvation and the custodian of the natural law.[76] In this the Church fulfils a duty primarily to her members but one which concerns all men even those outside the Church. All men

[69] Pius XII, Allocution on Christmas Day 1954, AAS 47 (1955), 25.
[70] Pius XII, Allocution, 1 May 1941, AAS 33 (1941), 197.
[71] Pius XI, *Casti connubii*, AAS 22 (1930), 541.
[72] Cf. O. v. Nell-Breuning, S.J., *Die soziale Encyklika. Erläuterungen zum Weltrundschreiben Papst Pius XI über die gesellschaftliche Ordnung*, III, Cologne 1950, 14 ff.; J. B. Schuster, S.J., in *Scholastik* 13 (1938), 399.
[73] Pius XI, *Casti connubii*, AAS 22 (1930), 541.
[74] Pius XII, Allocution, 2 November 1954, AAS 46 (1954), 672 ff.
[75] Pius X, *Singulari quadam*, AAS 4 (1912), 658; Pius XI, *Casti connubii*, AAS 22 (1930), 579; Pius XII, Allocution, 1 May 1941, AAS 33 (1941), 196.
[76] Pius XI, *Mit brennender Sorge*, AAS 29 (1937), 160; Pius XII, Allocution, 1 May 1941, AAS 33 (1941), 196; Allocution, 2 November 1954, AAS 46 (1954), 672.

are called to participate in grace.[77] Her activity as teacher of the natural law is all the more important when we consider that the human intellect is able to recognize this law, yet man's fallen state weakens his knowledge in various ways.

Both Pius XI in *Casti Connubii* [78] and Pius XII in his Encyclical of August 12, 1950, *Humani Generis*, drew attention as a recurrent theme to these questions of the natural cognition of morality. The relative necessity of Revelation and its proclamation by the Church[79] was repeatedly and insistently their motif.

[77] Pius XII, *ibid.*, 197.
[78] AAS 22 (1930), 579 ff.
[79] AAS 42 (1950), 561 ff.; cf. below Chapter VII

CHAPTER TWO

THE TESTIMONY OF THE BIBLE

Is the Church's teaching on natural law based on the holy scriptures which have been confided to her? One may certainly consider it this way. The Church offers scripture to us by the power of the Holy Spirit. Such an approach to the problem implies framing a question to the Church on the place of natural law in the Bible. We prefer in this context to consider the Bible as the word of God in the immediate sense. Consequently we shall be considering the Church's natural law teaching in its *biblical foundations*.[1]

Our inquiry is confined to the epistles of St Paul.[2] This special consideration of his thought arises primarily from his remarks on the knowledge of God and morality in the first two chapters of Romans and secondarily on his explanations of the Law and Christian liberty. This correctly assumes that we do not expect to find in his epistles an explicit and didactic treatment of the natural law in all its possibilities, validity or importance. St Paul's thought centres on quite other matters. For him, 'the natural law' is a self-evident domain which raises no problems as such. For us, it is legitimate to discover the notions of natural law implicit in his treatment of law, sin and grace. We confront the Church's teaching

[1] The problem as it is presented here does not deal with natural law in relation to salvation but rather with the reality itself and with the validity of natural law.
[2] A separate monograph might be devoted to all the Biblical texts pertaining directly to natural law. Several Protestant theologians have gone back to the Old Testament in their studies of it. If some authors have found an opposition between the divine and the human law in the Old Testament, it must be noticed that these human rights are not simply equivalent to our natural law. By human rights these *authors* understand *the historical fact of human rights*. Cf. E. Horst, *Naturrecht und Altes Testament: Evangelische Theologie* (1950–1), 253–73. For a short exposition on the *teaching of Christ* in regard to natural law see the Appendix to this chapter.

14

on natural law with St Paul's writings in order to find the extent
of her dependence upon them. Evidently we shall not look for a
Pauline usage of such terms as natural law or natural right. The
object of the inquiry is to discover whether the Church's use of
these terms can be grounded in St Paul's thought. Consideration
of such particular problems as natural law attributes will be subordinated to our main purpose of establishing the sense in which the
apostle acknowledges a moral and juridical order. This order
which is binding on every Christian will be considered in so far
it is assumed by the Apostle to be objectively founded in the very
nature and being of man. We must study the way in which he takes
it to be rationally discoverable in created nature. If the real substance of natural law defined in this way should be found in St
Paul's usage then our task is clear and simple. A modern nomenclature in terms of natural rights and natural law can then be applied
to his thought properly and accurately. This is but a matter of
technique and terminology.

Attestation of the natural law

If we turn to the classic text of Romans 1: 18–32 concerning
the natural knowledge of God it is obvious at once that St Paul
is not primarily concerned with either the natural law or with our
knowledge of God. His probing mind is preoccupied with the
religious and moral condition of the heathen world as manifesting
the need of redemption for mankind. He is concerned with the
importance of such a redemption by the grace of Christ. It is only
if they have a true knowledge of God that we may speak about the
religious and moral condition of the heathen as being culpable and
in need of redemption. St Paul was convinced that pagans have
this knowledge although God has not revealed himself to them
through the Law of the Old Covenant or through, Christ. They
know God by natural means. From the visible works of creation
and by the use of natural reason they have come to a knowledge of
their God. By indicating the source and power of such knowledge

St Paul conveys clearly that other possibilities such as a primitive and positive revelation were not entertained by him. He clearly has in mind a *natural* knowledge of God without Christ and without the Law.[3]

When writing of this natural knowledge of God acquired by heathens the underlying intention of this whole passage proves that St Paul is thinking of their knowledge of a personal God. Such knowledge includes a proportionate natural knowledge of religious and moral obligations.[4] It follows that, like their knowledge of God, this is derived by reason from the reality of creation.[5] Paul speaks of a duty of acknowledging God by giving him honour and thanksgiving. Man's awareness of this duty arises from his knowledge of God's existence just as certainly and naturally as does the pagan's awareness of God's personality, power and divinity. St Paul was conscious of the two determining elements of the natural law which the Church has in mind when she speaks in its terms: it has an objective foundation in man's essence which is to say that it is founded in his essential relation to God. It is a knowledge attained by the use of reason.

Of course St Paul does not speak of the 'purely natural' man but of the actual man of his time and of the real past. He knew very well the state of impotence, distinct from the state of pure nature, in which the heathens lived (cf. *Rom.* 5). According to St Paul man's weakness after the fall does not necessarily exclude the possibility of a natural recognition of God or morality. Neither is he unaware that the heathen as well as the Jew (cf. 1 *Cor.* 10: 4) is already influenced by Christ's grace. In fact he speaks of the fulfilment of the precepts of the Law by heathens (*Rom.* 2: 14–16) and of justification based upon this fulfilment (*Rom.* 2: 13). In Pauline theology all this presupposes the spirit and power of Christ (cf. *Rom.* 2: 29). The fact that the power of Christ's grace is already

---

[3] The hypothesis that a natural knowledge of God in itself possible is in fact only realized consequent upon a knowledge derived from a primitive revelation would probably not contradict our view. However, this seems *de facto* alien to the thought of the Apostle.
[4] Cf. G. Bornkamm, *Das Ende des Gesetzes, Paulusstudien* (BET 16), Munich 1952, 13 ff.
[5] In *Acts* 14: 15-17 and 26-31, St Paul speaks likewise of an obligation in natural law to orientate oneself on the Creator.

operative on the heathen alters nothing of the natural character of this acknowledgement of God. Their knowledge is an act of reason which bears on the visible creation. According to Paul neither the weakness of original sin nor the power of Christ's grace determine the heathen's knowledge of God's existence nor an acknowledgement of a moral duty to him. What does determine and characterize this knowledge is the heathen's *not possessing* either the Revelation of the Old Testament (the Law) or the Chirstian Revelation. This non-possession implies a knowledge deriving from the visible world.

St Paul does not explain the natural character of this knowledge or its ontological foundations. He does not examine our experience of creation for possibilities of any supernatural effects which might operate within it. For him there is a natural moral judgment bearing upon the created things which we experience. This is why he can write of the guilt of the heathens although they are without the Law and without Christ. He can speak accordingly of God's anger with them. In other texts the Apostle similarly accuses the heathens of their infidelity to God in the sense of Romans 1: 18, which is to say that they do not acknowledge God. (*Gal.* 4: 15; 1 *Thess.* 4–5; 1 *Cor.* 1: 21). The consequences of this basic religious and moral failure—at the same time a punishment permitted through the anger of God—is that heathens by trespassing against this moral obligation fall victims of all sorts of vices. (*Rom.* 1: 24–32; cf. 1 *Thess.* 4: 5). The moral order violated in this way was, for St Paul, equivalent to that called natural law by the Church now.

This is especially clear in his explanation of those unnatural lusts particularly stigmatized by him. In its opposition to nature and by introducing a contradition between human behaviour and natural being St Paul sees the sinfulness of sodomy. From this inner being, that is to say from human nature as the norm of human behaviour, sodomy is seen as immoral and ungodly. It is a denial of the acknowledgement due to God.

It is not only because they are contrary to the precepts of the Law or of Christ but as bad in themselves that St Paul castigates all those things the heathens do 'regarding disgraceful acts; versed in

every kind of injustice, knavery, impurity, avarice and ill-will;
spiteful, murderous, contentious, deceitful, depraved, back-biters,
slanderers, God's enemies; insolent, haughty, vainglorious;
inventive in wickedness, disobedient to their parents, without
prudence, without honour, without love, without loyalty, without
pity' (*Rom.* 1: 29–32). In this St Paul evidently drew up a catalogue
of vices objectively out of harmony with man's nature. According
to the Apostle the pagans were well aware of this lack of harmony
in their behaviour. The confusion into which God permitted them
to fall had basically nothing to do with knowledge but with concupiscence (*Rom.* 1: 26–8). He stated expressly: 'Yet with the
just decree of God before their minds, they have never grasped
the truth that those who so live deserve to die; not only those who
commit such acts but those who countenance such a manner of
living.' (*Rom.* 1: 32). The pagans have such knowledge *as pagans*,
without the Law and without Christ. This is to say that they
have it simply as men.

The classic Pauline text on natural knowledge of the moral law
is the passage on conscience in the second chapter in the Epistle
to the Romans.[6] It would be wrong to consider only the few verses
relating to conscience without reference to the thought of the whole
chapter.

The first verse not only indicates the content of the chapter;
it reveals the very foundations of St Paul's conception of the natural
law as he proceeds to use it in what follows. What is expressed is the
general subjection of both Christian and Jew to the same moral
order and to the same judgment by reference to its norms.

St Paul, from the standpoint of man-in-Christ, recognizes that
the Jew, man-under-the-Law, may pass just judgment on the guilt
of the heathen as man-without-Law-or-Christ: he recognizes, in

---

[6] The monograph of J. Quirmbach, *Die Lehre des hl. Paulus von der natürlichen Gottes-
erkenntnis und dem natürlichen Sittengesetz, eine biblisch-dogmatische Studie* (STS 7, 4),
Freiburg-Br. 1906, on the natural moral law in the writings of St Paul, refers only
to *Rom.* 2: 14 ff. A complete exposition however can be found in G. Staffelbach,
Die Vereinigung mit Christus als Prinzip der Moral bei Paulus (FTS 34), Freiburg-Br.
1932, 16–30. Cf. the study of the Pastor M. Lackmann, *Vom Geheimns der Schöpfung.
Die Geschichte der Exegese von Röm. 1, 18–23 und Acta 14, 15–17; 17, 22–9 vom zweiten
Jahrhundert bis zum Beginn der Orthodoxie*, Stuttgart 1952.

addition, that the Jew no less than the heathen falls under the same judgment because he commits the same works of iniquity. Good and evil are not determined by whether one is Christian, heathen or Jew. All will be judged by the same moral norms. Paul sees the heathen, who is the man-without-the-Law-and-Christ, as *man* simply speaking. It is therefore clear that for his thought the distinction between good and evil is founded in the nature of things. It is recognizable in and from nature alone. The verses which follow are to be understood in this sense when he states that judgment is effected not according to the 'person' (*Rom.* 2: 11) but according to the 'truth' (*Rom.* 2: 2, 8) and to 'good' and 'evil' (*Rom.* 2: 9, 10) and according to the 'works' (*Rom.* 3: 6). Not the 'person' but a certain way of behaviour (*Rom.* 2, 2 ff) decides the issue of how one shall be judged.

The Law of the Old Testament does not simply establish good and evil. It instructed the Jews on what was antecedently good and evil. That is why for St Paul it is just and reasonable that the Jews who were specially instructed about good and evil by the Law should wish to give 'guidance' to the heathens in their 'blindness' or lack of the Law. They should bring the pagans light in their ' darkness ' and teach those that are 'foolish,' educate those who are 'children.' They could do this because the Law was a privilege. It was no more than an embodiment of 'knowledge' and 'truth' (*Rom.* 2: 19 ff.) equally for all. It follows that stealing and adultery are evil simply in themselves and not merely because the Law decrees them to be so. It merely teaches us about them (*Rom.* 2: 21 ff.).

All this is even more evident when we consider that St Paul is aware of those prescriptions of the Law which are unknown to the heathen and do not bind the Christian. He admonishes the latter (the Galatian Christians) not to return under any circumstances to the observance of 'the days, months seasons and years' of the Old Dispensation. What is binding fundamentally and as an obligatory norm on heathen, Jew and Christian alike is that which is good in itself. This is no merely positive precept. It is clear and unquestionable for the Apostle—and this bears witness to his conception of natural law—which dispositions of the Law oblige man by virtue of the nature of things and consequently are not merely positive.

Since the Law does not *establish* the difference between good and evil but rather teaches men about what is already good or evil, St Paul can say that the good works of the heathen constitute a fulfilment of the demands of the Law. 'They do what the Law requires' (*Rom.* 2: 14) and they do it 'by nature' (*Rom.* 2: 14 vide 27). Although they do not have the Law of Moses (*Rom.* 2: 14) nonetheless ' what the Law requires is written in their hearts ' (*Rom.* 2: 15) so that 'they are a law unto themselves' (*Rom.* 2: 14). 'Their consciences and their thoughts, accusing or perhaps excusing them, bear witness to that' (*Rom.* 2: 15).[7] When Paul says accusingly that the Jewish violation of the Law is the reason why ' the name of God is blasphemed among the Gentiles' *Rom.* 2: 24 ff.) he can do this only because there is a natural relationship between the heathen and the Law.

This same chapter of the Epistle to the Romans states that neither possession of the Law (*Rom.* 2: 13) nor circumcision (*Rom.* 2: 25) is sufficient for God's grace or for justification (*Rom.* 2: 29 and 13) but that the fulfilment of the Law is required. This fulfilment does not necessarily come through the pedagogy of the Law. Even in the absence of circumcision it comes through that primitive knowledge which is the same reality that the Church calls natural law or natural right. Even the terminology of St Paul is not far from ours since the element of nature as norm and the element of natural knowledge are demonstrably and even expressly present. In stating that the heathens are a law unto themselves (*Rom.* 2: 14) it is clear that even the character of this law of real things is being exposed although, of course, it is a knowledge of the content of the Mosaic Law that is being emphasized (*Rom.* 2: 14 ff.; 26 ff.).

A further clarification of the Pauline concept of natural law or

---

[7] It is probable that St Paul does not place the special function of conscience in the Last Judgment but he adds that this conscience will manifest itself in the Last Judgment where he states, 'all this will come to light on the day on which . . .,' cf. O. Kuss, *Die Briefe an die Römer, Korinther und Galater* (*Regensburger Neues Testament* 6), Regensburg 1940, 32.

natural right comes from consideration of the seventh chapter of this epistle.[7] It deals with the difficult question of the relation between the Law and sin. The power of sin in man has been awakened by the Law. Sin has taken possession of the Law in order to bring it into the service of evil. It is important for our purposes to know precisely what St Paul meant in this context by law. There are many indications that he had in mind the positive law of God. He meant perhaps not only that given through Moses but also the law given to the original man as well. Man is confronted with this law and is able to judge it to be good by means of his reason (*Rom.* 7: 22 ff. and 25) and even to delight in it (*Rom.* 7: 22). Similarly reason judges the power of sin and declares it to be evil. It is clear from this that there is good and evil and that each is quite independent of the positive law. A parallel text in chapter five of the same epistle teaches explicitly that there was personal sin in the world even before the Mosaic Law. This sin was not of the same kind as the sin of Adam and Eve nor of the Jews under the Law. These latter were transgressions of the positive law and had bodily death as a punishment (*Rom.* 5: 13 ff.). The intervention of the Law only increased sin and did not establish it (*Rom.* 5: 20).

If we take the other interpretation of St Paul's use of the notion of law in chapter seven of Romans we shall see that the rational distinction between good and evil retains an importance. If he is speaking expressly of positive law but virtually of every kind of law in its relation to sin then he is, of course, including the natural law. It is by reason that we judge the positive law to be good and on this interpretation reason is still competent. The evaluations of reason concerning the natural law however would then be confined only to the processes involved in acquiring a knowledge of it.

With such a conception of natural right and natural law it is not surprising that St Paul seeks continually to base his moral exhortation to Christians firmly on the nature of things. A singular example is the thirteenth chapter of the Epistle to the Romans vv. 1–7. Here Paul quite evidently sees the State as 'a morality'

[7a] Cf. G. Staffelbach, *op. cit.*, 20 ff.

3

or natural institution corresponding to the will of the Creator. All things that Christians, Jews and heathens considered good he taught to his convert communities and lived out in exemplary fashion in his own life. It is part of the traditional moral teaching of the Church.[8]

Natural law and Christian liberty

We must carry our consideration of this fact very much deeper: what we call natural law belongs to the tradition of Christian morality. This profound consideration is particularly necessary in view of the Pauline teaching on *Christian freedom from the Law*. His notion of Christian liberty is fundamental for his doctrine. There is an impassioned defence of it in his Epistle to the Galatians. The Law was a tutor-guardian which brought men to Christ in such a way that, with the coming of Christ (*Gal.* 3: 24 ff.) we are no longer subject to its constraints. 'For, by freedom, Christ has set us free' (*Gal.* 4: 31). The Christian therefore having been 'called to freedom' (*Gal.* 5: 13) should not submit again to the servitude of the Law with its many obligations (*Gal.* 5: 1–4). Submission to the Law (by circumcision) is of no value in Christ (*Gal.* 5: 6). 'We are not sons of the slave but of the freewoman' (*Gal.* 4: 31). According to the Epistle to the Romans we are dead to the Law through the body of Christ (*Rom.* 7: 3 ff.) and the end of the Law is Christ (*Rom.* 7: 3 ff.). The law of the Spirit of Life has set us free of the Law of sin and death (*Rom.* 8: 1). Every Christian is dead to the Law with Christ in baptism.

We leave it an open question for the moment how far St Paul has each particular law obliquely in mind. He speaks in these texts directly of the positive law of the Old Testament. *We* must distinguish two affirmations: that the Law of the Old Dispensation has lost its validity and that the Spirit of Life has been given to us in its place. *For St Paul* these two in fact merge.

[8] Cf. for the following especially K. Benz, *Die Ethik des hl. Paulus*, (*Bibl. Stud.* 17, 3–4), Freiburg-Br. 1912, 83, and A. Kirchgässner, *Erlösung und Sünde im Neuen Testament*, Freiburg-Br. 1950, 29; cf. C. Spicq, O.P., *Vie morale et Trinité Sainte selon saint Paul*, Paris 1957, 65 (E. tr. *St Paul and Christian Living*, Dublin 1964): 'There is no question but that St Paul presumes the demands of the natural law and of common sense.'

The termination of the Old Dispensation is made clear in the vivid allegory in Galatians 4: 21–31. Paul contrasts the two Testaments. The Law given in the Old is holy, just and good (cf. *Rom.* 7: 12) and Paul can find joy in it according to the inner man. It has, all the same, lost its validity! Nothing shows this as clearly as the rejection of circumcision and his putting aside the observance of the Old Law's set times and seasons (*Gal.* 2: 1–14; Jerusalem and Antioch; 5: 2–6; 4: 10). To say however that St Paul is merely abolishing the ritual obligations while retaining the moral obligations of the Old Law is untrue. It is increasingly recognized that the reality of such a distinction cannot be proved (cf. *Gal.* 3: 23 ff.). It has even been shown that the Apostle refers very rarely to the Law or to the decalogue. For St Paul the Law of Moses has lost its importance.[9]

The end of the Law does not merely mean (for St Paul it does not even primarily mean) the end of its validity. A new principle has entered the world with the abolition of the Law. This principle has not come through the Law. It is the spirit of charity received as a grace. It inspires and enables man to do the good and *a fortiori* to do the works of the Law also. The Law included commandment and prohibition. It did not include the spirit of charity nor did it provide the power to carry out its own precepts. Man was left in his helplessness. The time of the Law was giving place to a time in which this impotence is overcome. The Law was the letter merely: Christ brings the spirit. The spirit is evidently the divine power 'that enlivens the faithful and fights against the flesh.'[10] The freedom of the Christian from the Law is not in the first instance a mere invalidation of the Old Covenant and its precepts. Much more and primarily, it means also a release of man from his impotence to do that which is good. Liberty in this sense is freedom to enter into communion with God (2 *Cor.* 3: 15; *Gal.* 2: 19 ff.). Where the spirit dwells there also liberty abides (2 *Cor.* 3: 17).

---

[9] P. Bläser, M.S.C., *Das Gesetz bei Paulus* (Neutest, Abh. 19, 1–2), Münster 1941, 227–30.
[10] P. Bläser, *op. cit.*, 212: St Paul's thesis on freedom has, therefore, no direct connection with the question of moral *obligation*. Cf. S. Lyonnet, S.J., 'Liberté du chrétien et loi de l'Esprit,' *Christus*, 4 (1954), 6–27.

In the Epistle to the Romans the letter of the Law is dead and carries death; it is replaced by the spirit (*Rom.* 7: 6) which is life-giving grace (*Rom.* 6: 14). Through it the power of love is given to us (*Rom.* 5: 5); by it we are enabled to fulfil what the Law had demanded of us (*Rom.* 8: 4).[11] Freedom from the Law is therefore a victory over sin and death [12] (1 *Cor.* 15: 56 ff.). This liberty is the reign of grace through righteousness and is effective of eternal life through Christ our Lord (*Rom.* 5: 20 ff.).

We have noticed already that St Paul always refers expressly to The Law of the old dispensation only. The question for us, *now*, is this: does this doctrine of Christian freedom from the Old Law have any importance for our study of what we today call natural right or natural law? It was to the reality of this that St Paul had testified. Let us leave aside for the moment any consideration of the question of freedom from impotence regarding natural law. It is of more immediate interest to ask whether the natural law has actually lost its validity for the Christian. The important thing is to distinguish two aspects of this Christian freedom from the Law of Moses. This is particularly so in view of our freedom from it as a valid norm. Its importance arises precisely because the lost validity of the Mosaic Law bears upon its moral precepts as well as its ritual obligations. This has already been indicated. St Paul sensed a danger. Twice he asked the daring question: 'Are we to continue in sin?' only to reply with an emphatic 'No!' (*Rom.* 6: 1–15).[13] He believed that he ought to put the Galatians on their guard against abuses of freedom by serving the flesh (*Gal.* 5: 13).

This twofold aspect of freedom from the Law of Moses does not signify that the Christian is by any means lawless before God (*anomos theou*). Rather it signifies that the Christian is bound to Christ and his law (*ennomous theou*) (1 *Cor.* 9 : 21). We may leave it open for further consideration what 'the law of Christ' does signify exactly. What is indisputably evident is that St Paul does

---

[11] See *Rom.* 13: 8–10, *Gal.* 5: 14.
[12] Freedom from death is equivalent to freedom from the Law; see *Rom.* 5: 17–21, 6: 21–23, 8: 21, 1 *Cor.* 15: 54–7.
[13] See *Rom.* 3: 5–8.

not wish the difference between man's condition under the Law and man's new being in Christ to be understood as obligation on the one hand and arbitrary liberty on the other. Belonging to Christ really means being owned by Christ (1 *Cor.* 3: 23). It means being bound to his service (*Rom.* 14: 18; *Col.* 3: 25) in true servitude (*Gal.* 1: 10; *Eph.* 6: 6; *Rom.* 6: 16–23). It means that there really is a law of Christ which makes real demands upon the Christian (*Gal.* 6: 2; 1 *Cor.* 9: 21). Christ's Spirit is not only charity and power; it is at the same time really law (*Rom.* 8: 2 and 4; *Gal.* 5: 13; 1 *Thess.* 4: 8). The condition of being bound to Christ signifies being bound to the will and law of God (*Eph.* 6: 6; 1 *Cor.* 9: 21). The reality of the new law of Christ is not merely and indeed not primarily *demand* 'but [is] grace and charity and the spirit of life' (*Rom.* 8: 2). This grace and charity lead to the achievement of the good which was truly demanded by the Law. It is in this sense that ' you are no longer under the Law (that was only a demand) but under grace which makes us hold to and accomplish the demands of the Law in a different way ' (*Rom.* 6: 14). ' The Law (in so far as it is a reality which makes outward demands and is not inward power) has not been laid down for the just but for the unjust' (1 *Tim.* 1: 9).[14] The precepts of the law of Christ and God bind the Christian but their obligation is related directly to the person of Christ himself rather than to the objective law as such. Consequently knowledge of the law of Christ is called 'knowledge of Christ' (*Rom.* 14: 14). This knowledge is our 'growing up into him who is the head' (*Eph.* 4: 15). The relationship between the Christian and Christ entailing obedience to the law of Christ, is at the same time a development of this 'being in Christ.' It is expressed in St Paul's writings by his well-known changes from the indicative to the imperative mood to demonstrate our communion with Christ.[15]

The fact that we are Christians attached to Christ and obliged

---

[14] Cf. S. Lyonnet, s.j., *La legge della carità in S. Paolo*, Rome 1954.
[15] Cf. A. Wikenhauser, *Die Christusmystik des hl. Paulus* (BZ 12, 8–10), Münster 1928, 86 and G. Staffelbach, *op. cit.*; see also *Gal.* 4: 19 '. . . until Christ be formed in you' and 2 *Cor.* 13: 5 f: 'Do you not realize that Jesus Christ is in you? unless, indeed, you fail to meet the test.'

to keep his law is a matter so grave that the Christian no less than the Jew or the heathen will be judged by his works. There is truly no acceptance of persons with God (*Rom.* 2: 11). Our redemption is not through our own merit. It comes entirely through the grace of Christ and we are thus entirely his work. Nonetheless we are 'created in Jesus Christ for good works which God prepared beforehand, that we should walk in them' (*Eph.* 2: 10). The Christian too will be judged according to his works (*Rom.* 14: 12; 1 *Cor.* 3: 12–15; 2 *Cor.* 5: 10; *Gal.* 6: 7–10) and he will be rewarded or punished accordingly (*Rom.* 2: 6; 1 *Cor.* 3: 8 and 12–15; 2 *Cor.* 5: 10 and 9: 6; *Eph.* 6: 8). Like the Jew and the heathen but referred to Christ and his law, the Christian must strive to fulfil the ideal. Paul proposes the example of the athlete and reveals that he has hardened his own body in order to be victorious (1 *Cor.* 9: 23–27). We must work out our salvation in fear and trembling (*Phil.* 2: 12) and in unceasing strife (*Phil.* 3: 8–14). We must take heed lest we fall (1 *Cor.* 10: 12). We may, on the other hand, hope for God's help in temptation (1 *Cor.* 10: 13). We know that he who moves our will to do what we ought also moves us to the accomplishment of what we will (*Phil.* 2: 13). God-given grace renders our negligence towards the law of Christ doubly punishable (2 *Cor.* 6: 1).

Christian liberty is anything but libertine. What then is the precise content of the law of Christ? We may here confine this problem to the question: does the moral reality which St Paul calls 'the law of nature' belong to the law of Christ? St Paul's characterization of the natural law makes the answer obvious. Freedom from the law means the abolition of the Law of the Old Testament as the norm of life and consequently does not present any difficulties. The *whole* Law including its moral precepts has indeed been abolished but the same precepts remain a binding norm for us independently of the Law. Therefore they bind the heathen as well. St Paul was of course justified in saying that even the pagans as part of the Law were ' doers of the Law ' (*Rom.* 2: 13) who 'did the works of the Law' (*Rom.* 2: 26). In the same sense he adds that the Christians also fulfil the obligations of the Law (*Rom.*

8: 4). In this context there is no difference in obligation between pagans, Jews and Christians. The catalogue of pagan vices (*Rom.* 1: 2–32) is consequently repeated for the Christians although they are freed from the Law and it is presented as a list of vices which exclude men from the kingdom of God. (1 *Cor.* 6: 9 ff.; *Gal.* 5: 19–21; 1 *Tim.* 1: 9–11). It is when the Apostle stresses that the Christians are dead to sin (*Rom.* 6) or that sin is out of the question for them (*Rom.* 6: 1 and 15), that the direction of his thought is most clearly evident. Being in Christ is precisely being free of those things which made the Jews and pagans sinners (*Rom.* 1 and 2). The thing which made them sinners is exactly this disregard for the order that binds both of them to its obligations. This is, as we have seen, a natural order.

It should now be very evident that for St Paul the exhortation to do what is good, kindly, natural and decent is an essential of the Christian exhortation. His admonition: 'Put on the Lord Jesus Christ' is interpreted by his own words: 'Let us, then cast off the works of darkness and put on the armour of light; let us conduct ourselves becomingly as in the day, not in revelling and drunkeness, not in debauchery and licentiousness, not in quarrelling and jealousy' (*Rom.* 13: 12 and 13). Generally he refers the moral demands of his preaching not to the Law or even to Christ but to the intrinsically moral nature of whatever action he requires of his hearers. Even when he seems to base his precepts on our communion with Christ it is often a matter of providing a new and additional incentive for living according to a natural moral order. There is seldom a question of establishing the primary distinction between good and evil. Indeed it is rather a matter of doing what is good in itself for Christ's sake. Typical of this is his warning against fornication (1 *Cor.* 6: 13–20). Paul proposes the motive that the body is meant for the Lord and for the resurrection and that it is a member of Christ and the temple of the Holy Ghost. These, however, are not the reasons why fornication is sinful. On the contrary it is a desecration of the sanctified Christian's body because impurity is a natural immorality. Fornication by a Christian is more malicious than the sin of non-Christians since even with these motivations he violates the natural law.

Law and justice in the *stricter* sense are also decisive for the
Christian as well as for pagan and Jew within the sphere of natural
law. Injustice by the heathen is a violation of the law of God and
is guilty unto death (*Rom.* 1: 29-32). Injustice under Christ excludes
from the kingdom (1 *Cor.* 6: 9 ff.). Outlawry and robbery are
contrary to justice for us as for the heathen, even though the
Corinthian Christian may not run at once to a pagan judge merely
because an injustice has been done to him (*ibid.*). St Paul himself
has the elementary natural right to eat and drink, to take a Christian
woman to wife and to pursue his apostolic activity without the
obligation to do any other work. For altogether good reasons he
does not in fact *exercise* these rights (1 *Cor.* 9: 4 ff.).

It is to a Christian community at Rome that he directs his explanations of the natural rights of the State and its demands upon their
obedience in the matter of legal obligations. (*Rom.* 13: 1–7).[16]

This place of natural law or natural rights in Christian morals
does not stand in opposition to the Apostle's classification of this
morality as part of the gospel and therefore subject to the faith.[17]
It proves that the natural law as conceived by him has been given
to us anew by revelation as a norm of life.

Freedom from the Mosaic Law whether we consider it objectively
in its abolition or subjectively in our deliverance from powerlessness
to obey it, does nothing to invalidate the natural law. Quite the
contrary! Because the Old Law has lost its validity as a positive
commandment of God's covenant, Christian freedom directly and
immediately signifies the power of fulfilling the natural precepts
which previously had been contained in the Law. It seems that
this must be St Paul's meaning. No other seems possible. The
positive requirements of the Law of Moses which are its ritual

---

[16] It is not the direct intention of St Paul to lay down here a doctrine of the State in
the light of natural law. His immediate intention is apparently to affirm that God,
in founding the Christian *ordo*, demands obedience to the public authority which
cares for the worldly order. Yet this demand of the Christian God does *not appear
as a purely positive commandment*. On the contrary the State, public authority and
obligatory obedience are all characterized as significant and necessary facts ultimately
rooted in God—not only in God revealing himself in Christ nor in God positively
commanding the initial setting-up of a public order. It is in this sense that the comments on the functions of public authority have, in all probability, to be understood.
[17] Cf. the exhaustive study by P. Bläser, M.S.C., 'Glaube und Sittlichkeit bei Paulus,'
in *Vom Wort des Lebens, Festschrift M. Meinertz, ed. E. Adler*, Münster 1951, 114–27.

precepts cannot be fulfilled any longer. It is abolished. Our freedom from the Law in the sense of liberation from our impotence in the face of its demands is now effective for the natural law also. Freedom from the Law *in the sense of its abolition* is restricted to the Mosaic Law. Christian freedom, in the sense of our liberation from the state of powerlessness, is demonstrated in the Mosaic Law but applied to every law. The fundamental theme of St Paul is that all men whether Jews or pagans, live in a state of weakness in which they become sinners under every law that binds in the sight of God. They are freed through Christ; natural law and natural rights have also been redeemed by him because man has been redeemed. Man now has the power and is thus free to do good. It is this freedom in which Paul is primarily interested. This is precisely the 'freedom from an existence that is death and sin, through the Law.' [18]

Natural law in the history of salvation

There is no state or stage in the history of salvation in which natural law is unimportant or valueless for St Paul. It constitutes a reality that transcends every situation in man's history. Certainly its position and importance change with the sequence of events. The three different states of existence, Jewish, pagan and Christian, are taken into account in his consideration of our salvation-history. The natural law is the valid order for the pagan who is without the Law and without Christ. The fulfilment of the natural law is what makes him good. Its violation makes him evil. His knowledge of its contents comes to him by use of reason. This indeed is difficult because of natural weakness and because of defective dispositions before God (*Rom.* 1). He has not the support of the revealed Law given by God to the Jews to work against the darkening of his understanding. He has not received Christ's Revelation. It is more difficult still for the heathen to fulfil the natural law than it is to

[18] Schlier, in G. Kittel, *Theologisches Wörterbuch zum Neuen Testament*, II, Stuttgart 1935, 492.

understand it. He belongs to the world of men into which the power of sin has entered with the sin of Adam (cf. *Rom.* 5 and 7). The natural law is not a positive law like the Mosaic. Yet it is also a commandment from without and not a power within which can overcome the weakness of original sin when man confronts his obligations. In this Jew and pagan are equal, excepting always the fact that the revealed law given to the Jew renders his violation of the natural law more culpable. Anticipating the power of Christ both heathen and Jew are already able to fulfil their obligations. Christ's coming gave the heathen freedom from helplessness. In fulfilling the law of nature by which alone he was guided in the absence of the Law of Moses (cf. *Rom.* 2: 10 ff. and 25–29) he became the subject of salvation in Christ as he had been the subject of the promise.

The Jew also knows the natural law from within his own native resources but in addition he has had it revealed to him in the form of the Law of Moses. The intervention of this Law does not bring with it the power necessary to fulfil it. The Jew in his own original sin is just as powerless as the heathen in face of the natural law which is contained in the Mosaic code. Certainly it is easier for him to understand the natural law but this results in a more intense experience of man's inner schism and makes his failures all the more sinful. Thus the Law of Moses instrumentally places a heavier and more accursed load of wrath upon man than the natural law alone could have laid upon him. (Cf. *Rom.* 5: 13; 4: 15; *Gal.* 3: 13). It is true that this stage in the history of salvation is but a transient phase. Man's indigence, already visible before the Law was given, was emphasized by the Law which was nonetheless to be the guide to Christ (*Rom.* 5: 20; *Gal.* 3: 29). Under it men were not merely sinners. They were also true subjects of the promise through that grace of Christ which was already active. The coming of Christ brought to the Jew, once and for all, that interior love and strength by which he was able to respond to the requirements of that natural law which was contained in the Old Law.

It is in the Christian that the natural law finds its most favourable 'situation.' He also has come to know the good from within and is drawn to it. For him God's Revelation in the Law of the Old Dispensation is a support for his understanding. St Paul cites the Law himself (1 *Cor.* 9: 9; 1 *Tim.* 5: 18; *Eph.* 6: 6). Notwithstanding all this, Christ makes the good known through his apostles. St Paul reiterates that he and the apostles preach the Christian way as given them by Christ.[19] This way contains the natural order. Generally speaking the natural law appears now as the 'Law of Christ' and not as in 'the Law' of the Old Testament. Through its relationship to Christ it has received a positive and a new *authority*. This does not imply that the natural law alone is the law of Christ. The salient fact is that the power to fulfil the law is bestowed in Christ. For the Christian man's state of indigence has been overcome. The Christian is dead to sin through baptism (*Rom.* 6: 3–25) and the non-observance of the natural law is sin. From now on the Christian is guided by the Spirit (*Rom.* 8: 14). To be a Christian to the full is to be free from sin (*Rom.* 8: 1) not only by way of its remission but by way of actually avoiding its commission and by doing all good works, including the natural law, by the power of the Spirit (*Rom.* 8: 4). With this new power, fulfilment of the natural law is a necessary condition for admission to God's Kingdom (cf. 1 *Cor.* 6: 9 ff.). It is an increasingly perfect participation in that Kingdom (*Rom.* 2: 6). The natural law in St Paul's teaching sketches a picture of the Christian life at least in its 'natural' basis. It forms the foundation of the rights of the redeemed Christian community (cf. *Rom.* 13). Fulfilment of its obligations by the power of Christ is now a divine service in the Kingdom of God founded by Christ (cf. *Rom.* 6: 12 ff. and 13: 4 ff.). Consequently, the Christian has a natural knowledge and inclination to (*Rom.* 2: 15; 7: 14–25) what is in truth an imitation

[19] Cf. 1 *Thess.* 4: 2 ff., 'For you know what instructions we gave you in the Lord Jesus. For this is the will of God, your sanctification: that you abstain from immorality . . .' Here it is not only a formal appeal to the authority of Christ but also a question of his teaching in its content. Similarly 1 *Cor.* 4: 17: '(I sent Timothy to you) to remind you of my ways in Christ, as I teach them everywhere in every church.' Yet this teaching is at the same time a moral demand. On the question of marriage, St Paul refers explicitly to the word of Christ (1 *Cor.* 7: 10). His words on the position of the wife in relation to her husband indicate that that which in his preceding sentences was shown to be in accordance with the natural law and the Old Testament, is part of the order of *creation* (and is not to be taken *directly* as *natural law*) or of the order of Christ.

of Christ (1 *Cor.* 11: 1) and a participation in his Kingdom. This renders possible our access to the Father (*Eph.* 2: 18).

Pauline doctrine considers the natural law only in connection with man's three states of existence in the actual history of salvation. Natural law in the historical state of the earthly paradise or in the hypothetical state of pure nature are not treated. His statements on these three actualized or historical states of man as pagan, Jew and Christian are sufficient all the same to allow us to understand his position on the natural law taken purely in itself. It is necessarily and beyond all doubt valid where-ever man exists. To posit an historical state of human existence without natural law implies the impossible notion of a real man existing beyond the realm of good and evil. The very problem is precisely the emergence of the inner law of human morality from the fact of human being. True this law is open to a completion from within, proportionate to the diverse situations of man's history. Knowledge of it is fundamentally possible to every man but the ability to acquire it can be obscured by his behaviour. God can support and make up this inadequacy by Revelation. Whether it is easy or difficult of fulfilment cannot be determined by any general principle; it depends on man's actual historical situation.

This natural law always represents for man a way in which he may express his love and acknowledgment of God. The fulfilment of its requirements indicates an openness to God's self-giving and self-revealing in the history of salvation.[20]

[20] Since the revision of this chapter, the book by F. Flückiger, *Geschichte des Naturrechts, Band 1, Altertum und Frühmittelalter,* Zollikon-Zürich 1954, has been published. On pp. 284–475, the author deals with the teaching of the Fathers and of the early Middle Ages (including St Thomas Aquinas) on the natural law. Flückiger defends the thesis that St Paul, and the Fathers, did not in fact know of a metaphysical natural law. What they did know is the natural law of the history of salvation, a natural law which is seen in relation to the *natura integra* on the morning of creation (cf. his article: 'Die Werke des Gesetzes bei den Heiden nach Röm. 2: 14 ff.', TZ 1952; 17 ff.). We have already discussed the teaching of St Paul on this point; cf. also O. Kuss, 'Die Heiden und die Werke des Gesetzes (nach *Röm.* 2: 14–16),' MTZ 5 (1954) 77–98. In any interpretation of the Fathers' thought more careful consideration should be given to the fact that metaphysical statements are by no means to be opposed to statements based on the history of salvation. However, not all Protestant authors agree with Flückiger according to whom the *praecepta naturalia* of St Irenaeus are to be interpreted in the light of salvation-history. Flückiger depends upon the fact that St Irenaeus juxtaposes, in another text, the two words, *natura* and *creatura*, to express the original state. Cf. for example V. E. Hasler, *Gesetz und Evangelium in der alten Kirche bis*

APPENDIX

Before we can understand Christ's attitude towards the natural law, it seems first of all necessary to go back to the statement of our Lord on the indissolubility of marriage (*Matt.* 19: 3–12, *Luke* 10: 2–12). The reason he gives for what it is good and proper to do in this matter gives, apparently, some indication of the essence or nature of marriage. It is therefore, to use modern terminology, based on the natural law. His remark that there was no dissolution of marriage 'from the beginning' and that this is consequently not now allowed, refers directly to the *historical* beginning, that is to the divine order. This, we know, was *not* merely a *natural* order. Christ's statement admits that the initial will of God must not be understood as positive will only, possibly corresponding to the preter-natural or supernatural mode of man's existence. Thus ' from the beginning it was not so (as it is now under the Law of Moses)' (*Matt.* 19: 8) is explained by the allusion to the statement in Genesis that the Creator made man 'male and female' and said: 'For this reason a man shall leave his father and mother and be joined to his wife, and the two shall become one.' From this Christ

---

Origenes, Frankfurt M. 1953, 43 ff. On the Catholic side cf. O. Schilling on the natural right of the State in the early Christian times (cf. below, Chapter V, n. 1); J. Stelzenberger, *Die Beziehungen der frühchristlichen Sittenlehre zur Ethik der Stoa*, Munich 1933; V. Giorgianni, *Il concetto del Diritto e dello Stato in S. Agostino* (Il pensiero medioevale, 2), Padua 1951.

Further studies on this question are urgently needed. A good survey of the problem of the natural law in patristic times has recently been published by P. Delhaye, 'Permanence du droit naturel,' (*Analecta Medievale Namurcensia* 10), Louvain, N.D. An excellent study on St Augustine has been written by K. Demmer, 'Ius caritatis: Zur christologischen Grundlegung der augustinischen Naturrechtslehre,' (*Analecta Gregoriana* 118), Rome 1961. B. Maes has completed an unpublished thesis on the teaching of St Ambrose on the natural law (Pontifica Universita Gregoriana).

concludes: 'What therefore God has joined together, let no man put asunder' (*Matt.* 19: 4–6). Thus our Lord refers to the will of God expressed in visible creation, the will of God expressed in the actual existence of man and wife. The law of the indissolubility of marriage is proved not only in general by reference to the will of God but more precisely by reference to the will of God expressed in the nature of the created human being.

In the same sense Christ, judging from a purely objective point of view, comments on the other commandments of the law of the New Testament. Thus his conception of the indissolubility of marriage is reflected in his remarks on the precept of the certificate of divorce, that 'everyone who divorces his wife, except on the ground of unchastity, makes her an adulteress, and whoever marries a divorced woman commits adultery' (*Matt.* 5: 31 ff.). Likewise does he add to the commandment: 'You shall not commit adultery' the comment (evident in itself): 'everyone who looks at a woman lustfully has already committed adultery with her in his heart' (*Matt.* 5: 27 ff.).

Corresponding to the conception expressed in the example of marriage, Christ presupposes in general (as can be found in St Paul) the knowledge of good and evil as objectively self-evident and therefore as subjectively known, for example, where he says in the dispute on the clean and unclean,' what comes out of man is what defiles a man. For from within, out of the heart of man, come evil thoughts, fornication, theft, murder, adultery, coveting, wickedness, deceit, licentiousness, envy, slander, pride, foolishness. All these evil things come from within, and they defile a man' (*Mark* 7: 20–23). He also presupposes the knowledge of good and evil when, after healing a sick man on the sabbath, he justifies his action by saying 'is it lawful on the sabbath to do good or to do harm, to save life or to kill?' (*Mark* 3: 3 ff.). Similarly in his words on the last judgment, 'and will come forth, those who have done good, to the resurrection of life, and those who have done evil, to the resurrection of judgment' (*John* 5: 29). Thus, Christ recognizes man's ability to judge by himself what is good at this moment (cf. *Luke* 12: 57)—in this context it bears upon the ability to judge correctly of Christ's own mission. In the formulation which impressed the eighteenth century so much and which is since known as the 'Golden Rule,' Christ points out the natural measure applicable by all to the love of one's neighbour, 'so whatever you wish that men would do to you, do so to them' (*Matt.* 7: 12).

Christ's attitude towards the natural law is also evident in his attitude to the Law of the Old Testament. He fundamentally acknowledged the Law (*Matt.* 5: 17). But he made it clear all the same that he had the power to give a binding interpretation of it, as when he explained how the law of the sabbath must be understood and kept (*Mark* 2: 28). Yet it is above all important that he had the authority to abolish the ceremonial Law (*Mark* 7: 15), whereas he intensifies and deepens the 'moral' precepts of the Law in his Sermon on the Mount. Given the intention of our Lord to intensify and deepen (and thus carry out a greater adaptation to reality), when we find the ceremonial laws are abolished and moral precepts remain have we not an expression of the objectivity and natural basis of the moral order on the one hand and of purely positive basis of the ceremonial laws on the other? (cf. J. Schmid, ' Das Evangelium nach Matthäus' [*Regensburger Neues Testament I*], Regensburg 1948, 71).

We do not intend to give here an interpretation of the ideas of the Sermon on the Mount. If *Christ* opposes the morality of the kingdom of God to the inclination and the attitude of the sinner, this is of interest for *us* in so far as certain statements of the Sermon on the Mount have a relationship to the order of the natural law. Certainly, Christ does not expressly deal with it. The 'naturally' thinking man, who is the subject of the Sermon on the Mount, is not the 'natural' man of the natural order.

The Sermon on the Mount is not opposed to the natural law. It is true that some of its statements, for example, on the renouncement of vengeance, give the impression at first sight that the natural legal order is being abandoned. The impression might even be given that the administration of justice, or at least a personal insistence on justice, is an absolutely forbidden or unchristian attitude from now on. Yet it must be remembered that Christ, in pursuing his ideal in the Sermon on the Mount, deals with the personal morality of man and this is primarily and basically from within. That which improves man's morals directly is his inner attitude, intention and disposition, even though they are expressed in single acts. In the Sermon on the Mount Christ speaks of everything that directly constitute man's moral behaviour, without referring explicitly to the significance of the various 'orders.' This does not mean that he rejects them. In other contexts he even makes it expressly clear that he accepts them as something quite self-evident, for example, in his word about the indissolubility of marriage, about adultery etc., or of the catalogue of vices already mentioned. A positive acknowledgement of the State can probably be seen in his words about the shekel (*Matt.* 17: 24–7), and about the tribute to God and to Caesar (*Matt.* 22: 15–22). His sermons reveal, however indirectly, that it is not these orders that are of primary importance for the inner moral attitude but man's disposition. The much quoted words of Christ on vengeance (*Matt.* 5: 38–42) offer therefore no real difficulty. They must be seen against the background of the *lex talionis* (eye for eye and tooth for tooth) which constituted valid penal law, though at the time of Christ it was no longer observed in its former vigour. Christ does not comment on this order but only on our inner disposition towards the fellow-man who does evil to us. It is here that he rejects the vengeance which is so easily connected with the *lex talionis*; he demands a readiness to forgive which may be considered in fact as part of the natural moral law. This is true although it is not conceivable as such by man whose thinking is in disorder through original sin. (Christ opposes this readiness to forgive to the behaviour of the Jews of the Old Testament, the tax collectors, the heathen and the sinners; (*Matt.* 5: 43–8, *Luke* 6: 32 ff.). Yet the condemnation of vengeance excludes neither the law nor its administration in every case. It often happens that the administration of the law without vindictiveness is even demanded and becomes a holy duty. Christ himself interpreted his own words when he justified himself saying: 'if I have spoken wrongly, bear witness to the wrong, but if I have spoken rightly, why do you strike me?' (*John* 18: 23). When the Jews called him a Samaritan and possessed by the devil, he contradicted this calumny (*John* 8: 49 ff.). When the Pharisees called him Beelzebub because he cast out devils, he sharply characterized their words as a blasphemy against the Holy Ghost, a sin that will not be forgiven either in this or in the coming world (*Matt.* 12: 24 ff.). With Christ's demand for absolute defencelessness did he seem to relinquish altogether the defence of all order? He quite evidently wanted to preserve it because he insisted on the observation of the commandments of the second table of the decalogue (*Matt.* 19: 17–20) (cf. T. Soiron o.f.m., *Die Bergpredigt Jesu: Formgeschichtliche und theologische Erklärung*, Freiburg Br. 1941, 291). Our Lord demands consequently the readiness to forgive and to abstain from revenge, a disposition that shall by no means remain an inner attitude without any action resulting from it. But he indicates likewise the limits that are set by the necessity to preserve order and justice. Both are demands of natural right; we must often forego *our* rights but we must be prepared to enforce *the* right. (Cf. P. Dausch, *Die drei älteren Evangelien* (*Bonner Bibel I*) Bonn 1923, 128.)

PART TWO

NATURAL LAW AND
THE UNDERSTANDING OF THE FAITH

CHAPTER THREE

NATURE AND NATURAL LAW

A strictly theological reflection on the data of our sources of faith is not necessary in order to provide a solid and intelligent foundation for natural law. An adequate although precise experiential notion of man, aware of his essential constituent elements, their necessary qualities and concomitant moral postulates, is practically and even scientifically sufficient. St Paul wrote of a natural knowledge of morals in the creation that can be known only by experience. He made no distinction between the natural or supernatural condition of that creation.

Scientific philosophy and *a fortiori* scientific theology may justifiably attempt a deeper analysis. The considerations which follow have a strictly scientific bearing. We are invited to this task by the Church's documents even as far as considering the natural in opposition to the supernatural. A noetic as well as ontological examination of natural law [1] fundamentals is an example of this properly theological work.

It is evident that these theological preoccupations are not peculiarly modern either in their noetic or ontological aspects. Several of the Fathers have treated the 'natural law' within the whole order of Christian morals. They, like the medieval theologians, spoke of a 'change' in the natural law as having taken place in the history of salvation. This fact of change is high-lighted as soon as we ask, for example, whether the natural rights of private property or the uses of coercion derive from original sin. We shall examine these particular problems elsewhere. In such cases we are treating of order to bring out the full intelligibility of the natural law. The properly theological questions in connection with Revelation in

[1] See above pp. 10–13.

strictly scientific legitimacy of placing the essence of the natural law
problem within the *totality* of our human nature is obvious.
Revelation teaches us that human nature is not merely natural.
It is not surprising that contemporary theologians choose as the
point of departure for their investigations of the natural law the
sense in which this law is ontologically as well as noetically natural.
To what extent is natural law more precisely determined by the
fact of man's supernatural life?

Protestant theology proceeds from an essentially different
conception of the natural and supernatural reality of historical man.
It tends to deny the validity of the natural law or perhaps tends to
regard it as law in a merely relative sense. The relationship of this
law to the total human situation within the supernatural order
seems to be the only profitable basis in which we might hope
gain Protestant understanding for Catholic natural law doctrine.

The theological concept of nature

Directing our remarks in the first instance to those of our readers
who are theologians we shall briefly summarize the Church's
teaching on nature and the supernatural.

In reaction to error the Church was obliged to define these
concepts more precisely.[2] Her achievements in this task revealed the
theological foundations of natural law. She had to deal primarily
with the theses of Baius. The basic principle of her case was that

[2] It cannot be concluded directly from the text of the ecclesiastical decisions what
qualification is to be given to each of the condemned propositions. In his essay, 'La
" nature pure " à la lumière d'encyclique " Humani generis ",' NRT, 1952, 337–54,
L. Renwart, S.J., concludes thus: the 26th condemned proposition of *Baius* (*Denz.* 1026),
according to which the original state is natural, should (considering the context) have
the predicate 'temeraria.' The same predicate should be given to porposition 21
(*Denz.* 1021) which states the natural participation in God's nature, and to proposition
78 (*Denz.* 1078) teaching the natural immortality of the first man. As for proposition
55 (*Denz.* 1055), stating that God could not have created man in the state in which he
is born now, the author believes it to have the qualification 'Suspiciosa.' The 35th
condemned proposition of Quesnel, teaching the necessity of grace for man in his
original innocence, is according to the same author 'temeraria.' The same proposition
laid down by the Synod of Pistoia is expressly stated to be 'erronea' (*Denz.* 1516).
In the Encyclical *Pascendi* against Modernism the word 'incauti' is used referring to
those who seem ('videntur') to hold the rejected proposition (*Denz.* 2103). The Encyclical *Humani generis* rejects the same proposition as 'erroneous' without giving it
any further qualification, AAS 42 (1950), 570.

the original state of man in the earthly paradise was not nature simply. In man as willed and created by God not everything is 'nature.' That is to say *not everything that he is derives from his composite being as body and soul.*[3] It is possible to call the totality of man in paradise his 'property' and his 'nature,' referring to his initial state. A distinction must be made within this totality between a natural sphere which is his own and another not necessarily connected with it. This latter owes its existence to a gratuitous love, not yet included in the concept of creator. In particular, participation in the divine nature is called supernatural. Such participation is not a constituent of that natural sphere by defect of which man would not be man. God in no way owes this participation to human nature as we have defined it even when we consider it under the aspect of original innocence and integrity. Absence of this 'supernatural' is indeed a state eminently defective if the basis of comparison is the state of man's existence in paradise. It is not, however, an evil in the sphere which we have called his 'nature.' This is to say that it is not a privation of something that is due to men so that each may attain his natural perfection. The Church therefore condemned the proposition that God could not have created man in the state in which he now exists. Of course this way of putting it quite overlooks the fact that man *in his present state* is born into a supernatural order and that from the beginning he is directed to a supernatural end. Nor does it take into account that in his present state he is, from the moment of his birth, subject to certain consequences of his supernatural situation in the history of salvation. He is subject, for example, to concupiscence. The phrase 'in his present state' simply signifies the absence of supernatural grace. Supernatural grace does not belong to the essence or nature of created man. His nature could exist without grace and this is a fact not only consequent upon original sin but also in virtue of God's creative act.[4]

---

[3] It seems hardly necessary to add to the above that here 'nature' is not to be understood as being opposed to 'spirit' or 'person.' The spiritual character is in a special way part of the nature of man as he is considered in this context.
[4] Cf. J. Alfaro, s.j., 'Sobrenatural y pecado original en Bayo,' *Rev. esp. de Teol.*, 12 (1952), 3-75, esp. 33-8.

It was in the sense of the condemnation of Baius that the Church responded to the theses of Quesnel and the Synod of Pistoia. These had asserted that the grace received by the first man was a necessary result of his created nature in the state of original innocence.

Similarly this is the problem taken up by the Church in her condemnation of Modernism although she is no longer concerned exclusively with the first man. She now articulates the general proposition that to speak of a true necessity in the supernatural order is erroneous. Further, in this condemnation the 'supernatural order' includes the basic orientation of historical man to a supernatural end. It is not confined as were her previous pronouncements to the concept of the 'supernatural' as signifying the life of grace. It now signifies a reality in which all men without exception and at all times actually live.

False and imprudent formulations of more recent date are answered on the same lines. The Encyclical *Humani generis*, for example, states that the gratuitous character of the supernatural order is impaired by the assumption that God is unable to create spiritual beings without directing or calling them to the beatific vision.

The theological distinction between a natural [5] and a supernatural domain in man must not be understood in the sense that as he actually exists he incorporates something purely natural that is not realized in a supernatural way. Neither should it be understood as something not yet assimilated into the supernatural. This is to say that we must not think of human nature as something that exists of itself and as having a complete existential signification in its own right. Man in his total existence is and always has been directed positively to a supernatural end. It is from this fact that he receives his significance. God's creation and providential knowledge has man in mind only as receiving his perfection in the inner life

---

[5] Within the supernatural (and in the following) it does not seem necessary to make a further distinction between the gifts which are in themselves supernatural (such as man's participation in the divine nature) and the gifts which are only preternatural yet closely connected with the supernatural state of grace and given to man because of this state. (Instances of these are the more complete control of the spirit over the senses, or freedom from death).

of the Holy Trinity. This is a finality to which man cannot attain
by himself. In fact there is no purely natural perfection of man's
real being which can be called 'nature.' Holy Scripture spoke of
man in God's creation and foresight in such a way as to allow the
Fathers to describe the total reality of man as his nature. The word
natura means man as he was in the beginning, deriving as it does
from *nasci* which means 'to be born.' It follows that in this sense
the supernatural is not accidental to man. It belongs to his definition
essentially. If nature is opposed to the supernatural it is undoubtedly
an abstraction but it is true abstraction taken from man as he really
and actually is. It follows that it is *realized in him in a true and
altogether proper sense*. It is a necessary consequence that the supernatural is also an abstraction from the total reality of man and must
be unhesitatingly and necessarily affirmed to be accidental to uatnre.
Nonetheless this nature is open to fulfilment by the supernatural
of its very essence. If we view it in the light of God's intention
and creation we must see it as existentially disposed to this realization and fulfilment by the supernatural. It receives its significance
from the supernatural. True, man's nature even in abstraction has
a significance in itself. This does not explain in what way it will
be actually manifested or find its realization within supernatural
reality.

As distinct from the supernatural, nature is but a part of that total
reality which is man and which we know exclusively from Revelation. This is the only source from which it is possible to know that
in the complete human being there is a 'supernature' and that
'nature' is open to receiving it. Likewise it is Revelation which
establishes what elements in man are connected with the supernatural. It alone can indicate what parts of our experience of reality
belong to the supernatural order and are conditioned by the
supernatural history of salvation. Some theologians justifiably
consider nature and its material content as a 'residual' concept
in the theological perspectives we are now describing.

There is no implication in all this that the man who receives the
word of Revelation does not already know the formal concept of
nature in the sense of the human essence. Conversely it does not

mean that he has no notion of himself as receiving the gifts of divine love. He can recognize in a general way the elements which make up the content of his nature. It is to Revelation also that we owe *inter alia* the distinction between natural and supernatural knowledge, especially where the supernatural is manifested in its effects in our experience. It is in this way that the concept of nature as a theologically qualified 'residue' may be entirely justified.

There is a further point upon which it is necessary to be clear. On the one hand we have no certainty that Revelation informs us of *all* the elements in our concrete human nature that either belong to or are conditioned by the supernatural order of salvation. No man knows the precise demarcation between nature and supernatural in his own individual and concrete reality nor can anyone be aware of the exact point at which his natural and supernatural obligations meet. On the other hand it can readily happen that, generically considered, a reality revealed as supernatural may be *at the same time* natural. Only the determinate form in which it is realized is supernaturally conditioned. For example the supernatural end of man and his moral duty to pursue it are clearly of the supernatural order. This never-the-less includes a generic element which belongs equally to nature and implies a relation to God as final end. So, of course, does the obligation to pursue it.

Taken in the sense of the total reality of God's design for creation (which is to take it in the sense of the nature of man in paradise)[6] the Church's usage of natural law is not founded in nature. This is why the Protestant theologian has such difficulty in understanding the Catholic theology of natural law. Since he does not admit a difference between nature and supernatural he cannot recognize a natural law which presupposes this difference. If the original state of man is *not* merely a particular realization of man's essence (certainly, willed and created by God) and *is* purely and simply the nature of man in all the ramifications of his being and if the effects of original sin destructively touch this integral totality, it follows that natural law cannot be affirmed of his present condition

[6] On this and the following point, cf. J. Fuchs, s.j., 'Situationsethik in theologischer Sicht,' *Scholastik*, 27 (1952), 166 ff., and by the same author, *Situation und Entscheidung, Grundfragen christlicher Situationsethik*, Frankfurt/M. 1952, 31-46.

nor can it be God's will for him. The law in this sense concerns human nature only in its original state. The Catholic conception presupposes this very distinction between nature and the supernatural. It understands nature only and precisely in as far as it is distinct from the supernatural.[7] This is the only sense in which it is *nature* and of which the Church can say that it was not destroyed but remains as the foundation of a valid natural law. The original *state* of man in its integrity was destroyed and does not survive into our present condition. Consequently the Church insists on the fundamental independence of our natural rights as being distinct from the Revelations of the Old and New Testaments.[8] On the other hand, we know of man's state in paradise and his supernatural condition generally only through faith in Revelation. Church declarations always place the natural and divine positive laws side by side. The former exists independently of God's supernatural historical action in man while God's positive law is based exactly on this action.[9]

We should now be able to formulate the question with precision: what exactly is this nature that is said to be the foundation of the natural law and that must be distinguished from the supernatural? Is it the *natura pura* as so many scholastic manuals of moral theology seem to indicate or is it our concrete and historical nature as constituted by all the actual elements of its existence? Again, is it rather 'human nature in general' differentially realized in all its

---

[7] Thielicke, in his work on theological ethics (*Theologische Ethik, Band I: Dogmatische, philosophische und kontroverstheologische Grundlegung*, Tübingen 1951), appeals to the essence of the 'creatio ex nihilo' in order to demonstrate the impossibility of distinguishing between nature and the supernatural, creation and redemption, and to establish their absolute unity (no. 753). Yet the fact that both come from God in an absolute manner does not exclude two spheres in man being traced back to their divine origin in very diverse ways.

From the Protestant anthropology to which we already referred (and from the relation of natural law to man's original state) connected with the first, there results in particular the doctrine of the relativity of the present natural law which we shall explain later on. Here, relativity is to be taken in the sense that natural law is none other than 'the will of God as it appears in the refraction caused by our peculiar state, and we may perhaps say, the will of God altered by the fallen universe' (*ibid*. n. 691). "The absolute 'goodness' of the original order now no longer exists, consequently the relatively 'best' in justice must be found " (*ibid*. n. 2015).

[8] See Chapter VII.

[9] The character of historicity present in the supernatural activity of God, is likewise attached to the original creation of the supernatural in the first man. This is so already, in sofar as this supernatural presupposes nature (though not in the order of time).

modes and in the multifarious situations of our supernatural
salvation-history?

Theology understands *natura pura* as the realization of human
nature in its natural existence without the supernatural gifts such
as sanctifying grace, immortality etc. The phase 'without the supernatural gifts' should be taken in the full and authentic sense as
meaning outside the supernatural order and without directing man
to supernatural grace or a supernatural destination. This thesis
which holds the natural law as referring in the final analysis to the
natura pura seems open to certain objections. The *natura pura*
is a certain mode of existence in human nature, even though this
may be a natural mode of such a character that its total reality
lies outside the supernatural. Some distinguished theologians hold
that the elements of man's natural mode of existence (*natura pura*)
cannot be found *in the same manner* in each mode of man's existence.
For example many believe that the moral possibility of observing
the natural law really belongs to the *natura pura* but not necessarily
after original sin. Others hold that the particular way of communion
with God as the final end of the *natura pura* and the consequent
obligation to pursue it, do not apply to the man of the supernatural
order. It has not been proved that all of what we call natural law
which is effectively valid for the state of *natura pura* is similarly
valid for every situation in the history of salvation. Do not some
moralists, basing their natural law teaching upon this concept, say
explicitly that such ethics are concerned with a hypothetical and
not a real man? It is certainly possible that certain natural law
principles based on *natura pura* can only be formulated validly as
applying directly to this mode alone. It is necessary to distinguish
these from the principles that have validity for any actual state of
human existence including our own. The same observation applies
without further distinction when we consider concrete human nature
as the foundation of natural law. We are convinced that the moral
imperatives of this law are not concerned with any hypothetical man.
It is certain that they bear upon man as he actually is. This requires
us to distinguish several levels in the law of man's nature as he
now exists and as he is involved in the actual economy of salvation.

The Catholic doctrine is that man's nature remains the same in all situations of salvation-history but is realized in each in a different manner. A distinction is therefore demanded which will indicate its changing and its unchanging elements. Our theological tradition teaches, for example, that the right to use force and, for many thinkers, the right to private property are imperatives of the natural law. Nonetheless they are so only consequent upon original sin as a fact of the history of salvation. Scientific theology then has the right and duty to undertake an analysis of man as he actually exists. It must work out the levels and structures of this analytical artefact and its subject-matter. Further, the distinction made by Protestants but attributed to us, between an absolute and a relative natural law requires an exact articulation. We must establish the sense in which we can accept it and the sense which we must repudiate it.

The precepts revealed in the different periods of the supernatural history of salvation [10] force us to consider human nature 'in general' as the principal foundation of the natural law. This 'human nature in general' possesses elements which are discoverable in all its various modes of realization. Further, nature remains open to yet other elements con-corporate with these constant ones in the actualities of history, particularly in our supernatural salvation-history. In a way to be determined, human nature requires the actualization of certain elements—no matter which—in a concrete mode of living. These elements, always concretized, are the basis of the natural law actively significant for any situation in the history of salvation but additionally and in a hypothetic way, the law establishes itself in the elements of *a* determinate salvation situation. These latter historically determined elements do not contradict the first and fundamental stratum of natural law. Rather they complete it.[11] Those elements which are always active

---

[10] But *not exclusively* the history of salvation.
[11] Cf. on this subject J. Funk, S.V.D., *Primat des Naturrechts. Die Transzendenz des Naturrechts gegenüber dem positiven Recht*, Mödling bei Wien 1952, 147: 'According to scholastic doctrine, the 'order' of private property is only *one* of many possibilities offered by the natural law, if man is taken in his specific essence in a purely abstract way, that is, without need to take the weakness of his nature resulting from original sin into account. The 'order' of collective property is (in this case) at least equally

in any situation can still include an indeterminate one which can be actualized *only in a special mode* appropriate to the actual salvation situation. An example of this is the orientation of man to God as his last end and his obligation to seek this end. These are realized in different ways in the *natura pura* and in the *natura elevata*.

The First Vatican Council [12] bears witness to this. It considered the ability of man to know God and his own moral obligations in a natural way and was aware of the conditional necessity of Revelation for man in his present state.[13] It's first formulation referred to nature as distinct from the supernatural but considered this nature as abstracted from any determinate mode of being, real or possible. During the Council an amendment was proposed which accorded the ability to know God and the natural law to man *in his present state*. Archbishop Gasser as leader of the discussion emphasized that the canon dealt with human nature in general (*agitur in genere de condicione naturae humanae*) and not ' with man as he actually exists.' [14] The Council had in mind only the noetic foundation of our knowledge of God and of morality. It did not speak of its ontological foundation.

A propos nature in general, it is proper to speak of nature as absolute in the sense that its content abstracts (absolutum) from the particular modes of existence within the different situations of salvation. In this sense only those obligations have validity and importance which arise from this absolute nature. The same is not true for the precepts which find validation in the particular and diverse situations of salvation, including the *natura pura*.

---

satisfactory. If we include the circumstances of original sin, the formulation of the 'order' of private property becomes immediately a principle of the natural law. (Cf. A. F. Utz, O.P., *Freiheit und Bindung des Eigentums;* Welty, *Die Entscheidung in der Zukunft.*) To be even more concrete, we can say that the principle of the 'order' of private property, in turn, makes allowance for exceptions. Thus, in the 'Indian Reductions' of the Jesuits in South America, circumstances presented themselves in such a way that the communist form of ownership was, for a brief period at least, the only reasonable solution. Cf. also Pius XI in the Encyclical *Quadragesimo anno, n.* 114.'
[12] *Denz.* 1785 ff.
[13] Cf. G. Sohngen, 'Naturliche Theologie und Heilsgeschichte. Antwort an E. Brunner,' *Catholica*, 4 (1935), 97–114.
[14] *Acta et decreta sacrorum conciliorum recentiorum. Collectio Lacensis,* 7, Freiburg-Br. 1890, 140.

The chapter on the history of natural law will indicate why we prefer to use this terminology rather than the nomenclature of many Protestant theologians.[15]

In Catholic theology the natural law concepts referring to nature in general or nature taken absolutely as an ultimate foundation, possesses qualities that have always been attributed to natural law. It is valid for every salvation situation and always has an actual validity and a possibility of being applied. It has these attributes because it is related to these absolute elements and is not conditioned by the particular situation. This is to speak absolutely but it has also a validity and a possibility of hypothetical application because it is related to elements that *are* conditioned by the particular situation.

In the concrete, therefore, natural law regulates all the elements by which human nature is actually constituted. This nature is certainly weakened but this refers only to that elevated existence which was man's in paradise and possibly also to the *natura pura*, as already indicated. Human nature 'in general' remains intact. It is this essence and its signification which determine its moral relationships to the particular elements of historical existence.

The reservation has already been made that we have no certainty of possessing a complete Revelation of all the elements of the supernatural, particularly in the case of the actual individual. A second reservation is now necessary. How is it possible to know and in what sense can we assert that these elements of nature, negatively described, belong positively and (more or less) necessarily to the essence of man's being?[16] True, Revelation informs us positively on many aspects of this problem but we find ourselves dependent in the main upon the resources of natural reason. In this work of reason revealed knowledge certainly comes to the aid of nature as

[15] Cf. E. Elter, *Compendium philosophiae moralis*, Rome 1950, 27, '. . . prae oculis habendum est: . . . 2° naturam humanam posse sumi vel secundum modum quo existit, sive a parte rei, sive in mente; vel absolute, praescindendo a modo existentiae; rationem normae habet non aliter, nisi inquantum absolute consideratur.' Elter, speaking as a philosopher, does not, however, make exclusive or express statements when he is dealing with the diverse situations of the supernatural history of salvation.
[16] On this problem, cf. the position of K. Rahner, s.j., *Theological Investigations*, II, London and Baltimore 1963, 219 f.; the same author, 'Bemerkungen über das Naturrecht und seine Erkennbarkeit,' *Orientierung*, 30 November 1955.

philosophy does to theology. In this way we can arrive at an
adequately comprehensive and accurate intellectual grasp of the
content of human nature and its concommittant moral and juridical
order.

The philosophical concept of nature

The theological point of view from which man's nature must
be understood as a 'residue concept' has already been mentioned.
On this level its content as the substratum of the supernatural is
abstracted from the total reality of man, known only through
Revelation. It can be understood as a matter of fact in the fullest
sense only within the total reality of historical man. This being
so our explanations should have conveyed to the reader that natural
and therefore philosophical knowledge of the law is possible. In
fact the Church does envisage a natural law in this way and since
she knows only one natural law there is evidently a theological as
well as a philosophical concept of nature corresponding to it. In
devoting a few lines to this philosophical concept we shall do so
from the standpoint of its theological rather than its properly
philosophical significance.

There is an immediate difficulty in the fact that man as a 'pure'
realization of absolute nature or nature 'in general' is not naturally
or philosophically knowable. We can know him only as he actually
exists here and now. In fact this man is part of the supernatural
order and indeed of an historically determined mode of that order.
What is natural and what is supernatural in him? Certainly the
supernatural known as such derives from Revelation alone but it is
possible that we can detect some of its effects without awareness
of their factual status as supernatural data, save under the guidance
of faith. Theologians who admit a positive inner ordination
to a supernatural end by means of a supernatural 'existential' [17]

[17] Thus K. Rahner, s.j., 'Ein Weg zur Bestimmung des Verhältnisses von Natur und
Gnade' ('Concerning the Relationship between Nature and Grace') *Theological
Investigations*, 1, London and Baltimore 1962, 297–317; also published in *Orientierung*
(30 June 1950). Following Rahner, H. U. von Balthasar, 'Der Begriff der Natur in
der Theologie,' ZKT, 75 (1953), 452–61; J. P. Kensy, s.j., 'Reflections on Human

must yet take into account a positive supernatural reality impinging on experience as a modifying mode of our natural being. Many are of opinion that the supernatural virtues have a proper formal object which is experienced in this way in its particular character. We do not propose to enter into this dogmatic question. Surely every theologian should hold as certain that we do experience a kind of concupiscence determined by the supernatural, without being required by the essence of absolute nature *to be so determined* or to be true for every mode of existence. Similarly, do we not experience the effects of grace without being aware that it is grace?

Natural law must take into account the realities deriving from the supernatural order and the history of salvation. In our present condition we must, for example, exercise a greater circumspection on sexual matters than was necessary in paradise where man had more powerful aids to stabilizing his faculties in harmony. The reality as we experience it and as we view it in its moral aspects is not simply and exclusively nature as theology uses the word.[18] Nor can the moral judgment arising from it be called *natural* law in the same simple sense and in all its elements as it may for

---

Nature and the Supernatural,' TS, 14 (1953), 280–7; L. Malevez, S.J., 'La gratuité du surnaturel,' NRT, 75 (1953), 561–86, 673–89; E. Brisbois, S.J., 'Le desir de voir Dieu,' NRT, 63 (1936), 1103–5 (quoted by Malevez, *op. cit.*). The judgments of theologians on this subject are still divided, especially on the question of a concrete determination of this 'existential.'

[18] It is to this 'more' as regards 'nature' in present man, who is the object of our experience, to which certain theologians attach a special importance. Thus K. Rahner, S.J., *art. cit.*, thinks that man as he here and now exists is directed exclusively towards a supernatural end. Yet, according to him, this orientation must not be understood as being merely extrinsic (*extrinsezistisch*). It is quite possible that the philosophical conception of man includes already something of the supernatural existential condition of man as he *de facto* exists. In his article 'Persönliche und sakramentale Frömmigkeit,' *Geist und Leben*, 25 (1952), 412–29 (also in *Theological Investigations*, II, London and Baltimore 1963, 109–33), he writes: 'One cannot object to this that (at least in general) the *empirico*-moral side of human acts for salvation belongs *only* to the domain of natural morality and that it cannot, therefore, be the 'outward appearance' of supernatural grace, since that side is possible even without saving grace.' (421, resp. 121). Even more emphatic on this point than K. Rahner is H. U. von Balthasar in *Karl Barth, Darstellung und Deutung seiner Theologie*, Köln 1951, 294 ff. In his article 'Thomas von Aquin im kirchlichen Denken heute,' *Gloria Dei*, 8 (1953), 65–76, he says succinctly: '. . . secondly, that in the concrete unity of created nature as it in fact exists, a detailed proof of the division made between the natural and the supernatural is not possible' (67). Both Rahner's and von Balthasar's thought originated in suggestions made by H. de Lubac, although they do not wish to simply identify themselves with de Lubac's idea (cf. H. de Lubac, S.J., *Surnaturel*, Paris 1946; 'Le Mystère du surnaturel,' RSR, 36 (1949), 80–121).

example in the principle that one must not lie. We are able to form
a natural judgment about the supernatural facts which we experience
by commencing with the general principles of natural law. We are
not necessarily aware that we go beyond nature in as far as nature
in the theological sense is the ontological foundation of natural law.
This must not obscure the more intimate and fundamental levels
of man's nature which transcend its purely residual character.
On the basis of natural law we can make a moral judgment on other
supernatural facts once they have been revealed, even though they
do not come to us through experience. In this way nobody would
dream of speaking about the true and purely natural law while
using the word nature in the strictly theological sense. In either
usage we have passed beyond nature as an ontological foundation.
Nonetheless we can come to a specific representation of man 'in
general,' with his concommittant moral and juridical order, by
means of concrete human experience. We can achieve a knowledge
of man's metaphysical essence in the strict sense of *definitio metaphysica.* From this point of departure and to the extent that we can
determine the physical content of human nature, the natural law
as pertaining to man with metaphysical necessity will be open to us.
Moreover, this *physis* of man is known, although not according to
its metaphysical definition which, perhaps, can never be determined
completely. But it was in this *physis* that the Creator willed that the
metaphysical essence should be realized. Therefore this *physis* is
also part of the foundation of the moral order. It is not impossible
that God created elements of physical nature in this way only
because he wanted to provide a substratum, patterned on the God-
man, for the supernatural reality which is the true end of his
creation. Nature, although conditioned by the supernatural,
remains nature and distinct from the supernatural. This is true
de facto and not by virtue of the *definitio metaphysica.*[19] We may
now see the way in which many theologians can raise the question
whether God could possibly have created such a nature as the
natura pura.

[19] The effects of the supernatural, on the other hand, which are the object of our
experience must be considered as elements of the supernatural domain, even in the
case of a nature created in view of the supernatural and of Christ.

It is important to keep in mind that the whole of man's specific essence, including his physical essence existing merely *de facto*, is circumscribed by what we commonly call metaphysics. The totality of the corresponding natural law is called metaphysical.[20] 'Metaphysical' natural law therefore, based on the specific essence of 'man in general,' signifies the human being created *de facto* by God.

From a point of view relevant only in matters of detail and perhaps to attain a precise and valid knowledge of the natural and juridical order, it may be expedient to determine whether a certain quality given in experience is based on the *definitio metaphysica*. It is of no importance in establishing an integral picture. The Church does not make any such distinction nor does she require us to make it. Where it is of importance to the moralist he should make it as accurately and, of course, use it as prudently as he would any other judgment.[21]

In this way we gain a wider comprehension, in the moral and juridical order, of man as God's creature. The minimizing tendency of certain modern theologians on this point is, perhaps, due to their too exclusive preoccupation with the supernatural reality of man in his present situation.[22] The philosophic concept of human

---

[20] It seems to us that not sufficient attention has been paid to this in more recent publications. Whenever it is a question of metaphysical natural law, it is always necessary to distinguish well and beforehand whether we are dealing here with the metaphysical nature in the sense of the *definitio metaphysica* or also with the *natura physica*. Thus, in the second hypothesis it is either *exclusively* a question of the specific nature or *also* a question of its *individual* peculiarities in concrete man. To prevent all misunderstanding as far as possible, we shall make use of this term in our further exposition with due caution.

[21] Cf. our brief remarks to this point in *Orientierung*, 15 June 1956, 127 ff.

[22] H. de Lubac considers it to be pure nominalism to attempt to find the same relationship of man to God (confidence in his Providence, love, prayers etc.) in the description of the man of the *natura pura* as in that of the man of Revelation (RSR, *art. cit.*, 89). It is indeed difficult to see any reason for this accusation of nominalism when it is possible to establish that already with nature there exist relations between man and God that remain and must remain valid in the effective order of the supernatural, though in a modified form. If one prefers to 'depart from the sublime,' why is it necessary to speak of nominalism, if we are able to affirm that our actual relations with God would be equally valid—in a modified form—in a purely natural order and that these relations have, consequently, their foundation in the real order of man's nature? (Whether this must be understood as *natura pura* or as *natura absoluta*, see H. de Lubac, *art. cit.*, 92.) H. U. von Balthasar too seems to limit too much the reality of the natural law. He lays particular stress on the fact that our nature *in its particular modality* is created in the perspective of the supernatural, thus in his book on Karl Barth,

nature includes more than the mere notion of creature. It is not altogether undetermined in its content. Consequently it is possible to establish genuine propositions regarding the essence, meaning and obligations of the human person just as well as we do for the human community. We can have an adequate knowledge of the meaning of temporal goods and their place in social and individual life; the meaning and order of sexuality, the essence and duties of marriage [23] are plainly known. So are the nature and order of social and political life. Equal precision of statement on man's relationship to God independently of personal revelation is feasible. Natural knowledge of God is not *per se* impossible, so a corresponding moral knowledge cannot be excluded. Man even without a personal revelation is, in fact, a personal being facing a personal God.

With the natural law in mind we can say that the concrete realities of our human life are truly accessible. If the specific absolute representation of man and the natural law of his being are fundamentally open to us, it follows from what we have said that they are not necessarily known in their precise lineaments. Not every single element of man as we do know him is explicitly in our awareness. Further, we do not know if these very elements belong to the permanent state of nature and natural law willed by God or whether we must in fact take into account the historical state of the subject in which they inhere. As already pointed out this is not important to the formation of a moral judgment. A provisional element of humanity in the concrete can, generally

---

especially on pp. 294 and 301. Cf. also the same author in 'Analogie und Natur. Zur Klärung der theologischen Prinzipienlehre Karl Barths,' *Divus Thomas*, (Fribourg 1945), 23, 3–56, esp. 27 ff. But is nature, as it is *de facto* created, not in reality *nature* in the sense of the *substratum* of the supernatural? And has not this nature truly in itself a *proper* meaning and a *proper* order, although this meaning and this order are not defined in all their details? However, we can leave aside the question of knowing how in fact God would have created a *natura pura* (and the order proper to this nature) as we have indicated already elsewhere). Cf. on this problem also E. Gutwenger, s.j., 'Natur und Übernatur. Gedanken zu Balthasars Werk über die Barthsche Theologie,' ZKT, 75 (1953), 82–97, esp. 92 ff.

[23] See, for example, the traditional teaching on sexual morality. It cannot be denied that the analysis of the physical and spiritual being of man and woman yields a fundamental knowledge of the sexual life and of the state of marriage which retains its validity in any and every situation of the history of salvation and in any supernatural mode of realisation. On the attempts made in the Middle Ages to establish such sexual morals based on natural law, cf. J. Fuchs, s.j., *Die Sexualethik des hl. Thomas von Aquin*, Köln 1949.

speaking, be articulated with sufficient accuracy to place it within the total human essence. In the few instances where this is not so, it is not a question of its belonging to a specific humanity. In this way we have indicated another delimiting area of doubt: empirical reality does not provide the intellect with any apodictic means of recognizing the supernatural reality which it in fact contains. Yet, despite all this, the concrete formation of moral judgments rests on the subject of *all* these elements. The philosopher runs the risk of an erroneous interpretation of the moral knowledge that he does really acquire. Without Revelation it is doubtful if he will, in fact, perceive the different modes of the being of this nature in the history of salvation or appreciate that his statements must be determined by them. He will incline to consider the entire being of man that can be experienced, with its significance and moral norms, as *the* human nature simply. It can hardly occur to him that his thinking transgresses philosophical knowledge in the strict sense. Possibly but not necessarily, the philosopher will reach the false conclusion that the concrete form of concupiscence with its moral norms is necessarily given with the nature of man. Revelation on the original state of man tells us otherwise. Again, he may make statements which he believes final and exhaustive about God as man's final end. His resources as a philosopher will only allow him to know God in a general way as the end of man. He must either leave the question of how this is so as a matter to be determined or by determining the relationship, he must suppose it to be realized in the pure state.[24]

In conclusion, neither the supernatural destiny of man nor our experience of supernatural realities in man in the concrete justify denial of the existence, knowledge and validity of a true natural law. Undoubtedly natural law statements are not exhaustive judgments on man as he actually exists. They are all the same true and valid.

[24] On these two examples, cf. Ch. Boyer, s.j., 'Morale et surnaturel,' *Gregorianum* 29 (1948), 527–543. In § 1 the author criticizes J. Maritain for calling moral philosophy a 'science subalternée à la théologie' (*De la philosophie chrétienne*, Paris 1933; *Science et sagesse*, Paris 1935). Cf. also Th. Deman, o.p., 'Sur l'organisation du savoir morale,' RSPT, 23 (1934), 258–80; J. M. Ramirez, o.p., 'De philosophia morali christiana. Responsio quaedam responsionibus completis et adaequatis Domini Jacobi Maritain,' *Divus Thomas*, 14 (1936), 87–122, 181–204; G. de Broglie, s.j., 'De gratuitate ordinis supernaturalis ad quem homo elevatus est,' *Gregorianum*, 29 (1948), 435–63.

The concept of nature, delimited in the ways indicated, relates to the ontological foundations with which we are now preoccupied but it is also relevant to the noetic element. We shall deal later with the *de facto* interdependency of human knowledge and divine Revelation.

The particular mode of being proper to nature in our state of salvation-history quite evidently conditions part of the moral order. There is nothing in our analysis to prevent calling this 'natural law,' at least in so far as the elements of nature that are conditioned by the supernatural are accessible to experience. Here we follow St Paul. In fact, regarding these elements subject to experience it is man's nature 'in general' which objectively determines the concrete judgment. This very judgment can issue subjectively from our reason without intervention of Revelation. As we have said, we remain conscious of the fact that this second sense of natural law in its ontological basis is not *natural* law in the same fundamental sense as the former.

CHAPTER FOUR

MAN AS GOD'S IMAGE
AND THE NATURAL LAW

The problem for us is to determine the precise sense in which man's nature constitutes natural law. In order to deal with it we must go back to the important theological concept of man's natural likeness to God.

Man's likeness to God as fundamental fact

It is decisive for the meaning and justification of natural law doctrine that we should be clear on this: man's 'nature' is not the work of sin.[1] The consequence of sin is the loss of preternatural and supernatural grace but this loss leaves nature as such untouched. The original man cannot now be recognized in nature, simply because in the original state he was entirely filled with the supernatural and stood in this relationship with God. Human nature has

---

[1] In view of the works of some Protestant theologians, one can justly raise the question of what in fact they mean by the destruction of genuine humanity through sin, if for them sin has to a large extent lost its historical personal character (and, thus, its character of guilt) in favour of a metaphysical and ontological reality. For this seems to be the meaning of sin which Karl Barth simply calls the fact of not being God, of being other, and of emptiness (cf. K. Barth, *Der Römerbrief*, 3 ed., Munich 1933, 149, 232 etc.). Does it not come to the same thing when for P. Althaus creature and sin are ultimately two different forms of thought, the idea of the original state being but a sign of what one wishes to express? (Cf. P. Althaus, *Theologie der Ordnungen*, Gütersloh 1934, 32). And even E. Brunner who strongly objects to a metaphysical attenuation of sin and its culpability, seems to fall into the same error (cf. H. Volk, *Emil Brunners Lehre von dem Sünder*, Münster 1950). F. Delekat (*Die Kirche Jesu Christi und der Staat*, Berlin 1933, 30) and likewise, R. Hauser (*Autorität und Macht. Die staatliche Autorität in der neueren protestantischen Ethik und in der katholischen Gesellschaftslehre*, Heidelberg 1949, 137) come to the conclusion that F. Gogarten's teaching on sin, too, is really a philosophical epistemology. Other theologians, however, object to such metaphysical explanations of sin; thus in his intention and words—as has been said already —E. Brunner, and explicitly G. Wünsch (cf. R. Hauser, *ibid.*, 218 f.).

not now ceased to be the nature of man, just as it was of the original man. Certainly man is now a sinner; original sin entered the first man and remains in all his descendants. We must be aware also of personal sin and of all the consequences of both, which mankind in the present economy has to bear. It is quite possible to distinguish, though not perhaps in every single case, between creation, sin and the consequences of sin. Since the fact of personality and the difference, say, between man and woman do not result from the Fall, the reality which we call 'nature' does not have its origin in the sin of man but comes directly from the hands of God. God speaks through it and reveals himself in it. It bears his features and it is his image. How could it be otherwise since nature is the creature of God?

It is in this manner that the salient elements in the problem of nature should be emphasized rather than saying that God and creature are utterly different or that, having nothing in common, they cannot be alike in all their unlikeness. After all, do they not already correspond in *being*, however differently being may be attributed to God and his creatures? The very principle of difference or specification in being must have its basis in God. Even in this the creature cannot be absolute and independent of his Creator. The complete superiority and absoluteness of God and the total dependence of man are precisely the bases for the solidarity of God and man in essence and existence. The notion of an independent creature would possess the distinguishing quality of the Creator, absoluteness. Being a creature always includes being God's image. For this reason the spiritual man understands himself and the world surrounding him as the word and work of the Creator. This is true not only for the word revealing God's being but also as revealing the divine will. The being of the spiritual man who is the image of God includes the obligation not to profane the divine, for this is likewise realized in the creature. By creating an image of himself God, through this image, gave a binding and necessary *in-formation* to the behaviour of the creature composed of body and soul. God's absoluteness communicates to creatures-as-his-image the character of absolute, normative moral power. Consequently, the elements of moral and juridical order stemming from man's likeness to God are based on God's being. Man cannot accept his life-norm originally and primarily from the outside. This is true vis-à-vis any legislator, even a personal God revealing himself and making his demands directly. Man's own being within the being of the world surrounding him, is indeed God's *demand*. Only in so far as the being of man is already actualized internally as God's demand is it possible to understand God's moral requirements from the outside. This relationship indifferently holds for man's obligations to civil or ecclesiastical authority or even for those demands of God which he has revealed to us himself. They are all truly divine and therefore impose valid moral imperatives. It is because the individuality of man's being must first render it possible and in fact does render it possible, that a positive moral demand of God or man can reach him at all.

Man's analysis of himself is therefore always and at the same time a vision of God's reality. Because of God's absoluteness it is also a vision of God's will. In the presence of the moral and juridical order which is based on the nature of the spiritual and personal creature and consequently on God's being itself, this will of God cannot remain indeterminate. Such analysis gives us a certain picture of the relationship between God and man, a picture of man's life as owing to God. It shows a binding scale of different human values. It brings to light the reality of the social character of man and the rules of social conduct. Family and State, politics and economics are developments of life that are prefigured in man's being. Because all this reflects something divine and absolute it is the apodictic norm of life, not in itself independently of God but as a free gift and image. The existence of human nature as God's image undestroyed by original sin is, moreover, the clear doctrine of Holy Scripture.[2] The Bible certainly knows that man's likeness to

[2] Cf. on this subject the very full exposition given by G. Söhngen in 'Die biblische Lehre von der Gottebenbildlichkeit des Menschen,' MTZ, 2 (1951), 52–76. On the Protestant side, cf. E. Brunner, 'Der Mensch im Widerspruch,' *Die christliche Lehre vom wahren und wirklichen Menschen*, Berlin 1937, Beilage I. Cf. also K. Barth, *Die kirchliche Dogmatik*, III/1, 2 ed., Zollikon-Zürich 1947, 205 ff.; cf. likewise, L. Berg, *Der Mensch, Herr seiner Rechte*, . . . *nach Thomas von Aquin*, Bensheim 1940; H. Hansen, s.v.d., 'Gottebenbildlichkeit, ein Grundgedanke der Moral,' *Festschrift* . . . *St Gabriel*, Wien-Mödling 1939, 45–104.

God has been lost through sin; it is this wonderful likeness to God which we regain in Christ through baptism. It is this which renders us like to him. Living in Christ, yet still in the flesh, we bear this likeness in us already so that it may radiate in the end in its full glory. Holy Scripture speaks also of a likeness to God that has not been lost with original sin and that remains in man independently of Redemption in Christ. It is in this sense that the words of St Paul, 'man is the image and glory of God' (1 *Cor.* 11: 7), and those of St James, 'all men are made in the likeness of God' (*Jam.* 3: 9) are very likely—though probably not exclusively—to be understood. Both statements of the New Testament evidently refer to the corresponding text in the account of creation (*Gen.* 1: 26 ff.). St Paul's exposition in the Epistle to the Romans is of special importance in this connection. In this Epistle he says that the nature of man without Revelation (*Rom.* 2: 14) is itself a Revelation of God and of his will. It therefore gives him a true knowledge of God and of the moral life and results in a genuine love of God.

There can be no possible doubt that St Paul spoke in this text of an ontological likeness to God. Modern Protestant theology, rejecting this ontological character [3] to a great extent, can of course find no access to a true teaching on the natural law, or at least it will find such a teaching very difficult.[4] For Protestant thought, man's relationship to God is *purely* actual, personal and dynamic.

[3] The denial of the ontological character of man's true likeness to God is taken for granted in modern Protestantism and can be found in Barth as well as in Brunner and —very recently—in Thielicke. The latter, especially, argues strongly against the ontological conception of Catholic theology, for example where he writes: 'Man's likeness to God is exclusively a teleological and not an ontological concept; or in other terms, we are dealing here with a state of relations not of being' (*Theologische Ethik*, I, n. 769); 'Man as imago Dei is only a mirror, not phosphorus' (n. 879); 'the question of the loss of certain ontic attributes is therefore neither to be affirmed nor is it to be denied; the question as it stands, is simply wrong. For we are always dealing merely with the preservation or the breaking up of a certain *relation*' (n. 792). Thus, Thielicke not only rejects the concept of a spiritual substance; he sees here a fundamental *theological* problem—as he formulates it—that every likeness to God which is based on being would be a *proprium* and not an *alienum*, that is, an attribute and not an exterior good of man. Yet in this way Thielicke's idea of 'God alone,' of God's exclusive initiative, would be called in question (cf. n. 1134). Cf. also E. Brunner, *Dogmatik*, II, Zürich 1950, 70: '. . . so that . . . man's likeness to God will be understood not as an independently existing substance but as a relation. And that this be rendered possible is of the highest importance'; cf. K. Barth, *Die kirchliche Dogmatik*, II/2, 3 ed., Zollikon-Zürich 1948, 589; III/1, 2 ed., 1947, 206.
[4] On the relation between the doctrine of man's likeness to God and that of the natural law, cf. H. Thielicke, *Theologische Ethik*, I, *loc. cit.*, n. 1014.

His likeness to God consists only in responsibility and in the fact of being called and in responding. This is to say that Protestant thought finds our likeness to God in a relation. The spiritual being and therefore also man's being composed of body and spirit, is understood as a substantial 'appeal' from God. If these propositions are true then the foundation for a real natural law does not exist. Does it not issue in pure nominalism if this likeness to God is merely a relation that tells us nothing about man and his being but, strictly and finally, only about God and the love with which he speaks to man? Certainly, man exists only through God's love. Man from his own resources alone has nothing of an image of God which he could offer to him in personal love. God's love *creates* its object—man. He is truly and in himself the 'love' of God and consequently not merely an indifferent correlative point. Rather he is the image of God's glory which God embraces in his love. Because man stems entirely from the love of God it is of small account that he has a particular being, a nature directed to God in its composition of body and soul loved by God. This does not stand over against the idea of 'God alone' properly understood. All that man can offer to God as creature and image of him is entirely 'love' of God. It is *proprium* and *alienum* at the same time. A pure *proprium* would exclude the created likeness to God and a pure *alienum* would imply a false nominalism. It would imply a denial of the earnestness of God's love.

Of course, nobody will (or indeed can) deny completely [5] that man's likeness to God has a relationship to the world of being. This does not justify any minimizing of man's being which would in fact deprive it of that very likeness to God which is essential to it. This is its direct and particular relation to God and constitutes its theological significance. Man's nature is no *profanum* having only an instrumental meaning for the reality of God's image. It is natur-

[5] Thielicke admits frankly that man's likeness to God has also an ontic aspect (cf. *op. cit.*, nn. 798-811, 1062 ff., 1105 ff.). Yet when Barth, opposing Brunner, calls this ontic aspect (spirit!) a trifle, a profanum, Theilicke follows him enthusiastically, saying that the ontic aspect does not in any way characterize man in his relationship to God, because this relationship exists only on God's side (1063 f.); it does not rise to the rank of a theological theme (1105). It is precisely on this point that Theilicke differs from Catholic theology (*ibid.*).

ally impossible to envisage it detached or separated from God's
activity and love. Precisely because it comes continually and entirely
from the hand of God and is therefore entirely his image it is
theologically powerful. The fact can only be denied if one does not
recognize creation *ex nihilo* as true creation. Every creation *ex
nihilo* is nothing in itself but is truly something through God.
It is precisely for that reason the image of the glory of the Divine
Being. It becomes with undeniable necessity the God-given norm
of the life of the spiritual man.

Human nature may be taken as a true residue of original man in
his pristine fullness as the image of God and consequently as something that is the image of God regulating man's life. 'Residue'
must be understood not as something changed and now different
or as the remains of something destroyed. It is a genuine work of
the loving hand of God. It has a theological significance not only
because it is a residue of the 'real' (i.e. original) man, even though
it is no longer man in the 'true' (i.e. original) sense; it really
represents man undestroyed in his natural aspect. To be a residue
does not only depict man according to his merely formal aspect.
It is not a restricted consideration of the possibility or even the
fact of his being called by God or his ability or disposition to
answer God's call. It envisages his material aspects equally with
these. The 'residue' is, in fact, the entire being of man as composed
of body and soul, including the *relations* between body and soul.
It takes into its intelligibility the relation between man and God
and those obtaining between man and man, both individual and
communal. It is open to the reciprocity between man and the
material universe and to everything human that is God's work.
It includes everything that belongs to man as God's image and
therefore represents the work of divine love and everything that
constitutes a divine demand. Every material and concrete content
of man's being must be understood in its intact natural character.
This natural character is understood, therefore, as part of God's
image, and consequently as the word and demand of God, in that
sense of 'demand' already indicated.

These deliberations of the revealed notion of the likeness of man to God lead to the conclusion, as far as a theological treatment of natural rights is concerned, that the entire order of natural law is based on God's *being*. It draws its strength from that source and whoever trespasses against the divine order offends God himself. This statement does not imply that every partial order of finality found in any creature is inviolable simply because it is based on God's being and reflects him in the manner proper to this creature. A fair example is a consideration of the sexual organs and their proper activity. The sexual act, has, no doubt, its biological finality. Are we therefore obliged to respect this finality? Here we must distinguish: biological finality can be referred not only to man but also to animals. We may ask whether man as a person has the right to induce an activation of the sexual organism of the animal, which is admittedly without personality, but is contrary none-theless to its biological finality. May this be done for the purpose of obtaining sperms for scientific research? No doubt, the answer is clear. But why? Because animal sexuality with its biological finality, as well as the animal in its totality, is subject to the free disposal of man. This biological finality, though based on God's being as a positive representation of the divine perfections in the animal world, is not its only finality. It participates in a finality superior to the animal, since it is ordained to man's utility. In so far as this is a superior finality it is based on God's being. The biological finality of *sexuality as such* does not therefore exclude the fact that one biological end may be checked in order to achieve another. The mere fact that the biological finality is based on God's being does not call for such a consequence.

What of the biological sexuality proper to man? Sexuality as such does not demand any other conclusion than the one already discussed. The obligation to respect the biological finality of man's sexuality derives first of all from the fact that man is God's image which is to say that it derives from man's spiritual and personal being. The requirement is morally mandatory because man as such belongs *directly and exclusively* to God. His being derives from God in such a way that he is obliged to live his life *as* coming from God. One part of this being is his biological sexuality with its particular end and this is not subordinated to any other end in the created order. Man is bound to respect it not because it is a biological sexuality with a finality based on God's being but because it is the biological sexuality of man *as God's image*. The obligation to realize one's own personal God-given humanity is directly based on God's being. The obligation to respect the biological finality of sexuality on the other hand, is based on God's being only indirectly in so far, namely, as sexuality is part of the totality of man's being. The relation of sexuality as such to animal sexuality specifically (which implies a human superiority with the right of disposal) is similarly based directly on man's God-derived humanity but only indirectly on God's being.

It seems then that it does not suffice for a demonstration of the obligatory character of an order or finality in creatures that we prove this order and this finality to be based on God's being. As the example of sexuality shows, it can happen that a creature, in spite of its likeness to God and perhaps also because of its difference from God, has a second finality differing from the one expressing itself in the biological nature of this creature. The finalities and 'orders' manifested in the spiritual and personal nature of man are all obligatory because they are part of *the being* (and not merely of the 'possessions') of the human person.

This does not mean that all orders of being and all finalities permit the ambivalence here indicated. One may ask whether there is an essential difference between the orders and finalities of the spiritual domain on the one hand and those of the material domain on the other. In fact the spiritual domain represents directly a completely different kind of image of God. The word image (imago) in opposition to 'resemblance' or 'similitude' to God can be employed directly only in the spiritual domain. The body is an image of God merely to the extent that it is part of the unity of the person. Faith, sincerity, justice, charity etc., are obligations that originate more profoundly and directly in God's being than, for example, obligations of the sexual order. Chastity, since we have taken this example, being part of the virtue of temperance establishes an order in sexual desire and therefore preserves human sexuality in the presence of disordered desire. It thus safeguards directly the magnitude and dignity of the spirit and its superiority over the senses. Respect for the biological sexual order *as such* does not have this signification.[6] Since God created man as we actually find him, all that is good for man is determined by God's nature and this remains the case as long as man remains man.

The theonomy of the natural law

If Revelation speaks to us of the likeness of human nature to God it follows that the natural law is the foundation of true *theonomous* ethics.[7] The doctrine of the natural law does not consider man as separate from God but as the work and therefore the word of God. All true ethics must be theonomous because God is good and what is good can be discovered only by turning to his Revelation. Revelation is possible through the *work* of creation either in its permanent duration or in its present reality as emanating from God and determined by him. It is found as well in personal *address* either to mankind in general or to an individual man. This is to say that it is ours either through Revelation in creation or through verbal Revelation. It is for God to decide in which way he wishes to reveal himself to us. It may be better to say: Revelation through creation is presupposed by all theonomous ethics, because verbal Revelation can only be addressed to the 'listening' man. This man is necessarily an image of his God and consequently is himself a Revelation through creation. The question is whether God wants

[6] It would be interesting to compare these considerations on the meaning of the material 'orders' with the various speculations of St Thomas Aquinas on the possibility of dispensations, granted by God, from certain precepts of natural law, including the *praecepta primaria*. St Thomas, relying on the facts of the Bible, thinks such dispensations possible: the Creator as such can in fact intervene in creation in a miraculous way. Or in other terms, by the very fact that a being, once created, finds itself placed within a new order and subjected to more elevated ends, then it is itself changed in its significance and thus the *materia mutata* requires the application of different natural laws. On this subject, cf. O. Lottin, O.S.B., *Le droit naturel chez saint Thomas d'Aquin et ses prédécesseurs*, 2 ed., Bruges 1931, 93–6.
[7] It would be a misinterpretation of the Christian doctrine of the natural law to believe that it presupposes a universe independent of God. Cf. this conception in W. Wiesner, 'The law of nature and social institutions,' *Christian faith and the common life*, (ed. N. Ehrenstrom) London 1938, (101–41), 106. This conception is sometimes found in Catholic authors.

to reveal himself through his word beyond the Revelation given in creation or whether he wants to confirm or explain more explicitly the Revelation given in creation. To accept God's word and will from positive Revelation only and to recognize as a theonomous norm only the moral norm received in this way, is erroneous. It contradicts revealed teaching on man's likeness to God.[8] A rationalistic conception of the natural law on the other hand, which does not conceive man as God's image and work and thus tries to determine morality by means of reason alone, can hardly be called theonomous. It is not based on listening to God's self-revelation but gives absolute value to man and to abstract ideas. Even though knowledge of morality by means of reason alone is objectively based on the work and image of God, it could be achieved without subjectively knowing this basic foundation and consequently without the docility due to God's word. This is in fact the attitude of the autonomous man.

The theonomous moral norms of the natural law imply that the definition of what is good is not taken directly from the word of God but from man and his world. The definition is drawn from 'things' and 'objects' as has been said.[9] If a sexual ethic is deduced

[8] To appeal exclusively to positive revelation is a symptom common to all who favour theonomous ethics yet deny any genuine revelation of the natural law, for example K. Barth. The same holds good for those who question the *absolute character* of natural law, resp. of 'the order of creation,' so for example E. Brunner; W. Künneth (*Politik zwischen Dämon und Gott*, Berlin 1954, 122 ff.) rejects any doctrine that appeals to orders which would be tantamount to a revelation outside the supernatural revelation. J. Klein likewise fails to see clearly the theonomy of natural law when he writes that 'the rationalism of natural law within the domain of the good which man has been ordered to practice, appears (theoretically) as normativism and (practically) as legalism. This collects man's entire activity in the numerous meshes of a net of commandments and presupposes (and wants to have actually prepared) an obligatory legal solution for every case. It can easily be seen how such considerations consider the good only in itself and independent of God. The connection with the will of God is purely external' (cf. 'Ursprung und Grenzen der Kasuistik,' *Aus Theologie und Philosophie. Festschrift F. Tillmann*, Düsseldorf 1950, 240). However, Klein seems to consider the practical subjective life of the individual rather than the ethical norm in itself. In this case he ought to have pointed out that this is only a danger and not an intrinsic necessity.
[9] E. Brunner, *Das Gebot und die Ordnungen. Entwurf einer protestantisch-theologischen Ethik*, New York (n.d.), 83. From this passage (83) it is evident, how little even Brunner values the doctrine of natural law of Catholic theology (in its content). He writes: 'According to the Aristotelian-thomistic way of thinking, the principle of good is, objectively, never the divine will and, subjectively, not the obedience rendered to God but " the suitability for human nature." Good is " whatever makes man more perfect in himself " . . . It is, furthermore, in accordance with this conception that " goodness and badness depends on the objects to which our will is directed," and this more

from the analysis of man's sexuality, economics from the analysis of the economic life, and the legal order governing the body and its life from the analysis of man's personality, such ethics have the appearance of autonomy and *apparently* lack theonomy. In discussion of natural law, should the concept of the 'conflict of rights' be used as if norms deriving from different 'objects' were at variance with one another, it would seem in this case also that theonomy had been abandoned; God can demand only one thing at a time. The natural law theorist, even before giving a definite solution, will certainly remark that all orders deriving from different 'objects' are connected with one another in a harmonious cosmos [10] of orders, and that therefore a true 'conflict of rights' is already excluded. He will tend to hold this without even looking for God's demanding will. Should we inquire in our ethical work about the *adiaphora* (that is, the possibility of indifferent acts) it would seem that man's theonomy had been forgotten. How could there be a question about man's indifferent acts in the face of God? Indeed, most natural law moralists will say that they do not in fact recognize the indifference of practical human actions if these actions really belong to the domain of subjective moral activity.[11]

---

precisely in the sense that " something is good for a being in so far as it harmonizes with its inclinations and abilities or is able to render them more perfect. All actions which correspond to the specific nature of man, are good.' Brunner has taken these quotations from the moral philosophy of Cathrein. He does not pay sufficient attention to the fact that, according to Catholic moral doctrine, the *material side* of morality has a corresponding *formal side*, which however is better revealed in the Augustinian than in the thomistic ethic. He can criticize the 'Aristotelian-thomistic way of thinking' severely only because he himself does not sufficiently appreciate its material side. *This is due to his insufficient conception of man's likeness to God.* He states that 'nothing is good but obedience to the commandment of God, precisely because it is obedience. No motive of material determination is here of any value' (46). 'All is neutral technique —except the setting into order of this technique by love. Nothing is purely technical and this is so precisely because all, even the smallest thing, is connected with the whole and borne by an idea' (104). 'Consequently, one can say both at the same time: there is no *adiaphora*, and everything is an *adiaphoron*—with the exception of love' (*ibid.*). We said above, that Brunner does not appreciate the material side *sufficiently*, because he does not see it from the standpoint of man's likeness to God. Nevertheless, he does value this side too because he knows that the will of God is established in the '*orders*' of being (cf. 109) and emphasizes that it would be religious fanaticism to try to experience God's will in every moment only by faith guided by the Holy Ghost, that is without the directives of the natural order (cf. 79). For further details on this question cf. Ch. VI.

[10] W. Elert, *Das christliche Ethos: Grundlinien der lutherischen Ethik*, Tübingen 1949, 110, states that natural law is 'not a seamless, uncontradicted system.' But he does not proceed from nature as the image of God but as 'possessed by a demon.'

[11] On these two questions cf. below p. 131 ff.

We have the right to speak of human autonomy, though only in a restricted sense. The norms of the natural law are not imposed upon man from the outside but are taken from man himself. One of the reasons for man's likeness to God is precisely the fact that he participates in the autonomy of God. Similarly the definition of what is good is not given us by God's arbitrary will but is taken from his being and nature. So, man can know what is good by analysing his own being and nature. Man's autonomy is a gift because God revealed himself by creating his image. It follows that man's autonomy is in the last analysis a theonomy that appears less heteronomous than does positive legislation. This is doubtlessly the danger of a rationalistic conception of the natural law as implying the absolute autonomy of man. The Christian doctrine of the natural law is not subject to this risk. For the Christian the search for and the possession of moral norms consists in listening to the will of God and in obedient incorporation into his creation.

Therefore in all genuine theonomy there is room for the good 'in itself.' This is the good which is discovered and recognized in man's nature. It is recognized by God because he has no choice but to recognize it as good. This is not to be understood as if God were merely the guardian of the good 'in itself,' a good facing God in its absoluteness. It has been said that God is not the guardian but the Creator of the good.[12] Yet even this can be denied: God cannot be said to decide arbitrarily what he wants to describe and present to man as good.[13] This would be nominalism. Christ says: 'God alone is good' (*Matt.* 19: 17). What is good cannot be defined according to something which is not in God—an idea for example; neither can it be declared alien to God by God's own arbitrary will. God *is* good. What is good, is, to speak in human terms, already good antecedently to God's will and *a fortiori* previous to all ideas and all creatures. The distinction between mastery of the spirit over the senses and mere observance of the sexual order was evident already in the fact that the sexual order can be violated without sexual desire or sensual pleasure, as is often the case with prostitutes.

[12] E. Brunner, *op. cit.*, 39.
[13] On moral voluntarism in the Middle Ages and in modern times cf. G. M. Manser, O.P., *Das Naturrecht in Thomistischer Beleuchtung*, Freiburg-Br. 1944, 41–50.

On the other hand, a failure in the mastery of the spirit over the senses does not necessarily bring with it a violation of sexual order. This is certified in the case, for example, of the natural but immoderate sexual use of marriage ('hedonism'). We can therefore continue to call God the guardian of the good, for in him there is no difference between nature and will and his will always approves the good that derives from his nature. We should say, and with good reason, that God is the Creator of the good. We can say so because the reality and consequently the existential validity of the corresponding order depend entirely on God's creative will. Creation and natural law are one. It is an essential necessity which is within God's discretion to decide for or against their *actual* existence and validity but he cannot separate them without changing man's nature in itself.[14]

The fact that the natural law is truly theonomous and at the same time relatively autonomous, indicates what God demands from man in obedience. He requires of us what is *suitable for man* and what will promote his perfection. To a theonomy which is not (or not also) based on man's likeness to God but which looks to a 'call and demand' issuing only from the positive Revelation of God, the question of what is suitable for man must seem blasphemous. For it, the essence of what is good is what God demands on the one side and our obedience on the other. Yet whoever knows the Revelation of man's likeness to God also understands that the natural law represents in fact a demand, though not one based on the will but on the being of God and consequently on man as God's image. Whoever accepts God must also accept his image. The perfection of man as God's image is objectively the adoration and glorification of God. The question of God's will for man includes always (or at least also) the question of man's perfection. An opposition between these two aspects would only arise if God

---

[14] Pufendorf, *Apologia pro se et suo libro*, Germanopoli, § 19, already made the following remark: 'If God were subject to an absolute good, then a principle would exist which is anterior to God, or, at least, eternally equal to God.' H. H. Schrey, 'Naturrecht,' *Evangelisches Soziallexikon*, Stuttgart 1954, 752, presents the doctrine of St Thomas Aquinas on natural law in a similar way, saying that the 'will of God is wisdom and as such is bound to justice and cannot free itself from this universal norm.' Seen in this way, justice could be conceived as being superior to God and not as being based on God's essence.

and man had nothing in common, if God were *wholly other*. God's
love and his nature have become visible in man; man's true acceptance of himself is always at the same time a true acceptance of God.
This acceptance is always at the same time an acceptance of one's
own self.[15] This is true objectively but man can overlook the fact.
He can also freely ignore God but in doing so he will ignore his
own true and complete self.

The righteous man, then, inquires about what is suitable for
him, what serves the true perfection of his being. He knows that
in doing so he inquires by implication about the nature of God
and consequently about the good. He does so not to distort his own
self but to bring it to perfection. He sees in it, finally, his dedication
to the good and to God. To discover this penetration and union of
God and man—God's image—to recognize one's own self as the
image, word, and demand of God, to conceive every element of
the natural law as God's guidance and personal message, is the
great and wonderful task of man's living. This is true above all for
the Christian to whom God has given the special Revelation of
his likeness to him. The man who, with full clarity, sees the true
theonomy of natural morality will mould his life alike on a 'purely
moral' fidelity as in a genuinely 'religious' reverence. He will
do this because most of the moral norms of life (such as those of
politics, economics, family, marriage etc.) are known to us as
expressions of the natural being of man, even after we have been
instructed about them by God's Revelation.[16]

Genuine theonomy bestows upon the natural law and its norms,
derived from the objective realm and suitable for man, its true
strength. This is the case not only subjectively but also objectively.
There is more than a 'purely moral' difference between good and
evil; this difference turns out to be an absolute, divine and personal
obligation. It is precisely by means of the recognition of theonomy
that good and evil become moral norms in the full sense. Love is

[15] Cf. the efforts of a Protestant theologian to disentangle the question of self-love in
N. H. Soe, *Christliche Ethik. Ein Lehrbuch*, Munich 1949, 147–50 (§ 25: 'May a
Christian love himself?').
[16] On the question of personal religious understanding of the natural law cf. J. Fuchs,
s.j., 'Situationsethik in theologischer Sicht,' *Scholastik*, 27 (1952), 161–82, esp. 172 ff.;
'Morale théologique et morale de situation,' NRT, 1954, 1073–85.

the form of all the virtues. It is because of a theonomy based on man's existential likeness to God that true moral obligations and true moral virtues exist. Only in this sense is it accurate to say that morality and religion are not identical, although they refer to one another and are connected with one another. If, on the other hand, moral theonomy is not based on man's existential likeness to God, love *alone* rooted in faith and manifesting itself in obedience has value but moral virtue as such loses its importance in the eyes of God.

Christ-centred morality and the natural law

Revelation of man's natural likeness to God has the last word also on the problem of how the Christian moral order is founded in Christ. It is impossible to say that Christian morality is exclusively based on the historical Christ, that is—on his historical epiphany. At least this cannot be asserted in such a way that all its elements in their substance result from and can only be known through this historical faith. Even without the historical coming of Christ—we speak in the abstract because the concept of the natural law implies a certain abstraction, as we have stated already—the belief in his likeness to God binds man and determines his actions to a great extent and with absolute theonomous necessity. This does not jeopardise Christ's place in the plan of creation: for this reason we used the expression 'the historical Christ' to indicate *the coming* into this world of faith in Christ. Neither does it controvert the opinion that certain aspects of human *nature* have been created merely for the reason that man was to be subject to the supernatural life and the image of the Word Incarnate.[17] Seen objectively, the natural law is evidently based on the Logos as the eternal Son of God. This in the special manner in which all things are created by the Father in and through the Logos (*John* 1).[18] Man's likeness to God is the mirror of the divine image

[17] Cf. J. B. Schuster, s.j., 'Natürliches und übernatürliches Sittengesetz,' *Scholastik* 13 (1938), 392–9.
[18] To this point attention has been called recently by J. Kraus, 'Zum Problem des christozentrischen Aufbaus der Moraltheologie,' *Divus Thomas*, 30 (1952), 257–72. In favour of a Christocentric approach, cf. F. Tillmann, *Handbuch der katholischen*

in which the eternal Logos portrays the Father. Human morality tends always to an effective assimilation with the Logos and thus with the Father as 'first principle.' What has been said above is of course equally true of the historical and pneumatic Christ in so far as he is the Logos. However, it applies not only to Christ as the Logos but also to Christ as the God-man. Scripture in fact tells us that in him and for him all things were created (cf. *Col.* 1: 15–17; *Eph.* 1: 9–23; 1 *Cor.* 8: 6).

From the subjective and noetic point of view the natural law is necessarily placed—as we have already indicated—along man's path leading to the God-Man Jesus Christ when man discovers Christ as the Way, the Truth and the Life.[19] The will to believe in Christ and to adhere to him signifies, in fact and always, a moral decision that must logically be previous to faith in Christ. Therefore it receives its objective expression in norms that are independent of this faith. The natural law indicates in what case and in whom we may believe and to whom one may or even must surrender oneself. Christ the Lord, as the prototype and the norm of man, represents a positive value for human nature; man's attitude towards this positive value is necessarily determined from the moral viewpoint by man's being. This is the natural law, even though its expression in natural terms remains hypothetical.

Yet, even after Christ has been given to us and has been accepted by us in faith the total content of Christian morality cannot be

---

Sittenlehre, III, 'Die Idee der Nachfolge Christi,' 4 ed., Düsseldorf 1953; and 'Um eine katholische Sittenlehre,' *Menschenkunde im Dienste der Seelsorge und Erziehung, Festchrift Müncker*, ed. W. Heinen and J. Höffner, Trier 1948, 9–19; A. van Kol, s.j., *Christus' Plaats in S. Thomas' Moralasysteem* (Bijdragen-Bibliotheek, Deel I), Roermond-Maaseik 1957; B. Häring, c.ss.r., *Das Heilige und das Gute, Religion und Sittlichkeit in ihrem gegenseitigen Bezug*, Krailing vor München 1950, 271–90; *The Law of Christ*, I, Cork and Westminster, 1962; I. Zeiger, s.j., 'Katholische Moraltheologie heute,' SZ, 134 (1938), 143–53; N. Krautwig, o.f.m., 'Entfaltung der Herrlichkeit Christi. Eine Wesensbestimmung katholischer Moraltheologie,' *Wissenschaft und Weisheit*, 7 (1940), 73–99; G. Thils, *Tendances actuelles en théologie morale*, Gembloux 1940; C. Robert, 'La théologie morale en Allemagne,' RSR, 23 (1949), 111–19; etc. In opposition to a Christocentric approach, cf. especially O. Schilling, 'Reform der Moraltheologie?', TPQ ,92 (1939), 451–56; J. Kraus, *art. cit.*, L. B. Gillon, 'L'imitation du Christ et la morale de Saint Thomas,' *Angelicum*, 30 (1959), 263–86.
[19] This is also the opinion of St Thomas when he says, 'Oportet quod prima directio actuum nostrorum ad finem (consequently the direction of all acts) fiat per legem naturalem (*S. Theol.*, I-II, 91, 2 ad 2); rationis prima regula est lex naturalis (I-II, 95, 2).

based upon Christ from the noetic and subjective standpoint without including considerations on the natural law. Christ's words on morality for man are not intended to be a system of Christian morality. Many questions on the concrete structure of human life are not even mentioned, for example, economic, political and married life etc. Neither does the appearance of the historical Christ allow us precise indicatives or rules. We must, therefore, take Christ's appearance in a purely formal sense, that is in his absolute surrender to the Father and consequently in his faithfulness to what is called nature. Nonetheless, man's nature must be analysed and from this, the necessary moral relations must be deduced in order to discover the actual content of Christ's rule of life. His life, like his words, can thus give valuable help to correct thinking and knowledge or serve as a confirmation of what has been discovered already. Christ's words, seemingly containing a formal assertion of natural morality, can be employed to supply the content of Christian morality by way of the natural law. Indeed it must not be overlooked that a formal assertion of the natural law binds us to it in a new (and this time), a positive way.

In the God-man the Father has given us the prototype of the Christian. Christ is the prototype of every man and above all the Christian, even regarding the natural sphere and the domain of the natural law. He is our prototype because he is truly man and realizes in himself the essence of man's natural being, no more and no less than we do. This applies to Christ in an absolutely individual manner.[20] Christ constitutes therefore the principle of Christian

[20] In addition a supplement taken from our *Theologia moralis generalis*, I, Rome, 2 ed., 1963, 101–3: 'Since all men were created and redeemed " in Christ," he, the God-man, crucified and risen, is the model of the Christian life (cf. I *Cor.* 8: 6; *Col.* 1: 15–19; *Eph.* 1: 3–10). For the scriptures seem to indicate that God's primary intention was that the Word should be made flesh, to be, as incarnate, the firstborn among many brethren. In taking flesh, Christ took to himself the whole of man (except for sin) and every man, putting himself at the head of them all.

Through him, and by being conformed to him, men are truly men and share in his supernatural life. Each man of course does this in his own way but even their individuality is rooted in Christ, the God-man.

It is true therefore that, objectively, Christ is the moral standard and measure for all men, both in the supernatural and natural orders. For if all created things, natural and supernatural, are rooted in him the same is true of the corresponding natural and supernatural moral orders.

But as in Christ human nature was intended as a vessel of the Word, so our nature

morality taken in the proper sense: but we are thus also obliged to accept Christ's human being precisely because we are dealing with the God-*man*. We must do this in all seriousness and recognize its natural likeness to God as the norm for us. Consequently man cannot but strive to acquire the natural knowledge of this norm; he may not ignore the help offered by Revelation.[21] The statement made above that Christ's humanity represents a new and positive obligation for all men regarding the natural law is equally valid for our being-in-Christ, the God-*man*. According to the way in which we conceive this union with Christ, the natural man in us (and thus the natural law) is confirmed in different ways peculiar to each of the two supernatural realities. For our part and following

---

seems to be meant to be a receptacle of the supernatural life: the consequence on the moral level being that the natural order, moral in itself, is directed towards the supernatural; more, it is part of it, since grace is the final perfection of man as created in Christ. Objectively, therefore, though not from our point of view, there is a natural law because of the existence of Christ's law; and Christ's law exists because in him all subsist. This remains true even though the natural law runs, and can be known by man, independently of Christian revelation, since all men were in fact created in Christ. Hence any breach of the natural law is, and always was, objectively and in itself, an offence against Christ and his law.

Christ is at once the most concrete and the most general moral norm. The most concrete—since he is a single person in whom, as God-man, all fulness dwells; he is the pattern for everything that exists, though for each thing in its own way. The most general—since all is rooted in him and measured against him: natural and supernatural moral laws, universal norms and the 'law' of each individual and situation, the teaching of the Church and each man's conscience.

So we can understand correctly what is sometimes said: that our moral life is regulated more by the person of Christ than by general laws: for these themselves are regulated by Christ; that in the same way the following of Christ is more important than the keeping of rules: since these belong to the norm which is Christ; that it is more true to say that 'whatever enters the kingdom of Christ is good' than to say that " whatever is good enters Christ's kingdom': for goodness is objectively grounded in Christ; that my own being as guided by Christ's grace, my situation " in Christ," is for me a practical directive in a deeper sense than any permutation of general laws; for all these are included in Christ's guiding plan.

It is important to note the following:

1. Since Christ is the firstborn of every creature and the head of his Mystical Body: (a) every moral act, even the observance of the natural law, has a social significance, an importance for the whole Body of Christ; (b) the natural social order, in itself, is only one facet of the whole social order founded in Christ: for the natural order is intended by God to be an integral part of the Mystical Body of Christ.

2. If all things are seen as created in Christ the Redeemer: (a) even the natural law, in itself, finds its fundamental meaning in relation to the redemptive work of Christ, and not the other way round; (b) and thus Christ's constant interventions—through revelation and grace—in our work of learning and fulfilling even the natural law can be readily understood.'

[21] On this possibility cf. Chapter VII.

the distinction made by theologians, we conceive it as a mystical but real bond with the Lord, a *character indelibilis*, the life of grace.

'Nature' is an abstraction but it is precisely for this reason that it gives us authentic reality. Christ is indeed more than nature although we are concerned here primarily with the signification of nature. We recognize also the unique and eminent prototype of all men in those aspects of Christ which do not belong to his nature. The Lord's message is not only concerned with our fidelity to nature but with those things in man that are more than nature. These are effected precisely through him and in view of him. Here the question arises whether Christ has not perhaps brought us another conception of morality, different from that of the natural law. If this is not so in general, is it not true at least in certain domains? We as Christians, finding the moral norms proceeding from the nature of man, must certainly take into consideration that nature is realized in the supernatural, as, for example, in the sacramental Church etc.[22] This does not yet imply an intrinsic modification of an absolute norm of the natural law. If, through the positive fact of man's need for salvation and through Christ's example, penance and reparation have received a new meaning and if, compared with the natural moral order, more penance is recommended or required, it follows that this does not imply a formal modification of the natural law but merely a material one arising from certain facts that are not given with nature. The natural law is capable of undergoing such a modification. It is already hypothetically[23] contained in the law from the beginning. It has been said,[24] that according to Thomas Aquinas, the natural virtue of temperance undergoes an inner modification. But in the text in question St Thomas does not seem to speak of natural law in our sense, and he himself states in the *Summa Theologica* that

[22] Cf. also below, 111 ff.
[23] Cf. Chapter V.
[24] J. Vermeulen, 'Moraaltheologie en natuurwet,' *Werkgenootschap van katholieke Theologen in Nederland, Jaarboek* 1951, *Voordrachten en discussies*, Hilversum 1951, 179-200. The passage in St Thomas runs: 'temperantia infusa exquirit medium secundum rationes legis divinae, quae accipiuntur ex ordine ad ultimum finem; temperantia autem acquisita accipit medium secundum inferiores rationes, in ordine ad bonum praesentis vitae.' It seems that St Thomas conceives in this passage 'temperantia acquisita' (= ordinis naturalis) differently from his usual conception of the order

the divine law does not lay down any new precepts for virtuous conduct that go beyond the natural law. Furthermore, if one points out St Thomas' teaching on the necessity of supernatural love in those moral acts evidently not required by natural law, two things must be remembered: first, that according to his teaching naturally good acts do not become intrinsically evil because of the absence of supernatural love. Second, that just as nature is essentially open to the supernatural so is the natural law open to supernatural supplementation. Even more frequently the attempt has been made to bring our Lord's Sermon on the Mount into contradiction with the natural law. We shall see later whether this attempt can be justified.[25]

Christological foundation of right and the natural law

Independently of Christ, man's likeness to God establishes not only an order of morality but an order of *rights* in the more specific sense of '*suum cuique.*' The ultimate reason for this is the existential personality of man in which his likeness to God is rooted. It is the concrete being of the individual, his 'being man' in relation to concrete circumstances, that indicates the rights he may claim. For example it is in this way that we can properly ask whether he has a right to his livelihood or the right to found a family. In both cases the moral obligation to look after oneself and a family, deriving from the likeness of his being to God, indicates already the rights in question. The reality of man which reflects the divine being contains and shows forth the natural order of rights. This order is by no means something purely profane.[26]

---

of the natural law. The latter contains, according to him, truly the consideration of God as 'finis ultimus.' It seems therefore that in this passage natural law and the law of Christ are not compared with one another. The second passage in St Thomas is taken from *S. Theol.* I-II, 94, 4 ad 1. On the question with which Vermeulen deals, cf. also L. Buys, c.ss.r., 'Onze moraaltheologie en de Bergrede,' *Theologische opstellen . . . aan . . . van Noort,* Utrecht 1944, 34–59, esp. 52–54. Cf. also N. Monzel, *Was ist christliche Gesellschaftslehre?* (Münchener Universitätsreden N.F., 14) Munich 1956.
[25] Cf. below p. 33 ff.
[26] Today attempts are being made among Protestants to overcome more and more the thesis of the 'profanity' of the natural law and to come to a genuine concept of this law. Cf. for example H. Liermann, historian of Ecclesiastical law, in 'Zur Geschichte des Naturrechts in der evangelischen Kirche,' *Festschrift für A. Bertholet,* Tübingen

One must therefore consider it a *one-sided* Christocentric or Christological attitude if, especially in wide circles of modern Protestantism, the foundation of the natural law is believed to be based on Christ. Yet this attitude is not too surprising. If sin has destroyed 'true' humanity and if the 'true' being of man takes its origin only from the renewal or new creation in Christ; if, generally speaking, only that is valid which has been granted to us in the historical and personal Revelation of God in Christ, then Karl Barth rightly raised the fundamental question years ago! 'Is there a relation between the reality of justification in the sinner through faith alone, accomplished by God through Jesus Christ once and for all, and the problem of human rights: an intrinsic, necessary relationship of such a kind that through it human rights, together with divine justification, become somehow the object of Christian faith and Christian responsibility and of the Christian confession of faith?'[27] The question of whether we are dealing with a *formal* foundation of rights or also with a material foundation may be left open here. Barth himself is certainly thinking of a material foundation of rights *as well* when he tries to find by means of analogical conclusions, the norms of the juridical life in civil society, in God's attitude to this world, as revealed in Christ. This is parallel to his earlier attempt to establish the foundations of Christian ethics. Protestant theologians were right in reproaching him for caprice in using such methods. They argued that 'from the same principle of analogy anything and nothing can be deduced: monarchy as well as republic (Christ the King), totalitarian State as well as a State of civil freedom (Christ the universal Sovereign, man as Christ's servant or even slave).'[28]

1950, 290–325; likewise E. Schott, TLZ, January 1952, 48 ff. See J. Heckel, *Lex caritatis. Eine juristische Untersuchung über das Recht in der Theologie M. Luthers*, Munich 1953.

[27] K. Barth, *Rechtfertigung und Recht*, 2 ed., Zürich 1944, 1.

[28] K. Barth, *Christengemeinde und Bürgerrecht*, (*Kirche für die Welt*, 7), Stuttgart 1946, 32–42; *Communauté Chrétienne et Communauté Civile*, Genève (n.d.), 41–53. Parallel text on Christian morals cf. K. Barth, *Christliche Ethik*, Frankfurt 1946. For Protestant criticism of Barth's thesis, cf. H. Thielicke, *Kirche und Öffentlichkeit. Zur Grundlegung einer lutherischen Kulturethik*, Tübingen 1947, 37 ff.; *Theologische Ethik*, I, n. 1241. E. Brunner, *Dogmatik*, II, 374; our quotation is taken from this work. Among Protestant theologians Brunner is considered as the foremost opponent of the foundation of rights

Emil Brunner advanced the question of Christian ethics in general terms: 'Does it mean that it is sufficient to know the Gospel of Jesus, the Messias, in order to regulate State, school, law, culture . . .? What does it mean to a lawyer who is working on a penal code " to recognize Christ's reign "? Is there anything in the act of reconciliation of Christ, who has himself borne the sins of *all men equally* and has taken *upon himself* the punishment for these sins, that allows us to say which criminal should be punished more severely and which criminal less and in general, whether anyone should be punished at all? To ask oneself these questions is to recognize these whole, socalled Christological ethics as a collection of phantasms which at best are of no use.' [29]

The fact that some Protestant theologians modify Barth's ideas and see man's rights as based on his *divine filiation*,[30] alters the already questionable usefulness of Barth's conception as little as the attempt to understand every right of man as a *right of grace*.[31] The development of Barth's opinion explains the Christological foundation of rights in this way: through sin man has lost his right —every right—and has found it once more in Christ. This is a difficult starting-point and cannot be easy even for Protestant theologians but needs further explanation.[32] What in fact is this right which we recover through Christ? Of course, it is somehow based on God the creator. Yet if that is so its foundation is no

on Christ exclusively, but he finds more sympathisers in America than he does in Europe. It has even been attempted to place him in the neighbourhood of Thomism; cf. R. Niebuhr, *Faith and History*, New York, 1933, 193. Cf. also P. Althaus, *Grundriss der Ethik*, 2 ed., Gütersloh 1953, 134; H. H. Schrey, 'Naturrecht und Gottesgerechtigkeit,' *Universitas*, 5 (1950), 429.
[29] Thus Brunner's question in connection with the exclusively christological attitude of the book by Visser't Hooft, *La royauté de Jésus-Christ* (E. Brunner, *Dogmatik*, II, *loc. cit.*, 374).
[30] Thus the 4th session of the General Assembly of the World Council of Churches held at Amsterdam, n. 21 (cf. *Herder-Korrespondenz*, February 1949, 237).
[31] This is the position held by H. Vogel, 'Die Menschenrechte als theologisches Problem,' *In memoriam Ernst Lohmeyer*, (ed. W. Schmauch), Stuttgart 1951, 337–49.
[32] The main initiator of this tendency is the French lawyer J. Ellul, who in this manner takes up and attempts to answer the question raised by Barth in *Recht und Gerechtigkeit* (cf. above); cf. *Le fondement théologique du droit*, Neuchâtel-Paris 1946. In the same sense writes Ernst Wolf, 'Naturrecht und Gerechtigkeit. Zum Problem des Naturrechts in evangelischer Sicht,' *Gottesrecht und Menschenrecht*, Munich 1953, 9–35. On the Protestant side this tendency (including K. Barth) has been criticized for confusing wordly rights and divine justification, the kingdom of this world and the kingdom of God.

longer entirely and purely a Christological one.[33] Is it through Christ that we recover the rights which were given to us originally by God the Creator? Or is that which is being restored to its original validity only a natural right which, as a historical phenomenon, is unquestionable yet subject to extreme variations? This natural right whose historical existence can be proved, could itself be conceived either as purely profane or as—more or less correctly understood—a right of creation. The latter indicates that in many more recent attempts to find the basis of rights in Christology, it is not sufficiently evident whether the situation of the creature, *as creature*, is originally the basis of the rights of man in a general and formal sense. Further it is not clear whether this situation is also materially the basis of each single right, at least objectively and 'per se,' yet in such a way that sinful mankind is apt to misinterpret these rights of creation in the course of history, or even to falsify them.

In so far as the foundation of rights in Christology is regarded as a question of *knowledge* rather than of rights, all attempts will be equally futile. The result will be either a return to the analogies of Barth, (and thus open to caprice) or a return to the words of the bible, which are unable to regulate directly the juridical life of man in its entirety.[34] Moreover, according to most Protestant theologians, the scriptural texts in question must be taken not as direct legal maxims but rather as general principles and instructions.[35]

The important thing is what has led to the different attempts at a Christological foundation of rights: the notion that the true being of man and his world has been destroyed by sin or has at least lost its likeness to God.[36] The question of the importance of

[33] This is hardly the position of Ellul who seems to take natural law as a purely historical phenomenon which receives its significance through Christ. The contrary position can be found in the essay *Kirche und Recht*, Göttingen 1950, published in the name of the EKD (Evangelische Kirche Deutschlands), which dissociates itself from Ellul's position.
[34] In the latter sense, cf. for example E. Wolf, *Rechtsgedanke und biblische Weisung*, Tübingen 1948; *Recht des Nächsten*, Frankfurt-M. 1958.
[35] *Ibid*. Cf. likewise E. Schlink, 'Das theologische Problem des Naturrechts,' *Viva vox Evangelii (Festschrift Landesbischof H. Meiser)*, Munich 1951, 256 ff.
[36] For further details on the question of the foundation of rights in modern Protestantism and in general on the contemporary Protestant position regarding the natural law, cf. the already quoted book by H. H. Schrey, *Die Wiedergeburt des Naturrechts*, in

Christ for man's rights is always preceded by the fact that there already exist valid rights, given with the nature of man. God's image is impressed upon man and can never be lost completely. It does not need to be and in fact cannot be restored in Christ alone. What has been said above presupposes man's existence and his ordination to his final end. This presupposition is doubtless true *de facto*; is it likewise true *de iure*, since sin has entered this world? Not only do Protestant but also a great number of Catholic theologians believe that after original sin God safeguards the existence of the 'homo viator' and maintains his rights only in view of his redemption in Christ. They conceive this to be so in view of man's divine filiation, precisely in the same way as God willed man's existence and recognized his rights in view of his supernatural union with him on the day of creation. In so far as the natural law is related to man *on his way to redemption* it is necessarily valid. To understand this no Revelation of God's intention is needed. It is correct to say that Christ the Redeemer is the foundation of the natural law. If, in the present order in which we live, the natural law has 'conservative' and 'Christological' significations, nothing more can be said about it when considered 'in itself' and 'abstractly.' What we have said above about the Christological significance of the natural law is likewise valid for natural rights in the strict sense.

Rights therefore simply belong to man independently of his salvation-situation. They are the property of the sinner as well as the Christian. They come to him directly through his natural personality as God's image and this is true in the same sense in which the reality of man's likeness to God itself comes *from* God.[37]

---

which an abundance of biblical references can be found. Cf. also J. P. Michael, 'Die Rückwendung der Evangelischen zum Naturrecht,' *Orientierung*, 15 March, 1953, 53–6. See likewise the more recent studies of E. Schlink, 'Gerechtigkeit und Gnade,' *Kerygma und Mythos*, 2 (1956), 256–88; H. Simon, 'Die kritische Frage Karl Barths an die moderne Rechtstheologie,' *Antwort. Karl Barth zum 70. Geburtstag*, Zollikon-Zürich 1956, 346–56; see the thesis of the same author, *Der Rechtsgedanke in der gegenwärtigen deutschen evangelischen Theologie unter besonderer Berücksichtigung des Problems materialer Rechtsgrundsätze*, Bonn 1952.

[37] To this we would like to add a complement which is taken from the article 'Christliches Rechtsverständnis' in *Vom Recht, Hannoversche Beiträge zur politischen Bildung*, III, Hanover 1963, 211–26: 'Man *has* rights—because of the fact that he is called to God. Yet it is precisely because of this call that these rights can be questioned, be they 'pre-positive' or positively protected and determined rights. And if man is unfaithful

to his vocation? We know that sin has come into this world: the sin of the individual and the all-embracing sin of Adam. Does man, in turning away from God and by being unfaithful to his vocation, retain the rights governing inter-human relations which are given to him by God? Even if his turning away from God in committing one sin has, possibly, not yet the character of a definitive and total decision of (this) man concerning himself, we have nevertheless the unmistakable word of Revelation that he cannot *by himself* change his aversion *from* God through sin into a conversion *to* him. The fact that he does not definitely go astray in his vocation through his sin—because rights presuppose man 'on his way' (*homo viator*)—is therefore founded on God's faithfulness to his call previously addressed to man. This faithfulness on God's part, which calls man even after he has sinned and gives him the possibility of returning and walking once more towards God, is realized in the present order *concretely* in Christ's gratuitous act of Redemption.

It is not decided whether God's faithfulness to man in spite of sin is necessarily a gratuitous act (as is man's *concrete* vocation in Christ) or whether it is to be regarded as something that God owes to man (because man can hardly come to a total and definitive decision concerning himself in one individual temporal act). In fact, the sinner remains for the duration of his life a 'viator' and hence 'in possession of his rights' because he participates in the gratuitous Redemption of Christ.

The fact that the world into which sin has entered does not constitute a meaningless and outlawed chaos but a human society with rights and a legal order is therefore really a consequence of God's faithfulness to man, a faithfulness which he has proved in Christ. The sinner has either accepted Christ's Redemption and started out on his way to God (thus enjoying his rights) or he is at least called by God through Christ to allow himself to be redeemed and to begin his ascent to God. In this latter case he retains the rights of human society which his Creator has granted him in view of his vocation and the possibility of striving towards God.

In spite of the presence of sin, our world does not have the appearance of a chaos, of hell. On the contrary, every living man has, permanently, a knowledge of his rights and of the legal order. Even Revelation speaks to us of the rights and the legal orders of this world. It states that man is fundamentally capable of recognizing law and justice and their respective obligations (cf. *Rom.* 1 and 2). Revelation demands the conservation of the legal order, but it knows at the same time that this, on the whole, is possible to fallen man only in sofar as it is the work and the fruit of the Holy Spirit sent to our assistence (cf. *Gal.* 5: 16–26). And yet it knows likewise that—because this justice is realized—the conservation of the legal order testifies to the love of God the Redeemer which is given to us. These rights of man in spite of sin, of which we know and of which Revelation tells us, are therefore truly the consequence, and hence truly the sign of our Redemption in Christ. The rights of man—including those of the sinner —have their immanent meaning as the environment of 'man on his way to God his Creator.' But in the present order of salvation this immanent meaning is embedded in its *transcendent redemptive* significance, because it is God who in fact sustains man 'on his way' and 'in his rights' in spite of his sin, *so that* we have contact with God through the Redemption in Christ—in time and eternity.

Hence, from the point of view of Revelation, the revealed truth of the Redemption and of the vocation of the sinner in Christ presupposes necessarily the existence of man in law and justice, because whoever knows himself to be called on his way to God in spite of sin, according to Revelation and under the influence of grace, knows also— in advance—that he is capable of being called and that he has the obligation to follow the divine call. How indeed would he, as man, be able to receive the revelation of his vocation, were it not already and always known to him that he is capable of being called and has the obligation to follow the divine vocation? Yet the capability of being called and the obligation of following his vocation are unthinkable without a corresponding domain of rights and freedom in the community life of man. It is therefore evident that the Revelation of Redemption and of the vocation of the sinner presupposes the personal 'man on his way' (*homo viator*) and his rights which govern all inter-human relations. Consequently, human rights do not constitute an intrinsic element of gratui-tous Redemption; they are not grace in the same sense as Redemption and Salvation

The Christian, too, possesses these natural rights because these rights are not purely profane. Even less are they consequences of sin. Attention must be paid to the fact that rights can be vindicated by force: does this not presuppose sin? Does it not imply the loss of original harmony and a lack of Christian charity? The fact that rights can be vindicated by force does not constitute the essence of these rights and is merely one of their qualities. Moreover this is not a quality of rights as such but only a quality of the rights of sinful man. It is a quality lacking the power of love to fulfil these rights. Not the rights but the fact that they can be vindicated by force, derives from sin. Nevertheless the possibility of using force is not simply a foreign element in these rights but rather a result of the intrinsic nature of the rights. In this case of a determinate situation of man, to wit our own, rights without the possibility of vindicating them by force becomes an absurdity.[38] We have now come upon the question of the historicity of the natural law and to this we shall devote the following chapter.

---

in Christ. Neither have they—as in the case of Redemption, grace and salvation—their origin in Christ. Rights are rather the " existential " of the created reality called man (" on his way "), which reality exists however de facto under the Lordship of Christ for the sake of the gratuitous Redemption of the sinner.

Christ as the *Son of God who became man* is the Archtype and the ultimate foundation of a man's living " rightly " for the sake of his Redemption. Christ accepted the appearance of man in spite of sin. The man of today is called by God in spite of sin, and thus remains in possession of his human rights. By offering salvation to man in spite of sin, Christ proved himself to be his Lord, demanding of man the acceptance of his salvation and—as a prerequisite—acknowledges man as " on the way " and as " having rights " as a creature. The Lord of the supernatural salvation is also the Lord of the reality of creation called " human right ".' Cf. B. Schüller, *Die Herrschaft Christi und das weltliche Recht. Die christliche Rechtsbegründung in der neueren protestantischen Theologie (Analecta Gregoriana,* 128,) Rome 1963.

[38] Protestant theology, on the contrary, sees law (and its enforcement) largely as a consequence of original sin and therefore as something non-Christian. Cf., for example, F. Delekat, 'Kirche und Recht, eine Thesenreihe,' TLZ, 74 (1949), 602; E. Brunner, *Dogmatik*, II, 357.

CHAPTER FIVE

NATURAL LAW AND THE SITUATIONS OF HISTORY

Human nature and its likeness to God are immutable in their essentials. In this sense the natural law too must be regarded as immutable and independent of time and history. On the other hand man endures through time and lives in history. The history of salvation, especially, knows nothing of an unchangeable historical concept but is instinct with the effects of the cataclysm that was decisive for man's history: original sin. How is the immutability of the natural law to be reconciled with this enormous tension between the original state of grace and the present state of original sin? The problem of the historicity of the natural law is primarily a question for us of its function in this violent change in the history of salvation. It is a problem that has been touched upon occasionally in the previous chapters. We shall now deal with it expressly and more fully.

The 'secondary' natural law in theology

The decisive difference between man's present state and his lost state in paradise (with an appreciation of its importance for the teaching on the natural law) is certainly not unknown to Catholic theology. Admittedly this difference was in sharper focus at a time when theologians thought more in terms of the history of salvation and less in terms of metaphysics then we do now or than theology has done in the last few centuries.

85

A certain parallel, quite familiar to the Fathers of the Church,[1] could already be found in the Stoa. Cicero and even more clearly Seneca, held that the original state was primitive and at the same time innocent. According to these writers the ideal order of man's state has been disturbed by his guilt and especially by his avarice. Seneca seems to have arrived at a notion of the ideal man by abstracting from the evil inclinations in existing mankind and projecting the resultant abstraction into pre-history. For him pure nature and the original state of man correspond to one another. There are consequently two orders: the ideal order of the original state and the corrupt order of the present state; although Seneca speaks very seldom of a twofold natural law based upon this dual order.

A similar theory was known to the Roman lawyers of later times.

The Fathers of the Church, being theologians of a religion based on Revelation, have a more precise idea of an earlier state very different from the present. Between these states lies the historical fact of original sin. Harmony in man is lost but this has no influence on their conception of the natural law. That it should modify natural law conceptions never entered the minds of the Fathers but they were well aware that it changes human institutions. The State, for example, is an absolute institution of the natural law. It would have existed in paradise together with the authority to govern. Man's freedom and equality would not have excluded an organic structure of superiors and subjects. Likewise for most of

---

[1] On the influence of Stoicism, cf. the exposition of O. Schilling, *Naturrecht und Staat nach der Lehre der alten Kirche*, Paderborn 1914, 4 ff., 10 ff.; on the later Roman lawyers, *ibid.*, 12. In this work Schilling deals also with the question of primary and secondary natural law in the Fathers; cf. also his synopsis *ibid.* 227 ff. These explications were occasioned by the corresponding theses of E. Troeltsch in *Die Soziallehre der christlichen Kirchen und Gruppen*, I, Tübingen 1912. Schilling was able to correct Troeltsch in many points. C. Weier, o.s.b., in 'Die natürlichen Ordnungen in ihrer schöpfungsgemässen und heilsgeschichtlichen Bedeutung. Zum Problem Naturrecht und Ordnungen,' *Die Kirche Christi*, (ed. O. Iserland), Einsiedeln-Köln (n.d.), 219, thinks Schilling's affirmation on the secondary law 'unnecessary and impossible' and contrary to the principles of natural law. It seems to us, however, that natural-law teaching is possible *only* in this way. Natural law which is not dynamic is impossible. On the question of a twofold natural law in the Middle Ages, especially in St Thomas Aquinas, cf. O. Schilling, *Die Staats- und Soziallehre des hl. Thomas. Versuch einer Grundlegung der speziellen Soziallehren des Aquinaten*, Freiburg-Br. 1932, 170 ff. Cf. also P. Tischleder, *Ursprung und Träger der Staatsgewalt nach der Lehre des hl. Thomas und seiner Schule*, M.-Gladbach 1923, esp. 37–45.

the Fathers, marriage and the family belong to the absolute order of the natural law and would not have been absent in paradise. The authority of man over wife and that of parents over their children would have been as much in accord with man's freedom and equality as any other relationship between authority and subject; they result from the differences of gifts in each person. There is one operative factor which gives a characteristic note to the State or to marriage and the family after the Fall, distinguishing them essentially from what they might have been in paradise. Man in the original state would have submitted to self-evident and necessary obligations in readiness and love. With the same readiness and love he would have met his neighbour in fellowship. This characteristic has been lost, with his inner harmony, through original sin. As soon as men began to fall into sinful egoism, the State, marriage, the family and other institutions could no longer depend on such unselfish love. They required *of necessity* certain means of coercion. They now need not only authority but coercive authority to be able to reach their natural ends under such changed conditions. Thus the State is, for example, on the one hand an 'abstract' institution of the natural law and therefore suitable for man in paradise. On the other hand its indubitable right of coercion is not an absolute right but became necessary following the alteration in man's state consequent upon original sin. The Fathers of the Church usually adopted a similar solution in explaining the fact of human slavery and the often slave-like subordination of the wife to her husband.

The Fathers then distinguish *in practice* a twofold natural law. Their consideration was not from the metaphysical but from the actual historical standpoint. Their thought took into account the law of the original state and that of man after the Fall. The norm of both is man's nature as the basis of different rights and different obligations in the various situations of man before and after original sin.

The teaching of the Fathers on *primary* and *secondary* natural law, as conceived in the light of the history of salvation,[2] has had

---

[2] Hence, 'primary' and 'secondary' must not be taken here in the sense attached to these terms when used to mark the distinction between diverse degrees of necessity or intelligibility appropriate to the principles of natural law.

a constant influence on Catholic thought in the centuries that followed. It had its effect even at a time when the new knowledge of Aristotle suggested a new way of thinking metaphysically rather than in terms of salvation-history. Although St Thomas Aquinas followed the lead of Aristotle he was never able to overlook completely the distinction taken from the history of salvation. He could hardly do so since it is absolutely necessary for the Christian theologian. St Thomas knew very well that the civil authority today must act differently from the Ruler in the original state. It is in this way that he, like the Fathers, looked for a justification of slavery —as *poena peccati*—and he believed that he could justify, in this way, institutions existing in his time and some of those that had been approved in the past. Of course, it cannot be denied that the vision of a twofold order and a twofold set of natural laws, as seen in the light of the history of salvation, is of far less importance in Aquinas than, for example, in Augustine.

The relativity of the secondary natural law

Could we not reasonably entertain the impression that the natural law seen in the light of Revelation does not finally represent an absolute and immutable value? Is it really possible to describe as a *natural* order that which is moral or juridical but does not provide a constant norm in an unequivocal and permanent manner? Protestant and Catholic conceptions of nature and man's likeness to God will necessarily differ on this point if they are to be consistent.

If Protestant theology is justified in saying that nature and the supernatural in man in the original state are indistinguishable and that there cannot be a natural *and* supernatural likeness to God, how then can there be a genuinely *natural law* in our present state? If the original state is, simply and indistinguishably, exactly the same as man's nature then the natural law is first of all related to this state and it remains an open question whether such a law is possible now in any true sense. If, with the Protestants, one should admit that the natural law has been modified in connection with the destruction of nature, so that the law may correspond with and do justice to the basically changed situation of man, what follows? By seeing in the natural order (taken as the order of man in the original state) an expression of the will of God, one has no choice but to determine the order of the present time, which is the 'natural law' of our era, as the *altered* will of God.

This is more or less true for all moral spheres. Contemporary Protestantism has underlined this especially for the domain of natural *rights* in the stricter sense. Emil Brunner may be quoted here as representative of many moderates in the eyes of Catholics: 'The temporal world, the life in which justice should intervene to preserve order, is not created simply by God. It is a world that has drifted away from the order given it by the Creator. What we know as the 'nature of man' is not simply created by God but is a nature which has, in its core and centre, turned away from God. That really is the reason for the ambivalent conception of nature in Christian doctrine, signifying the original and normative as well as the fallen state which involves opposition to the norm. This in turn must be of importance for the Christian conception of justice. There is a twofold justice: first of all there is a justice which is 'that which is just in itself.' This is based on man's nature as created by God and presupposes it; it is the absolute justice of the order of creation. There is, secondly, that which is relatively just which is to say that which is just in view of a reality no longer in accordance with creation.'[3] 'Morally " correct rights " do not exist . . . Yet the question that can and should be raised is that of the best possible rights in every situation.'[4]

In opposition to this relativism, necessarily arising from its basic principles, stands the almost literal unanimity of the Catholic doctrine of the natural law. Protestant theologians are mostly unwilling to recognize this uniformity of opinion. They raise a number of questions. Has Catholic theology not also and equally 'adjusted' the original order of creation (and thus the absolute natural law) to the needs of man in the state of original sin? Has

[3] E. Brunner, *Gerechtigkeit*, Zürich 1943, 116.
[4] E. Brunner, *Das Gebot und die Ordnungen*, *loc. cit.*, 255. Brunner sees, however, the rights in the *appearance of positive legislation*.

Catholic theology not 'transformed' the original order of creation
to the orders of the sinful world and to relative natural law? [5]
Does the so-called *application* of the absolute natural law to concrete
situations, of which Catholic moralists speak, imply in practice
any other than a 'making relative' of what is absolute? Is the idea
of valid and absolute natural law in the world of original sin realiz-
able *in any sense*?

The reader will notice that the Protestant argument against this
Catholic doctrine is based on a critical error from which everything
else follows. The objections pre-suppose a concept of nature which
determines the Protestant but not the Catholic doctrine of the
natural law. If our doctrine of natural law were based upon the
Protestant conception of nature (understanding nature as the original
state understood simply and without distinction) the Catholic
theologian would in fact have no right to speak of any uniformity
of teaching on absolute natural law. Our doctrine of the application
of this law to concrete situations would be merely camouflage for
the transformation of 'high voltage to domestic voltage.' [6]

We have established that the Catholic natural law teaching
does not proceed from the pattern of order in the original state.
On the contrary, its starting point is intrinsically independent of
any historical or other possible mode of human existence. It has
its foundation in nature 'in general' which *as such* is indeed only
an abstraction but in fact exists in every man in *any* situation in
the history of salvation. It is certainly open to misunderstanding
if Catholic theologians occasionally accept the formulation 'order
of creation' when speaking of the natural law. Nevertheless, it must
be noted that there is an essential difference at the root of the
two uses of this formulation in so far as the Protestant theologian
is thinking of the *entire* reality of the original man, whereas the
Catholic theologian thinks precisely of man's absolute and metaphysical nature.

Nature, taken in this sense is indeed something fixed yet remains
open in many respects to an accidental determination and actualiza-

[5] Cf. E. Brunner, *Das Gebot und die Ordnungen, loc. cit.*, 604–6, footnote.
[6] Formulation by E. Brunner, *op. cit.*, 606.

tion. Insofar as man's nature is something complete and fixed its meaning and corresponding moral and juridical order are naturally laid down permanently. Let us take an example: it is clear from sex-duality what forms of sexual behaviour are in conformity with nature, and what forms are not. The sexual order thus determined is valid whether it is applied to man before or after original sin, with or without Christ. It is valid because the underlying reality is the same in every historical situation of man. The obligation, for example, to beware of the *danger* of violating this order is another matter. It is an obligation of the absolute natural law to avoid every unjustifiable danger to the moral order. On the other hand, the essence of human nature does not permit us to say in general what precisely constitutes a danger to the sexual order. Only the concrete modes in the realization of man's nature can determine this, each in a different manner. To bring out this difference is exactly the purpose of the narrative of Adam and Eve for whom nakedness became a danger only after the Fall. Where preternatural forces make the preservation of harmony between body and spirit easy, the same realities do not always involve the same danger to the sexual order (explicitly) as they do in a condition in which the tension between flesh and spirit is felt very strongly and is never altogether mastered.

The order given us with nature *as such* can be called 'absolute' natural law. Part of it is the general principle which, though poor in content, remains: that man must avoid everything that endangers the whole moral order, including the sexual order. The 'concrete' forms of this principle in the different situations of our history— for example for man in the original state or in the state of sin— could accordingly be called 'relative' natural law. It is relative in the sense of being an *application* of the absolute natural law to a certain situation in salvation-history. It is relative but not in the sense of being a modification of an absolute order of the original state which would adapt that state *in the very mode of its being.* Yet the formal force of this relative natural law stems from the absolute law whose intrinsic openness to determination is actualised in a purely material way. Considered in this way the relative natural law which takes into account the particular situation of fallen man is, therefore, not a *transformation* of the absolute natural law but rather its genuine application to concrete circumstances. It is purely a material determination of formal moral enunciations. The principles of the absolute natural law do not change formally in man's changing states of salvation-history. They are changed materially according to the accidental changes of the various modes of being in human nature.[7] *The absolute natural law is realized in the relative law. Seen from a different point of view, it contains the relative natural law in a hypothetical yet truly original and essential way.*[8]

The Instruction of the Holy Office on situation-ethics insists, fortunately, on the distinction between *application* and *adaptation* of the principles of the natural law. It rejects adaptation, only to insist all the more on true application. All interpretations from the standpoint of a 'situation' are thus excluded. Happily the Instruction is in line with the patristic doctrine which we have examined already. It is in accordance with the teaching of St Thomas and St Bonaventure for whom a true application of the natural law implies a differentiation according to the diverse states known to man.

From this it can be seen that neither the patristic or medieval theories, according to which there are two sets of natural laws and a certain variability, nor our distinction between absolute and relative natural laws, touches the question of intrinsic truth. The statements of the natural law stand immutable. They do raise however, and they raise exclusively, the quite different question of its historical application and the problem of its actual validity in connection with the accidentally variated modes of being in human nature. When we consider the elements it admits in each situation of the history of salvation, human nature alone is the basis

[7] Thus also an expert on the natural law in the high Middle Ages, O. Lottin, O.S.B., 'Compléments de doctrine et d'histoire,' *Principes de morale*, II, Louvain 1946, 50–54. Cf. also I. de Finance, *Ethica generalis*, Rome 1959, 180 ff.
[8] Cf. the statement of Thielicke: 'The scheme of ontological thought prevailing in Catholic theology has done away with absolute decisions in favour of what is relatively possible.' This statement, too, is intelligible only in connection with the false relation set up between the absolute natural rights of which Catholic theology speaks, and the original state.

of an applicable and actually valid natural law. Regarding the specific elements of the different situations in the history of salvation *the same nature* is the basis of the natural law which is applicable and valid *only* in these situations. The moral formula, 'that human nature requires a specific mode of action in connection with specific elements in the history of salvation,' is as true and as immovable as those other statements of the natural law which derive from elements belonging to nature in an absolute way. The only difference between them is that these 'relative' principles, in opposition to the 'absolute' principles, have historically no possibility of being applied or validated in any other situation in the history of salvation.

St Thomas says: 'Human nature is not immutable as is the divine nature. And that is why the conditions of the natural law vary with the different states and conditions of man.' [9] 'What is natural for him who is endowed with an immutable nature must always remain identical; but the nature of man is changeable.' [10] 'The natural law received its determinations in agreement with the different states.' [11] St Bonaventure states the same: 'There are precepts that reveal themselves in nature as such, others in the state of created nature, others in fallen nature . . .' [12] For example, if one considers the right to private property as a right of the time after the Fall, one confirms that the right of private property is an actual application and therefore a value in the sense of an institution of the natural law but solely for the historical situation following original sin. At the same time one firmly holds to the principle that this right is a true right and is true in an intrinsic and immutable way. It is true because it is derived from human nature and therefore in the situation following original sin the institution of private property is obligatory. These two aspects respectively represent the historical and the 'metaphysical' aspects of the same truth.

Theological tradition likewise induces us to speak of an 'historical' and material rather than a 'metaphysical' and formal variability of the natural law. 'The just and the good . . . are formally and

[9] St Thomas Aquinas, *Supplem.* 41, 1 ad 3.
[10] II-II, 57, 2 ad 1.
[11] *Supplem.* 50, 1 ad 4.
[12] II *Sent.* 44, 2, 2.

everywhere the same, because the principles of right in natural reason do not change . . . taken in the material sense, they are not the same everywhere and for all men and this is so by reason of the mutability of man's nature and the diverse conditions in which men and things find themselves in different environments and times.' [13] This variability is not concerned with the content of truth in certain principles but with the law's validity and concrete application. Likewise it applies only to those 'relative' elements which undoubtedly do not belong necessarily to the concrete actualization of humanity *but to which nature is nonetheless open.* They are therefore regulated by nature through the permanently true, though as yet hypothetical, natural law. We think that in this way the fundamental difference between the generally accepted distinction of 'historical' and 'relative' natural law and the Protestant conception of relative natural law has been sufficiently brought to light. For many Protestants a valid and applicable natural law in the original state is, in its totality, an absolute natural law. They hold this in the sense that every relative natural law in a certain situation in the history of salvation necessarily implies an intrinsic and formal relativity to the absolute natural law. The traditional Catholic doctrine of the natural law knows only a *transition* from the relative natural law in one situation in the history of salvation to the relative natural law in another situation of the same history. The generally accepted distinction of primary and secondary natural law accounts for this 'historical' (and 'metaphysical') variability rather well. Both the primary and the secondary natural laws are *relative* natural laws in the sense indicated above. In a Protestant conception of morals the primary law is synonymous with absolute and the secondary law with relative moral laws. In Catholic theology the primary and the secondary relative law is always contained in the absolute law in a 'hypothetical,' 'latent,' and 'potential' way. This is precisely because of possible situations in the history of salvation. For Protestant theology the relative, secondary natural law represents the absolute, primary law but altered and therefore in contradiction to the true, absolute natural law.

[13] *Quest. disp. de malo,* 2, 4 ad 13.

If, for the purpose of explaining the traditional doctrine of secondary natural law, we speak of an actualization and application of the general and absolute natural law, it is evident that in the first place we are not thinking of a *psychological* process in which more general principles are actualized. Rather, we explain in this way the *intrinsic structure of various statements* about the natural law in which the law is presented objectively. Our explanations may give, for example, an analysis of the natural right to use force and of the anthropological reality on which this right is based. They demonstrate that this right is objectively derived from a concrete application of a more general principle of absolute and timeless validity. It is always an application of a general moral principle to a specific situation in the history of salvation. It would therefore create a confusion between the historical and 'metaphysical' points of view (both found in the traditional teaching) if we tried to interpret the application as well as the resultant variation of the actually valid and applicable natural law in the various successive *status naturae*, as an intrinsic and formal mutation of the truth of the natural law. The same immutable and eternal truth is being conditioned by *nature* to act in one way in this situation and in another way in that situation. It requires different measures in different situations: *diversa diversis mensuris mensurantur.*[14] We have already heard St Thomas stating that the formal *ratio justi* is immutable. He held that the way in which it is applicable and valid is historically modified according to the historical modification of man's nature.

Examples of secondary natural law

It was with good reason that the Fathers of the Church and the medieval theologians drew a distinction between authority and power,[15] that is between might and right, in order to demonstrate the transforming significance of the invasion of sin into man's

---

[14] I-II, 104, 3 ad 1.
[15] Some Protestant theologians do not make a distinction between (law) right and coercion because for them the (law) right is itself a reality resulting from the fall.

history. One may ask whether they did not unduly exaggerate the condition of sinlessness in paradise. If, in the following, we suppose the preternatural harmony in the original state to be established, we shall abstain from the difficult dogmatic question of the possibility of sin in the original state. For the same good reasons, the medievals were able to defend the immutability of the principles of the natural law in spite of the transforming force of sin. Human society, marriage, family, State, all belong to the absolute natural law. This is to say they are independent of the specific modes of realization of human nature. Questions whether the State can reach its goal with or without the use of force and coercion etc. belong to the particularities of the different stages of the history of salvation. If the gift of grace given to the original man made possible a State *without coercion* and required its actual existence as a State-without-coercion, then this fact constituted relative natural law for this particular State. Nonetheless it resulted from the absolute necessity in natural law to have a State—but for men for whom coercion was superfluous. As soon as sin disturbed the harmony of man, the State *with the right of coercion* became the relative natural law in this condition of man. The absolute natural law demands, on the one hand, the existence of the State for any human condition including the present. The natural destination of the State, on the other hand, cannot be achieved without the use of coercion; thus the absolute natural law itself is the foundation for the realization of the State as exercising the function of coercion in man's actual condition. Coercion as such is not evil or sinful but is quite in accord with the nature of fallen man. From the standpoint of the history of salvation it is indicative of sin in so far as a State without coercion was followed by a State with coercion and in so far as the State without coercion is primary and the State with coercion is secondary natural law. From the *metaphysical and absolute* point of view the State is in fact simply an institution of the absolute natural law which must be realized relatively. This means that it must be realized in relation to the realities of man's situation, before and after the Fall, as a State without and then with coercion. It would therefore be incorrect to call the State without coercion (primary natural law) a case of the absolute natural law and the State exercising coercion (secondary natural law) a case of the relative natural law. Coercion is not something which, when we take the divine and human essence into account, should *simply not be there at all.* Only a certain circumstance excludes its existence, the original state of man. This is precisely a question of relative and not of absolute law. Admittedly, coercion was not included in the primary plan of creation and was not contained in the original creation of the original state. Human society in its full harmony made coercion superfluous and therefore unlawful. The fact must not be ignored that coercion was, all the same, conditionally part of God's plan of creation. It was part of his plan in so far as human nature provides for a State exercising coercion—*as in the present condition.* Coercion is a result of sin from the historical and not from the metaphysical point of view.

The fact that coercion is a result of sin is probably most strongly felt in the right of the State to impose capital punishment. It is especially in the application of capital punishment that the qualities of force, coercion and violence inherent in the situation after original sin are evident. It is here too that the importance of the distinction between primary and secondary natural law is clearest. In this, a right which is primary in time and in God's plan (voluntas antecedens) is being changed into a secondary one; whereas the absolute natural law retains all its validity and even places capital punishment at the State's disposal in its function of safeguarding human rights and society itself. Even this is not true in an absolute manner but is true exclusively for the situation in which rights and society are endangered by the violation of the law and by human egotism.

The right to kill in self-defence is likewise a phenomenon typical of the era after original sin. In the gracious original state of love, peace and order, such a right made no sense and had no validity. The same natural order which recognized no such right of self-defence in the original state, grants this right with intrinsic necessity in the state in which harmony has been destroyed by sin.

In line with what we have said above, the doctrine of the just war must also be considered as belonging to the secondary natural law. This is evident in the case where a clearly defensive war turns out to be an exercise of the right of self-defence. It is likewise evident whenever war is justified, hypothetically speaking, as an enforcement of one's own rights or as a punitive measure. This may be the case in the absence of a competent and efficient authority superior to both parties. It is true especially for the killing of a single enemy, no matter whether he is formally or only materially an unjust aggressor and whether singly or as a member of an unjustly aggressive State. Nevertheless it is equally true that war is not in contradiction to the principles of the natural law. Precisely from this law, war finds its justification for man in the fallen state. The absolute natural law, in this state as distinct from the original state, is invested with the garb of the law of war.

A parallel case to a certain extent is the right of the people to resist a despotic government. According to the absolute natural law, the civil community requires an authority serving this community and having the duty to promote its welfare by directing all individual energies towards this end. Only care for the common good justifies the existence of public authority. In the sinful state of man, the danger cannot be completely excluded that authority may pervert its office from the benefit of the common good. Still, the people have the right to expect that authority be used for the good and not for the ruin of the nation. The people may and, under certain circumstances must, resist authority in conformity with the idea of the State as designed by the absolute natural law. Moreover, in the light of this concept of the State, that is in the light of the absolute natural law, the people have the right (in this case a right of necessity) and sometimes the duty to provide a new and genuine authority in the service of the common good. The absolute natural law creates this relative natural law in the present state. Violence (and what is ostensibly revolution) are no more sinful or evil than any enforcement of rights in general or the execution of a criminal or the defeat of an aggressor. All this is permissible in order to allow a publicly organised community-life in a sinful world. It would nevertheless be sinful if the original state, in which such reactions have no place, signified an absolute order together with an absolute natural law. None of these 'orders' of the secondary natural law—although they point to the existence of sin—represents an order of sin, necessity, conservation, substitution or wrath in the meaning many Protestant theologians give to these expressions; nor may they be understood in the diminished sense of orders; of orders, that is, that do not embody an authentic value; they are, on the contrary, in virtue of absolute natural law, true, divine ' orders,' based upon the exemplar of God's essence.

One may indeed ask whether it is only a despotic government, in the commonly employed sense of the term, that renders resistance and apparent revolution lawful in case of extreme necessity. If it is the common good which ultimately declares a government legitimate it could, at least *in abstracto*, be asked whether other non-despotic governments or forms of government can become so harmful to the common good in given circumstances that a progressive evolution and, as an *ultima ratio*, a revolution would be justified. In answering this question in the affirmative, for a case of extreme necessity, one goes beyond the well-known theory that condemns every uprising as in itself unlawful and immoral and finds in the impossibility of restoring the *status quo* the only justification which allows or demands the maintenance of the state of affairs produced by the revolution. This conception would not imply a violation of the absolute natural law because this law would, in its absolute demand to care for the common good, be the foundation for the legality of violent change, especially when this is urgently indicated by the common good in the case of extreme necessity. The relative right of a case of necessity would thus have its foundation in the absolute natural law. Even such a rigorously theoretical consideration is sufficient to explain the nature of the secondary natural law as relative law, without falling into relativism.

The relative natural law of man after original sin does not signify a transformation but rather an application of the absolute natural law. This is the case because it is not man's original state but his nature 'in general' to which the natural law is fundamentally related. This fact is especially evident in those spheres of life in which the original state itself needs a variable *application* (and not

a transformation) of the absolute natural law adjusted to various
situations and (in this sense of application) *changing* with them.
Also, in those spheres in which the absolute natural law allows
general statements requiring a more precise determination and
realization by applying this law to certain situations, there is a
need due to the sinful state of man now. There was also a need
of determination due to the changing conditions of man before sin.

Often questions are raised about the ideal State, an ideal economy,
ideal laws, etc. The absolute natural law has certainly something
to say about them but its statements are relatively general, formal
and poor in content. This calls for a more precise determination
produced by the historical situation. The question of the ideal
State is usually raised, above all in Protestant theology, from the
point of view of man in the state of sin. That it cannot be solved
definitively is regarded by some theologians as an indication that
there is consequently no absolute natural law governing man in
his sinful condition. But is it possible to believe that there is a
definitive answer to the question of the ideal State in the original
condition of man when we consider that this order is absolute
according to Protestant theology? Even in the original state certain
changes and developments would have existed. One has only to think
of the fact of an economy and one must think, necessarily, of law.
We have no reason to think of a sinless mankind as being unener-
getic or undifferentiated. It follows necessarily that the general
norms of the absolute natural law would have to be applied to
changing situations. Within the 'primary' natural law the changing
relative law would still exist without enabling us to speak of a
transformation of the absolute law. In exactly the same way the
general statements of the natural law regarding the State, its
economy and its rights must be applied to the special and con-
tinuously changing situations of sinful man. This application would
be made without implying a transformation of the absolute natural
law. The only difference would be that this situation is partly (and
only partly) brought about by sin and the sinful egotism of man.
There can be no doubt that from this point of view the situation
after the Fall is a great deal more obscure than the situation before

the Fall. This does not imply, however, any essential difference in their regulations.

It will be worth while investigating especially the variable form of the *positive law* which existed in the original state as well as in the state after the Fall. In the state of sin positive law appears in such surprising forms in order to take the true situation of man really into account, that one is understandably (but wrongly) induced to think of a genuine transformation of the absolute natural law. Does it not seem as if the relative and secondary natural laws of man do make possible a legislation that contradicts the natural law? If so, it really means that the relative and secondary natural laws permitting this would constitute a truly transformed natural law. A contemporary example is the civil permission of divorce and the subsequent contracting of a new marriage. Does not the natural law permitting such a legislation seem to be a transformation and *not* a genuine application of the absolute natural law? It will be necessary to distinguish between the different possibilities or perhaps impossibilities of legislation and examine them one by one.[16]

Let us begin with the question of the right to dispose of anyone's body and life. From the viewpoint of natural law it is unlawful to take innocent life, be it born or unborn. Likewise is it unlawful to practise or permit sterilization if this is not required by the whole organism of the patient for whose benefit and well-being the members and functions in question exist? Has the legislature or government the right to *order* the taking of innocent life by interrupting pregnancy, executing hostages, or the sterilization of certain people? We say no! Such actions would on the one hand contradict the natural law and permission for such actions would have to be given on the other hand by the natural law, although even then only in concrete and difficult circumstances. The moral possibility of such legislation would represent a true transformation of the absolute natural law. This is precisely the reason why it is certain that no relative and secondary natural law justifies such actions; the secondary natural law implies a definite application and not a transformation of the absolute natural law.

[16] Cf. J. Fuchs, s.j., 'Naturrecht und positives Recht,' SZ, 163 (1958), 130–41.

8

Let us return to the example of divorce. The civil law legitimizes an order according to which two people united by the indissoluble bond of marriage are, by the decision of the State, no longer publicly regarded as husband and wife. They are legally free to contract a new marriage with other persons and this union is publicly recognized as a marriage. Yet the first marriage continues to exist from the viewpoint of the natural law and bigamy is opposed to this. Nobody is, of course, forced to make use of the legal institution of divorce or the implied legal permission to re-marry. But many will use this legal possibility and the permissive law is evidently a means to something that is in contradiction to natural law. Because the law offers merely a *possibility* and allows for the expected immoral exploitation of this possibility but *does not itself order something immoral to be done*, we are dealing only with a material and not a formal co-operation in an action that is unlawful. One aggravating fact must however be added. In some cases one of the spouses is forced to accept a divorce decree. The latter is only being deprived of protection against infidelity by the other; his wife is not being taken from him. It is therefore only a question of material and not formal co-operation in the injustice done to the unwilling spouse. Such a co-operation can be justified in certain circumstances because it neither includes nor causes actual separation of the spouses. The justification could lie in avoiding an otherwise great damage to the common good. Care for this is a demand of the absolute natural law. In fact, legal exclusion of divorce in a State in which the majority of citizens do not recognize the intrinsic indissolubility of marriage would hardly be possible without such a damage to the common good. In other words, in a democratic State, if one does not wish to risk an eventually very liberal law of divorce, then such a law limited by the common good can hardly be avoided. Approbation of a moderate law of divorce can sometimes in certain circumstances be formally equivalent to the avoidance of greater evil as a desirable good. The secondary natural law by no means gives any right to the legislator to promulgate positively immoral laws, but only the right to create, for important reasons, legal institutions that are undoubtedly open to the immorality and the injustice of sinful man. They represent merely a material co-operation and *not immorality itself* and approve of the good that is gained by avoiding greater evil. This implies a change by comparison with the right of legislation before the Fall but not regarding the absolute natural law. On the contrary, this is no more than its concrete application.

The same is true for those legal institutions that are opposed only to the rights of some or even many citizens, for example, education-laws in collision with parental rights. Such laws cannot, of course, take away the rights of parents. But a Christian representative can, in certain circumstances, vote for such a law *if* a refusal to do so would bring about an even greater evil. Parents thus hindered in their rights cannot reasonably claim their exercise; by their obligations to social justice they must be prepared to have their parental rights restricted for grave reasons bearing upon the common good. The natural law does not thereby permit a legal suppression of the parental *rights*. This is intrinsically impossible. Natural law does require a mere co-operation in the legal order for grave reasons concerning the common good even though this should restrict *the exercise* of parental rights.[17]

[17] Cf. to the previous explanations the following passage from an allocution of Pope Pius XII given on 6 November 1949 (AAS 41 (1949), 602 ff.): 'We know well, beloved sons, how conflicts not infrequently arise in the conscience of the Catholic jurist, desirous of remaining true to the Christian concept of law, especially when he finds himself in the position of having to apply a law which his conscience condemns as unjust . . .
Therefore, we take this opportunity to enlighten the conscience of Catholic jurists by enunciating some fundamental norms:
(1) For every sentence passed, the principle holds good that the judge cannot purely and simply disclaim all responsibility for his decision . . .
(2) The judge may never oblige anyone by his decision to commit any intrinsically immoral act, that is, an act which is by its nature contrary to the law of God and of the Church.
(3) He may in no case expressly recognize and approve of an unjust law (which, in any case, would never constitute the basis of a valid judgment before his conscience and before God). He cannot therefore pronounce a penal sentence which would be tantamount to such an approval . . .
(4) However, not every application of an unjust law is equivalent to recognizing and approving it. In this case, the judge may—and sometimes, perhaps, must—let the unjust law take its course, when that is the only way to avoid a still greater evil. In order to avoid harm or to ensure a good of much greater importance, he may inflict a penalty for the transgression of an unjust law if it is of such a nature that the person involved is reasonably disposed to endure it, and provided the judge knows, and can prudently suppose that such a sanction will be readily accepted by the transgressor, for superior reasons. In times of persecution, noble priests and laymen have permitted

We have thus raised the question of right and justice. This question belongs in great measure to a domain which implies change in the original state as well as in the state of sin. What does *suum cuique*—to every man his due—mean? It is true that the state after the Fall tends to give answers to this question that are not immediately evident, but are required by the exigencies of this state; it tends, that is to say, to admit apparent changes in the general principles of the natural law. Here again it is not a question of changes in the absolute natural law. As consequences of sin very peculiar and difficult situations are possible. Man's intellect is weak to such an extent that, without preternatural aid, solutions are possible which are anything but readily intelligible. Fundamentally we are in the same case here as in the original state: the determinations of the absolute natural law, poor in content and relatively formal, are being applied to concrete and actual nature. They take the firm form of the relative natural law in this case as in the former.

In comparing the states before and after the Fall, or the primary and secondary natural law, the difference must not be widened to form an abyss that makes a comparison practically impossible. For example, it is not correct to identify the concepts of justice and equality and to regard absence of equality today as a sign of injustice consequent on sin and opposed to the original state. The

themselves to be sentenced, without offering any resistance and, even under Catholic magistrates, have paid fines or been deprived of their personal freedom for infraction of unjust laws. They have suffered these things when by so doing it was possible to preserve for the people an honest magistracy and ward off much more terrible calamities from the Church and the faithful.

Of course, the more grave the consequences of the juridical sentence the more important and general must be the good it aims to protect or the evil it aims to avoid. There are, however, cases in which the idea of compensation through the attainment of superior benefits or the banishment of greater evils cannot apply, as for instance in the death sentence . . .'

Cf. also the parallel passage in another Allocution of 6 December 1953, on tolerance: 'Above all, it must be stated clearly that no human authority, no State, no Federation of States (whatever their religious standpoint may be) can give permission to teach or to do something that contradicts religious truth or the moral good . . . A second, essentially different, question is . . . whether it is permitted to assume the attitude of not preventing or tolerating . . . , and whether therefore the positive suppression is not always demanded . . .

Firstly, what contradicts the truth and the moral norm has no right of existence, no right of propaganda or of activity. Secondly, the attitude of not preventing through unjust laws and penal measures can nevertheless be justified in the interest of a superior and more comprehensive good.' (AAS 45 (1953) 798 ff.).

extent of inequalities (not merely inequalities without foundation in reality or surpassing any reasonable measure), may, perhaps, be understood as a *sign* of sin in this world. Justice by no means necessarily implies equality. It does imply equal treatment of the equal: unequal treatment of the unequal. That is why man in the original state—the absolute state for the Protestant theologian— knew his duty to find the 'suum,' that which was just for him.

Justice, moreover, must not be taken in an individualistic sense. There is not only a *justitia commutativa* but also a *justitia distributiva et legalis*. Man always exists in relation to a community. The *suum* can be defined only by taking into account the incorporation of the individual into the community. This involves a close consideration of the necessities of the community of which the individual is a member. The rights of the individual (or their justified exercise) are limited if, by pursuing these presumed rights, the common good would suffer a disproportionate damage. The individual considered as a member of the whole would then contradict himself in action. Besides, the limit is very often set, not by the preservation of the existing order but by the necessity of *establishing* an order that serves the common good. Only by taking this incorporation of the individual into the whole fully into consideration, is it possible to define what the *suum* stands for. The individual can in certain circumstances be obliged to give up what was formerly a *suum*. He may indeed even lose it by the decision of authority. It is likewise possible that the *use* of existing rights can be limited either by legal obligation or because of other moral ties such as motives of charity, pity and obedience.

What is just must be determined, in the original state as well the present one, in accordance with the relations of equality and in-equality imposed by the social well-being of the moment. It may demand, today above all, a difficult and not always accurately achievable effort of intellect. But basically the *suum* or in other words what the absolute natural law requires (having regard to the demand) today, above all, is a difficult and not always accurately achievable effort of intellect. But basically the *suum* or in other words what the absolute natural law requires having regard to the concrete realization of human nature, is determined 'objectively' by that concrete realization of human nature.

The general and formal 'suum cuique' can be given its material content and can be actualized for certain situations. It is, all the same, important to notice that such concrete legal statements are valid only in identical situations. These are situations which correspond exactly to the conditions for which these statements are meant. As soon as certain situations contain elements that are not allowed for in the statement, it must be expected that this statement does not give a solution of problems applicable to the concrete reality. If therefore St Thomas states that such statements are valid only 'ut in pluribus,' that is in a majority of cases, he has in mind a too general and imprecise formulation.[18] A man giving a sword into custody has per se the right of restitution. Because he is a member of the community his right is limited and valid only within the limits of the common good. His right ends where the common good is endangered by such restitution. This is a well-known example given by St Thomas. From the viewpoint of the absolute natural law this case is in no way different from the original state. It is a true application of the absolute natural law. The original state however excludes such a situation and the present state makes it difficult for most people to recognize the inaccurate formulation immediately or to see through its limitations.

It may be wise to illustrate these considerations by two examples taken from the recent past with all its peculiar misery typical of man's state after original sin.

The first example is the 'black market.' Without consideration of the common good, that is in a liberalistic and individualistic way, a just solution is impossible. The necessity of the common

---

[18] I-II, 94, 5c: '(Lex naturalis) potest tamen mutari et in aliquo particulari et in pauci-oribus propter aliquas speciales causas impedientes observantiam talium praeceptorum, ut supra dictum est.' St Thomas refers here to art. 4 where he states that the principle, according to which an object given into custody must be returned, is valid *ut in pluribus*, but that it is invalid where there is reason to think that the object, once it is returned, might be used to do harm to others, because this particular circumstance is not envisaged in the formulation of the principle. 'Apud omnes enim hoc rectum est et verum, ut secundum rationem agatur . . . , irrationabile, si deposita reddantur; puta si aliquis petat ad impugnandam patriam; et hoc tanto magis invenitur deficere, quanto magis ad particularia descenditur: puta si dicatur quod deposita sunt reddenda cum tali cautione vel tali modo' (*ibid.* 4c). Cf. *In III. Sent.*, 1, 4 ad 2 et 3.

good limits the right of the individual to free contracts or to free disposal of his goods. Yet, under certain circumstances it may justify actions contradicting the law, if this law is unable to regulate the reality which is overpowering the established order. This implies that observance of the law would damage the common good. The common good can impose severe restrictions on freedom of the individual on the one hand and on the other permit actions which seem to contradict that established moral and juridical order which seems to act only according to strictly legal decrees. *What does happen* in this state of chaos is fundamentally different from *what ought to be done* in every situation of man's existence. That which is just at any given time must be determined in accordance with the position of the individual in the whole community. The degree of deviation from correct behaviour in less chaotic situations merely makes visible the varying destructive force of sin at work at this given moment. Sin does this not by allowing unlawful acts to be committed but by creating situations which in the light of the absolute natural law, condition men's behaviour. It deviates from the conduct prescribed in more settled conditions to the same extent as the force of sin increases. It was, in those war-affected times, anything but easy to see clearly what participation in the 'black market' would have been permitted, if necessary, in spite of all prohibiting laws. Where it seemed permissible there arose a new difficulty: how were the high expenses of black market transactions to be met, so that life itself would not be endangered on their account? A serious question this and one which can arise occasionally in other circumstances. Very often a solution was only possible by adopting an attitude towards the authorities that could at the first sight easily be branded as a lie. Deeper insight into the matter makes it clear that such an attitude cannot always be called immoral. Have we not thus arrived at the point where, because of the disorder, we permit in case of extreme necessity what is absolutely forbidden, namely lying? Does the end, then, justify the means? We say no. By a lie we mean a statement that contradicts the innermost consciousness: but the meaning of a word can only be understood by considering the situation in which it has been spoken. This again is not peculiar to man in the state of original sin. True, it can be found more often and more clearly in this state than in the state of harmony. Must we not ask similarly whether the positive law must principally be fulfilled at all times (and in every condition of man) by making use of *epikeia*? In other words it is to be fulfilled by taking the reality of the situation into consideration, so that under certain circumstances it is allowed or even necessary to act against the literal meaning of the law. This is no peculiarity of the present state of man. It will be more frequent and more noticeable under chaotic situations than at ordinary times.

Our second example is that of the right to appropriate enough of another's goods to alleviate one's own extreme need. Here again, it is not a question of a transformation of the absolute natural law but of its genuine application. It is true natural law that the goods of the earth are there to support the life of mankind. If the actual distribution of the goods of the earth as private property—itself a natural right—threatens to frustrate this original order, this itself is only an indication of the fact that this actual distribution has no absolute character. It cannot hinder a man in extreme need from taking what is necessary to alleviate this need. That such situations of extremity occur may be taken as a sign of the fallen state of the world. That these situations should be met in this way is itself a demand of the absolute natural law *for such cases of necessity*. The prohibition against taking the property of another must be taken, not simply as the absolute natural law, but only as its proper application to more or less 'normal' situations. We must always consider the original purpose of all material goods. Consequently, the appropriation of another's goods in extreme necessity is not an alteration of the absolute natural law.[19]

[19] We have chosen these two examples in connection with Thielicke, *Theologische Ethik*, I, *loc. cit.*, nos 2055–61. Thielicke deals with the first example in his controversy with F. zu Löwenstein, s.j., 'Fragen um den schwarzen Markt,' SZ, 142 (1948), 37–49. In particular he asserts against zu Löwenstein that by participating in the black market one is 'actively obliged to lie and to deceive,' and that consequently bad means are justified by the good end. ' . . . if therefore the common good must not excuse an active lie, the subsumption of the case of " the black market " under the criterion of natural law of " common good " is more than doubtful. This doubt is based upon the cleavage of the world *ante et post lapsum* " (no. 2056). The second example was taken by Thielicke from the famous sermon by Cardinal Frings of Cologne on pilfering. Thielicke asks the question how the Cardinal can allow this, when (in this very way) others are

By choosing a variety of examples we have demonstrated the reality of the secondary natural law. Let us finally draw the reader's attention to a general principle of the secondary natural law that influences man's moral decision again and again. This principle whether it be reflexively conscious or not, is necessary. Without it life in a world of sin would be impossible. It is the principle already mentioned which justifies purely 'material' co-operation in doing what is wrong if grave reasons support such an action after the conflicting goods in question have been considered carefully. This principle does not in fact permit us to agree to the evil either by internally intending it or by externally co-operating in it. It does permit us to do something not evil in itself which becomes involved in the unlawful action by the malice of the principal operator. Thus allowance is made for the possibility that, without my intention but with my knowledge, someone will use my indifferent action for his evil purpose. This allowance can be justified for the sake of a good that would not otherwise be accomplished. It is evident that this is a principle of the secondary natural law, for it presupposes the existence of sin in this world. It does not permit evil to be done but, because it is the duty of the absolute natural law to help good in this world to victory, it justifies and under certain circumstances demands permissiveness in another's evil action.[20]

Natural law under the influence of grace

The phenomenon of the secondary natural law, though very interesting from the point of view of the history of theology and the theology of history, causes the Christian theologian to question

driven into even greater need or privation. The answer is that this fact too must be taken into account when considering 'whether', 'how much', and 'from whom' (one may take) in every individual case. Moreover, 'pilfering' must be considered as something that has the *appearance* of theft (taken in the meaning the word has in 'normal,' 'usual' circumstances) yet is not real theft (as Thielicke thinks), though only within the limits of absolute necessity. If the 'original norm' instead of the *natura absoluta* were to be taken as the respective fundamental norm, as Thielicke expressly states in no. 2060, then the permission to 'pilfer' would not constitute a subsumption of natural law but its alteration.

[20] Cf. the allocution of Pope Pius XII on tolerance, footnote 17 above.

whether a parallel development coming from the Redeemer can be pointed out. The question must be answered in the affirmative: there is not only a natural law conditioned by the effects of original sin but also a law influenced by the effects of grace. Side by side with the relative natural law that makes the force of sin in this world visible, there exists a law that shows clearly the reality of grace. The effects of the salutary power of grace are always experienced together with the reality of the world of sin. The so-called secondary natural law constitutes the order of the world after the Fall and this order is at the same time already under the influence of grace. The stronger therefore the influence of assisting grace, the less will be the chaos in the world after the Fall. It follows that the corresponding relative natural law approaches more and more to that of the original state. In a family, for example, or in a State in which men by the help of grace are good and well disposed, the element of coercion cannot and may not be developed as strongly as in a family or State existing under different conditions.

Here, as in connection with the secondary natural law, one can with good reason speak of an order of *nature*, because man experiences his nature only under the influence of original sin and the auxiliary grace of Redemption. The chaos after the Fall and the effects of grace are accessible to his intellect without the help of Revelation; they can be taken as realities actualizing nature 'in general.' [21]

The conditioning of the natural law by time and situation

The problem of the relative natural law, in the sense of an altered or transformed law in the history of salvation, appears as a peculiarity of Protestant theology. It is virtually unknown in the Catholic theological tradition. Nature (*natura absoluta et metaphysica*) and the various states of nature *status naturae*) must be carefully distinguished.

[21] J. David rightly insists on the fact that among the exigencies of natural law which are susceptible to modification, the most profound and immutable exigencies of this law are in constant action. Cf. 'Wandelbares Naturrecht,' *Orientierung*, 31 August 1956, 171–5, esp. 174.

Even within each stage of salvation-history there exist continuous and accidental changes in human nature. This applies to our present state no less than to the original, as we have pointed out in a previous chapter. Where St Thomas Aquinas in the texts quoted above [22] underlines the mutability of human nature and consequently admits a variability of the natural law (in a historical and material although not 'metaphysical' and formal way) according to the principle '*diversa diversis mensuris mansurantur*,' [23] he has in mind not so much the different situations in the history of salvation as the different situations of periodic history.   Even within the situations of *salvation*-history and their *periodic* situations, there are constantly changing situations in our *individual* history. The absolute natural law demands a consideration of the historical peculiarities of society, that is of certain peoples and groups in human community. It must take cognizance, for example, of the special social and human situation of the working class today as well as the pecularities of the individual and his respective singular situations. Although the main subject of this study is the natural law in connection with the various situations of the history of salvation, it does not seem proper to pass over in complete silence the similar question of the natural law in its relation to the situations of periodic and individual history. Both cases are excellent examples of the *historicity* of the natural law. We shall explain this briefly by means of the peculiar situation of the individual.

If the starting point were the Protestant concept of nature, a true historicity in the natural law would be practically impossible. A nature destroyed by sin cannot constitute a norm for men nor can it do so 'purely within certain limits.' Only God's will, freely creating its demands in each situation, could be regarded as the true norm in this case.

Catholic theology on the contrary, based on the concept of nature 'in general,' proposes a different teaching. According to St Thomas, human nature 'has a common character not because it can be found in a particular individual but because it is abstracted from all the particular individuals—the object of pure contemplation; for it can be found in all individuals.' [24] This nature not only allows the application of statements deduced from this notion to particular situations; it even requires such an application. In itself it is only an abstraction and thus always exists particularized within every individual reality. The same must naturally be said of the 'relative' principles of the natural law in a given historical situation, where they have a concrete value in a particular situation. The word 'application' can have a twofold sense. On the one hand it may be that a particular case, as far as the external act is concerned, is purely and simply the realization of a factual situation envisaged in a given proposition by natural law. Here, in the majority of cases, it is a question of negative commands. One might take as an example the case of pathological conditions in childbirth together with the prohibition of the direct destruction of human life. There is *moreover* the possibility that the facts, indicated by the statement of the natural law, *are* given in reality but under circumstances which are not taken into account by the general statement. Here 'application' means something different to anything discussed so far: by analysing the situation we must discover how the general statement can give norms for the more concrete situation. The concrete situation, which is related to the more general principle, is determined and made more concrete and in consequence more precise: the principle retains its native validity and force. It cannot exercise its normative function by itself. It can only do so in combination with the normative force of the other elements of the concrete situation in order to act as a norm. The more general statement of the natural law contains indeed the more concrete facts but only when considered under certain aspects. It needs to be completed by another element of human nature that either in itself (and thus revealing its equal descent from the natural law) or by positive disposition, has a normative character. The particular circumstances have evidently a normative power of their own only in so far as they are related to man. Human nature is the primary foundation of all norms. It serves therefore as the foundation of all norms

[24] *S. Theol.*, III, 2, 5 ad 2.

differentiated according to the peculiar character of different circumstances which, as a result, influence the normative power *to this same extent*. It is a question of terminology whether one prefers to speak of an application of the natural law, a derivation or deduction from this law, a valuation of the concrete reality in the light of the law or a prudent estimate in the light of basic moral and legal norms. If one prefers the term 'prudent estimate' and does not conceive it as an arbitrary process intrinsically independent of the norms of the natural law, then one does not come into conflict with those who prefer to make deductions from the general norms of the natural law in order to apply the law to the situation. These are 'estimating' its significance in view of concrete reality. With this restriction it is quite correct to say that the right thing to be done must be decided upon in the concrete situation.

Already we see that the first way of applying general statements of natural law can be quite difficult in certain cases. It is very often not easy to see whether certain facts correspond exactly to the pre-supposed reality envisaged by the statement of the natural law in question. The task of applying the natural law to more concrete facts in the second way is often more difficult. Here, the moral and juridical force of very concrete particular elements must first be found. A strict and complete analysis of very concrete or even actually existant facts sometimes defies every sincere effort. This is true to an even greater extent in the attempt to understand the normative importance of particular elements. The obstacle in this case is not only the weakness of man's intelligence in the present dispensation but also the restriction of this intelligence by fixed habits, inordinate inclinations etc. But this is merely a subjective difficulty, peculiar to man in the state of sin. Objectively, from the view point of reality, the natural law is able to go beyond general principles and master the absolutely unique historical situations in all their variability.

We emphasize now, as we have done previously with the actual application of the law to the different situations of salvation, that here again we are dealing with the analysis of facts objectively given and not with the psychological processes of understanding. Human

nature is objectively actualized by particular qualities and by a
relation to concrete exterior circumstances. It should be noted
particularly that it is not the exterior circumstances but *the relation
to them which is inherent in man* that indicates the individual destiny
of a human being. Nature thus actualized is objectively the foundation of a norm of behaviour which corresponds to this concrete
being in its totality. Man must live according to a realization of
the nature that God has given him. This 'individual norm' contains
the actualization of the natural law, itself expressed in universal
norms. Moreover, regarding individual situations, there always
arises at the same time a question of the objectivity of the *personal
knowledge* that man has of these situations in their concrete individual elements. This question is identical with the problem,
frequently treated, of the objectivity of prudential judgments by
which man dominates the individual situations and comes to know
which general norms must be applied in these unique and unrepeatable circumstances, *hic et nunc*. This is a judgment on the intrinsic
and extrinsic circumstances and how to apply the norms. Such a
judgment of prudence, in so far as it represents an *aestimatio* and
ponderatio of the elements of existing facts, occurs not only in our
estimation of an individual situation but also in the subsumption
of a less general *norm* under one that is more general. It is evident
for example, in the subsumption of the lawfulness of a capital
punishment under that right of punishment which was granted to
civil authority after the fact of original sin.

We think it necessary to point out that in traditional theological
expositions the prudential application of norms to concrete cases
has been understood in divergent ways. Some seem to have the
following conception: one tries to gather a complete account of the
true situation; then one forms one's conscience by making use of all
the elements of the objective moral order, the sum of which constitutes the total norm for the present situation. Others consider
what is very much the same process but under another aspect.
Having consolidated a complete account of the true situation, one
grasps the implications of certain more general principles for this
concrete reality. This judgment of the intellect, determining the

principle more precisely, introduces itself as a knowledge of the objective norm which is contained in human nature for such circumstances. The first group being more static, ask themselves the question: from whence does the concrete and final moral judgment come? The second group try, in a more dynamic way, to discover how one is to proceed in the formation of a judgment by starting with a more general principle and then moving towards particular knowledge. However, according to all traditional theologians the final criterion of concrete moral truth—in all the elements of the judgment—is the objective moral order based on being to which the diverse general, particular and individual norms are attached.

The historicity of the natural law is especially evident in the distinction we have used between absolute and relative natural law, as application and not as 'alteration-transformation.' It is true that the principles of the absolute natural law are in themselves metaphysical principles which dominate the person and his situations. They receive their existential significance only from the physical reality, the particular human person and from the individual situation. Adopting a language more Aristotelian than Platonic it can be said, vice versa; that everything in the physical and particular situation of a human person which can be recognized as *natura absoluta* and can be abstracted from it by reason, constitutes the basis of the general and absolute principles. In exactly this way it becomes evident that they are indeed metaphysical principles, in their abstract and general validity, dominating the person and his situation but in such a fashion that they are valid for the person and the reality of his situation, in their existential validity.[25] The absolute natural law is connected with this 'personal-

[25] Thielicke is entirely correct when he recognizes in the Catholic doctrine of natural law a 'character which transcends the person' (*Theologische Ethik*, I, n. 1889). Yet he misinterprets this character when he says that natural law 'is not only *independent* of the " chance " of meeting with the word of God but also independent of *the* " *chance* " *of personal attributes or certain situations* (*ibid.*). G. Wünsch, too, has a wrong conception of the Catholic doctrine of natural law when he believes that both denominations try to extract the good from reality, but with the difference that Protestantism tries to extract it from the immediate reality, that is, from (natural) being, whereas Catholicism attempts to extract it from supernatural being. According to him Protestantism knows only the Bible and reality, while Catholicism believes in " idealistic whims," an ideal intermediate domain, a supramundane prototype. In as far as Wünsch merely says

and-situational' reality to such an extant that not even positive human laws specially made to grasp the *historical* reality could be more existential. On the contrary, according to the true conception of *epiky* as the correct attitude in observing the positive law, the concrete reality is always a stronger normative power than the positive law. It follows that in a case of dispute the wording of the positive law is not decisive. This is in itself quite evident because the principles of the natural law refer in fact to the *true* historical reality whereas the positive law envisages the reality only *in so far as it is conceived* by the legislator.[26] In so far as Protestant theologians deny the validity of natural rights in the strict sense, or in case of dispute prefer the positive law, except in the matter of tyrannical civil authority, the Catholic doctrine of the natural law testifies to a greater historicity of this law than the Protestant conception.[27] If Protestant theology repeatedly reproaches Catholic theology with a rigid and unhistorical attitude in her teaching on the natural law,[28] this has two causes. The first is the erroneous idea that the Catholic conception of the natural law proceeds from the idea of the original state as man's nature. The second is an actual

---

that the knowledge of general statements, being an abstraction from reality, is possibly subject to error, we refer the reader to our explanations on the knowledge of the natural law (below, Ch. VII). Nevertheless, the question remains whether the knowledge (and valuation) of individual *being* does not create greater difficulties than the knowledge of an abstract and consequently (in its content) poorer statement. This is to say that, consequently, the 'immediate' knowledge and valuation of the individual being faces both Protestant and Catholic as the more difficult task. A preceding general statement can, however, be a great help in acquiring an existential knowledge. This is especially true in view of the fact that a general knowledge can possibly proceed more impartially and more objectively than the probably more 'interested' knowledge of the individual being. Cf. G. Wunsch in his review of R. Hauser: 'Autoritat und Macht,' TLZ, 77 (1952), 241–4.
[26] To the notion of *epikeia* and its signification cf. J. Fuchs, s.j., *Situation und Entscheidung, loc. cit.*, 47–68; R. Egenter, 'Über die Bedeutung der Epikie im christlichen Leben,' *Philosophisches Jahrbuch*, 53 (1940), 115–27; J. Giers, 'Epikie und Sittlichkeit (Gestalt und Gestaltwandel einer Tugend),' *Der Mensch unter Gottes Anruf und Ordnung* (*Festgabe für Th. Müncker*), Düsseldorf, 1958, 51–67.
[27] Cf. E. Brunner, *Gerechtigkeit, loc. cit.*, 11; 'Das Menschenbild und die Menschenrechte,' *Universitas*, 2 (1947), (269–74, 385–90), 388 ff.
[28] G. Wehrung believes that natural law is static and 'does not take account of upsetting emotions, of discontinuity or violent change, of transforming continuation and transformation to a higher level. It knows probably only a purifying return to itself' (*Welt und Reich. Grundlegung und Aufbau der Ethik*, Stuttgart 1952, 203). According to him only our own concept of the nature of man (in its likeness to God) guarantees (besides the static element) the dynamism rightly demanded by Wehrung, without leaving doors open for the unexpected.

subjective difficulty in understanding the objective natural law adequately. We shall return to this point later on.

Here it becomes evident why Catholic theologians give a varying extension to the natural law. There is good reason for relating every objectively gained moral or juridical estimate of a concrete *situation* to the natural law. Very concrete solutions of various cases can be considered as principles of the natural law, yet one can restrict oneself unduly by relating only general (or the most general) principles to the natural law and by calling all other possibilities mere applications of the law. Consider the dispute over workers' rights in participating in commercial or industrial enterprise, in their relation to the natural law. No serious sociologist would call such a right a general and permanently valid demand of the natural law. Whoever defends its foundation in the natural law (whether rightly or wrongly does not concern us here) proceeds from a general principle regarded as a natural right: that certain social circumstances or a certain degree of the social and personal development of the worker, justifies this right of participation. If these conditions seem to be fulfilled in the present situation then the general principle can be applied to this actual situation. Thus, either the principle alone, serving as starting point, is called a natural right and the actual demand for a right of participation in enterprise is understood as a consequence of a norm of the natural law, or the actual demand for the right of participation is called a natural right precisely because it is deduced from a general norm.

The examples which follow can be considered as natural law in particular. Take first the most general principles, for example, to do good, to give every man his due; secondly the primary 'consequences'—that is the primary applications to objective individual spheres of nature 'in general': not to kill, or steal, or lie etc. just as one likes; thirdly, the application to more concrete facts which, however, presuppose to a great extent a certain state in the history of salvation: for example, the question of the interruption of a pregnancy in extremely difficult circumstances. Finally we must consider the application to particular concrete situations. It is a good sign that there is a tendency in recent times to depart more and more from a restriction of the natural law to the most general principles.[29] If we understand by natural law that law that is naturally, that is with intrinsic necessity, connected with nature and which takes into account all the actually existing elements of man's being that are perceivable, then *not only the absolute but also the relative* natural law is included. *So also is the relative law that is related to particular situations. For man's nature, being substantially unchangeable, is accidentally in constant movement.*

The historicity of the natural law explained in this way corresponds exactly to the way in which God is working in this world. Deism, unaware of the constant dependence of the world on God, is certainly an aberration. Equally little justice is done to reality by a concept of God as *deus actuosus* who preserves his character of *deus solus* only by avoiding the creation of a stable human nature (based on being and therefore accessible to us) and thus, correspondingly, avoiding the creation of a permanent and accessible law. Man and his world are existential and permanent. This permanence of existence does not cease, nevertheless, to depend for its very being on the creative power of God. It receives its actual mode of being at every moment from God, even to its actuality and disposition, in precisely this situation. It is truly in accordance with the permanent being of man, given anew at every moment and therefore absolutely unique, that the existential demand of the natural law is addressed to me by God at every moment. It remains true that it contains exactly what is suitable for my present God-given nature in this unique situation. The natural law possesses historicity in the same way in which human nature is historical and unique and peculiar at every moment.[30] As nature is not violated but is actually determined in virtue of an inner possibility by the supernatural and by original sin, so the supernatural and the Fall of man do not invalidate the natural law. They represent elements

---

[29] This is emphasized by A. F. Utz, o.p., who follows St Thomas, in vol. 18 of the German edition of St Thomas, 1953, 432 ff., 401–8. He distinguishes in natural law between *lex naturalis* as general immutable norm and *jus naturale* as concrete right, susceptible to modifications. Cf. also A. Auer, o.s.b., *Der Mensch hat Recht*, Graz 1956; J. Funk, s.v.d., *Primat des Naturrechts*, *loc. cit.*, 133–8; W. Rauch in *Rheinischer Merkur*, 21 January 1950; C. O. von Soden, 'Das Naturrecht in der Situation,' *Hochland*, 32 (1935), 488–500.
[30] For further details cf. Ch. VI.

which determine the norm of reality together with the law of unviolated nature, ever valid in its integrity.[31]

Natural law and the order of Redemption

The historicity of the natural law is such that all modes of human existence are regulated from the metaphysical and noetic points of view by man's nature. This is true also for the supernatural reality of the redeemed Christian. Redemption is not an escape from man's nature but from the effects of a certain mode of being. Nature is the foundation for a new mode of existence to which this very nature is open. Redemption represents a new state of the *natura humana*. For this reason human nature must be lived in the light of the gracious reality of Redemption and the fact of Redemption must be made visible in our lives as being the Redemption of *man*. It is in this sense, as we have seen already, that the consequences of original sin, as well as the effects of grace, can be 'mastered' with the help of nature and of the natural law. The same is true for all other realities of the order of Redemption: the *natural law, on the one hand, takes them up to put its mark upon them and is itself more precisely determined by these realities.*[32] However, although we were able to speak of a more precise determination of the relative natural law through the effects of original sin and grace —in so far as determinate nature is *experienced* through these effects—this terminology is not suitable to describe other supernatural realities because we know of them only through Revelation.

The importance and meaning of the natural law for the supernatural and Christian world become even more evident in the light

[31] While insisting on the historicity of natural law in every human situation, we do not intend to favour an exaggerated extension of natural law, a danger to which W. Schöllgen rightly draws our attention ('Die sozialen Grundlagen der katholischen Sittenlehre,' in F. Tillmann, *Handbuch der katholischen Sittenlehre*, V 3, Düsseldorf 1953, 286). Natural law admits, within the framework of the permitted and the ideal, a multitude of ethical forms (*ibid.*, 289, notes 1 and 2). Cf. W. Schöllgen, 'Um den Sinn und die Bedeutung der Kardinaltugenden,' *Theologie und Glaube*, 46 (1956), 26–39; 'Konkrete Ethik,' *Wort und Wahrheit*, 14 (1959), 85–96.
[32] Cf. also our explanation on the definition of *Christian* morals from the standpoint of natural law, p. 73 f.

of Holy Scripture. It tells us that all things have been created in Christ the Redeemer (*Col.* 1: 15 ff.; *Eph.* 1: 9–23; 1 *Cor.* 8: 6; *John* 1: 3 and 14; *Heb.* 1: 2; *Apoc.* 22: 13). Consequently in the objective order, known to us only through Revelation, Christ the Redeemer is the measure of all natural creatures and not vice versa. But philosophy, either because it ignores Christ as the measure of creation or because it abstracts from this fact, comes necessarily to the opposite conclusion. For the philosopher it is in fact metaphysically necessary to take nature as the measure of all supernatural 'additions,' even though he fails to recognize that nature is created for the purpose of *receiving* the supernatural and Christian order.

At best, one is right in speaking of a 'natural law of the supernatural' or of a 'supernatural natural law' as has been done by those who followed the teaching of the Salmanticenses ('naturalis quodammodo') and Suarez ('connaturalia gratiae').[33] In fact, self-evident moral demands and laws result from the *supernatural being* of man, known to us through faith, in the same way as from nature. But this formulation indicates sufficiently already that these commands are supernaturally revealed in so far as they result from the revealed supernatural reality of *man* and are thus revealed in the light of the natural law. Natural and supernatural reality are but one reality in man; they penetrate and complete one another. It is the *total reality of man that regulates his behaviour. The Christian moral order is neither that of nature nor that of the supernatural but an order constituted by nature* AND *the supernatural together*. Both 'nature' and 'the supernatural' taken separately are mere abstractions.

Consequently, to take an extreme example, so truly Christian a doctrine as that of the evangelical counsels does not stand like a 'foreign body' in the orientation of man's life, distorting or overpowering his nature. The influence of original sin on the state of fallen man indeed promotes revolt. For 'fallen nature,' *in so far as it is fallen*, these counsels are incomprehensible. For that view

[33] J. Mausbach—P. Tischleder, *Katholische Moraltheologie*, I, Münster-Westf. 1941, 101–6.

of man's nature which establishes the absolute natural law, the evangelical counsels have significance in the light of the Redemption and the supernatural realization of human existence. The historicity of the natural law signifies the *continuity* of the natural and supernatural orders. Nature as such is open, even to the surrender of natural values, in the existential mode of the fallen and redeemed man and proves moreover that such a renunciation is in itself the better solution in this state; so far nothing has been said of the value of such a renunciation in the original state or that of the *natura pura*; yet these states are precisely not the *natura humana* but merely a certain condition of it.

Anticipating here what we shall explain in a later chapter, we may be permitted to draw the reader's attention to the new significance of *natural orders* in the state of redeemed mankind. It is evident that in the state of man that has been positively founded by Christ, natural orders like marriage, family and the State receive a new significance and a new purpose.[34] All of them must take into consideration what has been accomplished in this world by Christ. There is a necessary relation between them and Christ's work which was not set up side by side with the orders of this world but was incorporated into these. Marriage, the family and the State are in the service of the supernatural destiny of mankind and its accomplishment through Christ. All natural orders are meant to render this possible.

This has practical consequences, for example, in the relation between Church and State. As soon as the Church, as a positive institution of Christ, has to fulfil certain duties in this world, the State cannot simply pass over this institution of God's will and creation by appealing to the natural law. This is not the place to deal in detail with questions concerning education of the youth, of public cult etc.[35]

It is in a similar sense that the natural law regulates the Christian reality wherever Christ has positively appointed the bearers of

[34] Cf. the thorough study of C. Weiser, o.s.b., *Die Natürlichen Ordnungen*, *loc. cit.*; likewise J. Funk, s.v.d., *Der Primat des Naturrechts*, *loc. cit.*, 141 ff.; G. Bornkamm, *Gesetz und Schöpfung*, Tübingen 1934.
[35] Cf. also the discussion on the relationship of Church and State in recent years.

certain functions in the community. Thus, the absolute natural law certainly demands an order and a custodian of order in public religious cult without positively indicating who is to be the bearer of such office. Consequently the question has been solved differently at different times and among different peoples before or outside Christianity. With Christ's foundation of the Church, God himself appoints the holder of this office. This does not imply a change in the absolute natural law but previous positive regulations are being replaced by those of Christ. It is in this sense that the rights of the Church in the sacrament of marriage are to be understood; the elevation of marriage to the dignity of a sacrament implies the appointment of a human institution that is competent for the ordering of marriage. The State is not being ousted from an absolute natural order; the natural law is not being abolished. The reality, marriage, is being completed and developed beyond its natural existence and this process is not without consequences for the social order. This happens with equal necessity when the order of marriage acquires new attributes in the process of completing its natural existence. The new sacramental and supernatural character confers on it a new and greater stability.

The historicity of the natural law through which the new reality of the order of Redemption is gathered and metaphysically and noetically established as a normative reality for man, *is in some measure the same law* according to which licit human regulations are accepted by men in virtue of the natural law. Since there can be no valid human rights that contradict the natural law, so can there be no contradiction between the natural law and the demands of the reality of the Redemption.[36]

---

[36] We do not of course overlook the difference between the 'openness' of nature to the supernatural intervention of God and its 'openness' to social authority.

CHAPTER SIX

THE ABSOLUTE VALIDITY
OF THE NATURAL LAW

In the perspectives of the history of salvation, as well as from the viewpoint of the individual, the natural law has the power of mastery over all aspects of man's reality. We have seen how this is so. There is no situation that can escape its compass; it is true for *every* particular situation. The absolute natural law is always valid; the relative natural law proper to our state in the history of salvation knows of no exception for the duration of this state. *Any principle of the natural law remains efficacious in every situation that realizes the facts involved by this principle.* For example, it can never happen that the prohibition of a direct destruction of unborn life—a principle of the natural law—could cease to be an absolute demand even in a difficult concrete situation, or out of charitable consideration for a mother and her family.

The validity of the natural law and the notion of nature

An extreme interpretation of the natural law from the standpoint of situation-ethics which would question the law's absolutely demanding character is impossible when considered as true natural law. An erroneous concept of it is always liable to promote further misinterpretations. Nearly all Protestant theologians, in their desire to give the natural law a real chance, are none the less unable

to avoid an interpretation, in the sense of situation-ethics, that has
a touch of relativism.[1] Moral formulations based upon the natural
law are statements on man's essence and thus on his archetype,
Christ (*Col.* 1: 15 ff.) and on God himself. We were able to establish
that they express in fact 'what is good in itself,' *that which cannot
but be good.* Finally it is the absolute nature of God himself that
morally excludes, *in any situation*, opposition to a true demand of
the natural law.

Real interior moral goodness, on the other hand, pre-supposes
that the original state does not represent man's nature simply.
If it did, the present natural law would be in some measure 'altered'
or structurally adapted natural law. This would reasonably lead
us to question its claim to general and absolute validity, precisely
on the grounds that it would not reflect God's original and authentic
will. How are we to counter an assumption which no longer necessarily implies execution of the demands of such a 'natural law' if
it should lead to painful solutions or if it should run counter to
concomitant obligations and values? The same problem could be
formulated in this way: if the natural law, constituting the present
world of man, does not only reflect God's creation understood as
nature but always and at the same time the reality of sin, how can
such a natural law constitute an unconditional and absolute moral
demand? Yet, to the extent that formulations of the natural law
seem to represent God's original will in the sense of the original
order of creation, it remains to be seen whether they are able to
regulate sinful reality in every case. Must divorce and a new marriage
be denied in extreme cases? Must an abortion of unborn life (in
order to save the life of the mother who is needed by her family)
be denied if the discrepancy between nature (meaning the original
state) and the natural law on the one hand and the present reality
on the other is so great? *Already the notion of nature is decisive
in finding out whether the natural law, if it is considered to be of any*

---

[1] This point is very clearly brought out in the (already mentioned) work by R. Hauser,
Autorität und Macht. For details, cf. our bibliography in *Scholastik*, 27 (1952), 162.
It will become clearer in the course of our explanations that the tendencies to a situation-
ethic in Protestant theology do not spring from one source only. However, we shall
not here examine the influence of philosophical existentialism. (For the philosophical
bases of extreme situation-ethics, cf. E. Griesbach, *Gegenwart, eine kritische Ethik*,

Halle 1928; to this cf. E. Brunner, *Griesbachs Angriff auf die Theologie*, (*Zwischen den Zeiten*, 6), 1928, 219–32; Th. Steinbüchel, *Die philosophische Grundlegung der katholischen Sittenlehre*, I (in F. Tillmann, *Handbuch der katholischen Sittenlehre*, I, 1), 4 ed., Düsseldorf 1951, 237– 57). What can be (and actually is being) presented as situation-ethics *on the Catholic side*, does not—in so far as it is truly Catholic—amount to such an interpretation of the natural-law norms in the sense of relativism. Cf. also the instruction of the Holy Office of 2 February 1956 (AAS, 48 (1956), 144 ff.); the allocution of Pius XII of 23 March 1952 and of 24 April 1952 (AAS, 44 (1952), 270 ff. and 413 ff.)—cf. J. Fuchs, s.j., 'Morale théologique et morale de situation,' NRT, (1954), 1073–85 and 'Ethique objective et éthique de situation,' NRT, (1956), 798–818, where further references may be found. Cf. B. Häring, *The Law of Christ*, I, 294 ff.; Y. Congar, o.p., 'Au monde et pas de monde,' *La vie spirituelle*, Suppl. n. 18 (1951) 243–70; E. Ranwez, 'Morale de situation,' *Rev. dioc. de Namur*, 9 (1954), 155–71; K. Rahner, s.j., 'On the question of a formal existential ethics,' *Theological Investigations*, II, 217–34; 'Prinzipien und Imperative,' *Wort und Wahrheit*, 12 (1957), 325 ff. Since the publication of the instruction of the Holy Office on situation-ethics of 2 February 1956 many books and articles have been written on this subject, cf. the author's article mentioned above, in NRT, (1956), 798–818; F. Hürth, s.j., in *Periodica de re morali, canonica, liturgica*, (1956), 137–204; Y.-M. Le Blond, s.j., 'Sincerité et vérité,' *Études*, 292 (1957), 238–56; R. W. Gleason, s.j., 'Situational Morality,' *Thought*, 32 (1957–58), 533–58; F. Scholtz, 'Situationsethik und situationsgerechtes Verhalten im Lichte der jüngsten kirchlichen Verlautbarungen,' in R. Hauser–F. Scholz (ed.), *Der Mensch unter Gottes Anruf und Ordnung*, Düsseldorf 1958, 32–50. Cf. also the monographs: A. Poppi, o.f.m. Conv., *La 'morale di situazione,' esposizione e critica*, Roma 1957; J. M. de Lahidalga y Aguirre, *La llamada 'Moral Nueva' a la luz del Magisterio de la Iglesia*, Vitoria 1957; A. Perego, s.j., *L'etica della situazione*, Roma 1958; D. von Hildebrand, *True morality and its counterfeits*, New York 1955; J. Kraus, *Situationsethik als pastoral- und moraltheologisches Problem*, Mainz 1956.

Examples of how situation-ethics is being applied can be found in recent declarations of certain bishops made to their clergy 'on the authority and following the mandate of the Holy See' on the subject of the theory and the practice of treating psychoneurosis (cf. *Analecta voor het Bisdom Haarlem*, annus 3, num. 1, 183):

'6. Ut therapeutae vel directores spirituales in hoc stadio liberationis aegrotum a quovis metu vel anxietate liberent, sunt qui psycho-neuroticis suggerere immo inculcare non desinant, ipsis in re sexuali fere omnia (excepta tamen copula extra-matrimoniali) esse licita; alii autem tuta conscientia false existimant se aegrotis dicere posse: 'Si tu hoc facis in tuis circumstantiis, tu non peccas' idque eo fine ut psycho-neuroticus absque scrupulo vel anxietate morali actiones objective malas, quibus passiones suppressae erumpant, provocet perficiatque.

7. Tandem non sine gravi scandalo animarumque periculo docetur personas plane sanas propter caritatem christianam sese praebere posse psycho-neuroticis ut eorumdem actiones sexuales objective illicitas in semetipsis recipiant, quin tamen malo morali ipsae consentiant.

8. Frequentissimi sunt casus, ubi psychosi laborantibus uno alterove modo suadentur pollutio provocata, accensus ad domos publicas, visus tactusque inhonesti, desideria voluptuosa, relatio adultera; immo ubi sacerdotibus vel religiosis consilium datur videndi personas alterius sexus plane nudas atque cum iis amicitias sexuales habere eo fine ut sive a tensione sexuali sive a curiositate morbosa liberentur.

Ex altera parte quod ad vitam asceticam spectat, conceditur libertas talis ut multi psycho-neurotici sese prorsus exemptos existiment a praeceptis ecclesiae, regulis, exercitiis spiritualibus, vita communi, non sine grave detrimento totius communitatis religiosae.

Quae omnia quam reprehendenda sint, in aperto est. Accedit quod multi boni medici catholici sint scandalizati: multi sacerdotes jam dubitare incipiant de principiis traditionalibus theologiae moralis; quod tali therapia, ad quam psychoterapeutae et confessarii simul suam ferunt opem, creantur consuetudines pravae, deformationes conscientiae, complexus inferioritatis moralis, immo suppressiones conscientiae, quibus majores disturbationes psychicae provocantur quam illae quae essent curandae.'

importance at all, can and must be interpreted in the light of situation-ethics or not.[2]

Our concept of nature does not allow us to attribute to the natural law a mere organizing function in this world. It would be inadmissible even if it were assessed as a function of importance for this sinful world. It would, on such an assumption, represent a general obligation according to the will of God, yet would not be binding in a definite and unconditional way. It is not sufficient to attribute to this law a *directive* character and refuse it a truly *demanding* character.[3] We cannot be content to take the directives of the natural law into account as an extra consideration merely in order not to lose complete touch with the reality of creation. We should thus fall victim to our own powers of fantasy. Some Protestant conceptions of 'natural law' do as much, in our view. We cannot

[2] Cf. E. Brunner, *Das Gebot und die Ordnungen, loc. cit.*, 110: 'We know of no other world than the world of the sinner, that is, we know God's creation always only as *broken* by sin, and in consequence the will of God comes to us through this world only indirectly, never directly. There is nothing real in this world which God does not want, but there is likewise nothing in this world which God does (not not want, that is) want.' Thielicke sees in the existence of a natural law always a crisis of the concept of history (*Theologische Ethik*, n. 697). According to him it is impossible to regard the law as *the* will of God, 'it is rather God's will *quoad nos*, the will of God as it appears in the " refraction " of our peculiar situation, and if it is permitted to say so, the will of God altered through the fallen state of the world' (n. 691). But also G. Wünsch who, less concerned with the sinfulness of the reality, wants to see moral activity radically determined by reality, is unable to escape situation-ethics in its extreme form. He takes every moment as a completely new and unforeseen creative act of God and thus, fails to recognize the being which underlies all created things and persists through all situations. Cf. *Evangelische Ethik des Politischen*, Tübingen 1936, 16, 29, 38.

[3] In the essay *Kirche und Recht*, Göttingen 1950, published in the name of the Protestant Church in Germany, allusion is made to 'signs (Richtungsweiser) in air traffic.' Already before this publication E. Brunner had borrowed from Thurneysen the simile of the spokes of a wheel, which although they all point into one direction, in fact do not meet in the centre (nave) (*Das Gebot und die Ordnungen*, 99). No doubt, one can conclude exactly what these examples want to express: the measure in which the *general* norms do not indicate in a concrete way that which should be done in a concrete situation. Cf. C. Nink, s.j., *Metaphysik des sittlich Guten*, Freiburg-Br. 1955, 32, n. 25, 'Ethics does not determine directly what should be done in a given conjunction hic et nunc. Its principles have absolute value even for the obligation here and now, without always being able to express the unique character of this obligation in the singularity proper to it. It is precisely this singularity which man, in his action, is bound and forced to recognize with preciseness by means of the principles, before he passes on to the execution. This discovery is and must be practical. It is also necessarily different from the abstract discovery of a mathematical principle.' *Ibid.* 77, 'The application of a principle of natural law or natural rights in the case of a particular moral act is essentially different from the purely logical application of a general principle to a particular object belonging to the same category. Logic proceeds in a purely formal manner in assimilating an object to a general principle. In doing so it abstracts from the particular

take these natural law directives into consideration and yet reserve to ourselves the ultimate right to break them if we believe this to be justified or even demanded.[4]

It has been pointed out, especially in the juridical domain, that it matters little whether or no we execute the *absolute* right and do what is *absolutely* right without fail. It has been contended even, that we are not presumed to be capable of intending so absolute a course but must be satisfied with 'what is possible' here and now. Of course, the impossible never represents right or justice. A right is always something demanded in a concrete situation, in the light of general (or the most general) principles and in this sense the contention is valid. It is likewise true if it merely intends to indicate the difficulty of how to *find* what is right at this moment by the processes of reason. In this case we have to be satisfied indeed with what is 'possible.' Quite different however, is the task of *executing* what has been recognized as right. We speak of what is right in the present situation of salvation and as a genuine application, therefore, of the absolute natural law to the reality which is man now. To use the phrase 'as far as possible' as *conditioning* the

---

individual and existential character of the object, a character that is absolutely necessary in reality and which is consequently always present. The principles of natural law and natural rights, on the other hand, are not only *relevant* to all man but also *valid* for all, applicable to every individual and valid for each man. They are such in an absolutely necessary manner, yet determined in the individual form by the historical situation. Taken formally, or in their practical consequences, these principles then express the obligation to be fulfilled by every individual in an ever personal way according to its reason and end. Thus, in applying a principle of the natural law in the case of a morally good act, man never accomplishes this morally good act by means of a purely formal and dialectic assimilation; he does so always by means of an individual and existential execution. In this execution man, placed within a historical context and its exigencies, acts according to his reason and end in a manner that corresponds to his individual and existential character. And this is precisely what the natural order demands of him. It is in fact impossible for man to act with moral rectitude in any other way. Consequently, there is no case in which a principle of natural law or natural rights can be applied in a purely formal manner, just as in the case of a principle of positive law or positive rights.' *Protestant* theologians, however, will go further and say that there can be particular cases in which the general principle of natural law is simply not applicable.

[4] Also E. Brunner is greatly disturbed by the kind of fanaticism which disregards all order (for example *Das Gebot und die Ordnungen, loc. cit.*, 79). K. Barth, on the other hand, is unable to see what significance Brunner attaches to these orders, cf. *Die kirchliche Dogmatik*, III, 4, Zollikon-Zürich 1951, 20. Still, according to Brunner, the proper (relative) significance of the laws makes allowance for their infringement (not their being passed over) and even seems to demand just this by virtue of the commandment of God received in faith (*Das Gebot und die Ordnungen*, 127).

foundation of moral action presupposes the natural law to be the order of the original state and as incompetent in the moral order of the present state.[5]

It may not be amiss to draw special attention to the fact that a conception of the natural law in the light of situation-ethics must necessarily forego the absolute and metaphysical notion of nature and, consequently, the fundamental distinction between the natural and supernatural orders.

The validity of the natural law and the notion of God

The interpretation of the natural law from the standpoint of situation-ethics strikes more profoundly into its foundations than any problem of the definition of human nature in the state of original sin. We are asked if the Catholic conception of the natural law and its absolute validity does justice to *God's Revelation in the Christian religion*. What the philosophers were able to understand only in an obscure way has been brought into the fullest light through Revelation: that our God is a *personal* God and as such dominates his creatures in sovereign freedom. As men we are not merely obliged to behave according to certain objective moral *norms*. God personally commands everyone in every immediate situation. What is being asked (and doubted) is whether a natural law that is not only a general directive but is an absolute demand, is extensive enough for the God of Revelation and his ever actual freedom. The question is whether absolute and objective moral norms do not deprive him of the possibility of laying free and unlimited claim to the individual at every moment. Karl Barth absolutely rejects our

---

[5] In this sense, for example, E. Brunner writes: 'To establish the necessarily best possible, after what is truly good has been found to be beyond our reach, is by no means equivalent to sacrificing what is absolutely just . . . The establishment of the best possible is determined only by the will to help—as far as possible—in the realization of what is truly good, within the framework of the de facto given limits' (*Gerechtigkeit*, *loc. cit.*, 119). Thielicke's position, in this question nearer to Barth than to Brunner, is more emphatic: 'The absolute " *good* " of the original order no longer exists. Therefore, it is necessary to strive for the relatively " *best* " in justice' (*Theologische Ethik*, I, n. 2015). 'Thus we are again confronted with the decisive and fundamental problem of natural law, that is to say with the question of the extent to which sin is really a total break and this makes it impossible for us to accept, simply speaking, an *ordo* in the fallen world that would reflect the original *ordo* and which could therefore be governed by the norms of this *ordo*' (*ibid.* n. 2056, cf. n. 1216).

doctrine of the natural law. According to him it is God's action in the history of salvation and not the natural law that points out ('in general') the way to be followed by the Christian. But even he who attacks so vehemently the idea of God's being delivered into the hands of man through the natural law has to submit to the criticism of other Protestant theologians as having bound the free and personal God of Revelation. This is sufficient to indicate the extent to which the Protestant notion of God complicates an unconditional interpretation of the natural law, even without the implications of situation-ethics. *A fortiori*, for this kind of outlook, recognition of the Catholic teaching on the law [6] becomes increasingly difficult.

The answer to these problems has already been anticipated by what was stated above concerning man's likeness to God and the theonomy of the natural law. God's personality and freedom do not exclude but presuppose that his own essence is 'given before' all personal and free volition. It therefore constitutes the 'measure' of everything. God, precisely because he is God, cannot deny or give up His own essence. Likewise, He cannot deny or give up the *image* of his essence which is man. Man is the expression of the personal and free will of God who is man's Creator. He is this expression not arbitrarily but according to the measure of God's glorified and divine essence. The same is true of the natural law.

There is then a valid and more or less exactly formulated natural law that must be conceived as permanent and having existential

---

[6] Brunner expresses the same thought in this way: 'There is nothing good but *obedient* action, the obedient will. Yet this obedience is rendered, not to an unknown law or principle, but solely to the free and sovereign will of God. To do always what God requires in every particular circumstance, constitutes the good' (*Das Gebot und die Ordnungen*, 69). 'Consequently, the commandment cannot be known in its content in advance, like the law; it is communicated to us in each case through the word of the Spirit' (*ibid.*, 97). By this, Brunner does not mean only (as we do) that the concrete application of a general *law* in a particular circumstance is God's *commandment* requiring actual obedience. For him, this commandment of God which demands obedience cannot correspond to the general law. K. Barth uses similar formulations, 'The commandment of the living God . . . is given to man precisely and not merely in general and formal terms but in concrete fulness and determined in content' (*Die kirchliche Dogmatik, loc. cit.*, III, 4, 11). However, in Barth this carries a much stronger connotation of relativism than in Brunner (cf. *ibid.*, 20). Against a 'fixation' of God by means of an *analogia fidei*, as proposed by Barth, cf. for example Thielicke, *Theologische Ethik*, I, n. 1241.

demands. But it must indeed be more than a general law to which
a 'certain' validity is to be granted. *The natural law becomes historically, in the concrete situation of man's life, a concrete demand by God
here and now.* In this sense it is true that the demands of the personal
God are always demands on the present situation and are directed
to man as he is at this instant of his action. It is precisely in the
perspectives of the general natural law that the individual to whom
his demands are addressed *really* is an individual distinct from
everyone else. It is the same general natural law which ensures
that this situation of his life is not confused with that of other
persons, that it is different from all others. It is the guarantee
that the situations of the individual's own life, arising one
after the other, are in fact to be taken individually and as being
different even from one another.[7] The individual meets the respective demands of his God in each individual situation. Only thus does
our conception correspond to a correct philosophical notion of God
and to the Revelation of God in Christianity. This does not necessarily imply a pure, interior inspiration but rather a knowledge
of God's will through the concrete reality of the given situation.
This knowledge is derived from the application of the natural law.
However, the unique and peculiar character of the individual man
and the individual situations of his life, do not by any means
contradict the general and absolute character of the principles of
the natural law. The general thing, 'man' and many more or less
universal human attributes, exist in fact in each individual man
and in his unique situations. They can do so, of course, only in a
unique and individually particular manner. This is precisely the
reason why the statements of natural law on human being and its
attributes are truly and absolutely valid for every single man in his
unique situation. God's concrete demand, which we call a demand
of the natural law, is absolutely unique and actual. It is this: *that
the individual should correspond and do justice to his unique reality
in the concrete situation in which he finds himself.* This obligation
can be presented in the negative form of prohibition in which

[7] To this proposal cf. the quotation from Nink, p. 126, footnote 3. In regard to the question of the knowledge of this particular circumstance cf. above p. 113 ff.

any action of man against his own being is forbidden. Alternatively, it can be said that man's being imposes the duty of finding out the significance of general and more formal demands for the concrete situation, in order to give these demands a fuller content and to actualize them. For example, it may oblige us to find out what efforts should be made here and now to save another man from danger.[8]

We are again confronted with the problem of the *conflict of rights* and the *adiaphora*.[9] We are asked if the conflict of several demands of the natural law, which are supposed to be interpreted as absolutely valid, does not contradict the absolute validity of this very law. In a concrete moment God cannot, by an individual appeal to me, demand what in fact contains a contradiction. How can there be a morally indifferent action while a personal God dominates every situation of man's life through his demands? Yet, the content of these same actions is in itself morally indifferent from the standpoint of the natural law.

The answer to these questions is that the difficulty of a conflict of rights can easily be solved if one understands that there are no heterogeneous orders and demands of the natural law placed side by side without any relation to one another. There exists indeed *an order* of goods and values, of commands and demands through the very nature of things, so that there can be no true conflict of rights but at most an apparent conflict. The two obligations concerning a pathological birth, to preserve the life of the mother and not to kill the child, only seem to contradict one another. There is in fact no commandment to save the mother at all costs. There is only an obligation to save her in a morally permissible way and such a way is not envisaged in stating this given situation. Consequently only one obligation remains: to save the mother without attempting to kill the child. Likewise there is only an apparent conflict of the two demands to remove the mother's appendix and to avoid the danger of a miscarriage caused by the operation. There is only

---

[8] Cf. above, p. 110 ff. J. Mausbach gives the following formulation, ' The correct act is the individual modulation of what is good, and not the modulation of what is individually good' (*Die kirchliche Moral und ihre Gegner*, 4 ed., Cologne 1913, 181).
[9] Cf. above p. 69 ff.

an obligation not to permit any danger to the child without grave reason in the treatment of the dangerously sick mother. But the danger may possibly be unavoidable in the course of an appropriate and necessary treatment. This then is no longer a question of mis-using medical knowledge. It is rather the consequence of an insuperable medical difficulty here and now. Only *one* obligation which is derived from the cosmos of values and orders by virtue of the natural law, is the object of the unique and absolutely concrete requirement of God in this situation.

Considering the *adiaphora* we may say that some actions may perhaps be considered morally indifferent if taken abstractly and in connection with their object. Many actual and concrete activities of man take their position below the line dividing what are really only 'acts of a man' from those activities that are truly 'moral' actions. When man rises spiritually above this dividing line, where his actions are truly conscious and free, it becomes possible not only to state in general that God lays claim to man in every instant of his being; we must say also that the morality or immorality (never the amorality) of an action can be traced *per se* from the standpoint of the natural law, by considering man's concrete cir-cumstances or his subjective intention.

Moreover, to emphasize this explicitly it is of vital importance from the moral and religious point of view that we conceive the demand of the natural law in the concrete situation as the personal demand of God to the personal man.[10] The spiritual encounter of man with his own being, the confrontation of his interior and exterior worlds, is in fact an encounter with God. It is an encounter not only with God as Creator but also as preserver. The doctrine of the *preservation* of the world states indeed that all reality of the moment exists here and now because of God. It is therefore God who is before my eyes in creation and, through it, he addresses the world of his creation in me, and in this very moment. He reveals, through the existence of the actual reality, not only his glory and above all his love but also his claim on me. To this we must add

---

[10] Cf. J. Fuchs, s.j., *Situationsethik in theologischer Sicht, loc. cit.*, 173–82; 'Morale théologique et morale de situation,' *loc. cit.*, 1073–85.

God's *providence*: the content of the present given reality does not come into existence without God's providence and permission. The demand of the natural law of this moment is a personal appeal made directly by God to me. It is truly given to me at this instant and is destined in its content. In the light of such personal understanding of reality and the natural law, it becomes more evident that the doctrine of the absolute validity of the natural law in no way contradicts the statement that God appeals to the individual and give his commandments in an individual and personal manner. A contradiction would arise only if it were assumed that God could lay claim on us through his individual and personal appeal in a manner contrary to the universally valid and intelligible demands of nature. This is impossible because this, my nature in a concrete situation, is the word and image of God.

One objection against this view points out that Christ is also the *Lord* of all orders of being, dominating them and therefore able to renounce any obligation to observe them at any given moment. One is led to expect from this view that Christ, through the Holy Ghost, can make it known in the heart of man that the obligations of the natural law are not decisive at this moment, and that his commandment is not to obey them here and now.[11]

It is evident of course, that we must be prepared for the intervention of the Holy Ghost in our lives here and now. This intervention is a very important and decisive element of the Christian life. This is precisely the teaching of St Paul where he speaks of the freedom of the Christian! Indeed, for him, Christ enlightens us through his Spirit and urges us in our hearts to do that which is good. It is therefore, at least primarily, this inward law that is the law of the Christian. Great theologians like St Augustine and St Thomas have developed this doctrine in a splendid way and the masters of the spiritual life insist on it unceasingly. Yet the primary purpose of the intervention of the Holy Spirit is to lead us to a correct understanding of the existential situation. Its demands, interpreted in the light of the natural law, are made upon us 'at

[11] Cf. E. Brunner, *Das Gebot und die Ordnungen*, 182 ff., 'Not " Man " must serve God but " you " . . . this personal call is the word of the *Holy Spirit* . . .' Cf. above, p. 129, footnote 6.

this moment.' Whoever is willing to admit that there exists a
'qualitative individual factor' in every man and, circumstances
permitting, a corresponding obligation which cannot be proved by
generally formulated principles [12] of the natural law, will see it as
the work of God's Spirit to make known the demands of this situation to the understanding. This demand is seen not in opposition
to the general natural law but as possibly surpassing it. This is so
because the natural law must be considered, not as the sum of
external universal laws, but as *internal* law comprising the totality
of that moral norm which corresponds to the totality of man's
being. It is this objective law that judges *all* that is in man, even
the most individual spheres of his being and action. The possibility
cannot be excluded [13]—it must in fact be considered as *fundamentally*
possible—that God gives us his moral directives through the Holy
Ghost in a completely personal way. This is indicated in what we
have already said. These directives can be proved neither by a
generally formulated natural law nor by the above-mentioned
individuale qualitativum. Such divine inspiration would then have
to *manifest itself clearly as such*: We have no right to regard as an
inspiration of the Holy Ghost a merely personal opinion that a
prohibition of the natural law in a concrete situation (for example,
direct interruption of pregnancy) contradicts the commandment of
love and is therefore not obligatory. In the *content* of such an
inspiration, a contradiction to the demands of the natural law
would be totally impossible because it would imply a contradiction
of his own essence by God himself. For this reason, the Holy
Office, in the Instruction on situation-ethics which we have already
quoted, insists on this point as certain: a feeling or inner judgment
of any man cannot be the norm deciding ultimately the objective
correctness of an act. The *only* deciding factor is the objective moral
order based upon being. God could, through his inspiration,
demand an act of the individual which is not *given* with the onto-

[12] Cf. on this subject J. Fuchs, S.J., *Situation und Entscheidung, loc. cit.*, 76 ff.; 'Ethique
objective et éthique de situation,' *loc. cit.*, 808 ff. 812; H. Hirschmann, S.J., ' " Herr,
was willst Du, dass ich tun soll? " Situationsethik und Erfüllung des Willens Gottes,'
Geist und Leben, 24 (1951), 300–4.
[13] J. Fuchs, S.J., *Situation und Entscheidung*, 77–92; H. Hirschmann, S.J., *op. cit.*,
loc. cit.; R. Egenter, 'Kasuistik als christliche Situationsethik,' MTZ, I, 1950, 54–65.

logical reality of the concrete situation. Is it permissible to think of a *dispensatio impropria* in questions where the traditional moral theology considers a modification of the obligation by which God, as its author, could change the 'matter' on which the application of the principles of the natural law is based? This, of course, would have to be proved in each case. We think here especially of questions concerning natural *rights* in the stricter sense. It is possible that God changes, not these rights themselves, but the fundamental relations of these rights, such as the right to life, property etc., of which he is Master as he is Master of all men and all things.

Such an apparent modification of the natural law would be possible, not only through personal inspiration, but also as *universal* revelation. Thus Christ, by positively instituting the sacramental Church, has given her the ordering of, say, cult and marriage. This is a new order for which no natural provision was made but which is, all the same, not excluded by the natural law.[14]

The validity of the natural law and Christian liberty

The Christian relationship of man's affiliation to God does not justify an interpretation of the natural law in the light of the situation-ethic, no matter whether this relationship is called 'christian' because Christ *has brought us the good tidings* or because he *initiated* it. It can, in fact, be noticed that those theologians who are generally in favour of extreme situation-ethics (and who are committed also to an interpretation of the natural law from this point of view) do not intend to propose in the end a specifically *Christian* idea but rather ideas that are based upon philosophical and anthropological views *employed to prove distinctly Christian arguments*.[15]

One of these invokes above all the Pauline teaching on the *liberty of the children of God*, saying that there is no longer any

[14] Cf. above, p. 122.
[15] We have demonstrated this affirmation expressly concerning E. Michel in *Scholastik*, 28 (1953), 314. E. Michel speaks with preference of the *partnership* of man with God, and especially of the relation of the child, called to freedom, and its father. Cf. his books, *Der Partner Gottes. Weisungen zum christlichen Selbstverständnis*, Heidelberg 1946; *Renovatio. Zur Zwiesprache zwischen Kirche und Welt*, Stuttgart 1947;

merely legal obligation for man but only a personal bond with
Christ and his Father by which God-given love can and will do
what is right in every moment. The same is expressed in the formulation which states that we men, according to Christ's teaching,
are subject to God alone. They mean that there is a personal
subjection without a binding intervention of an impersonal and
impartially binding law. The expression of man's *partnership* with
God has the same meaning. According to this view man is not
uniformly bound by God's law but, as a partner before God and
almost *with* God, he seeks and finds what is right. It seems that he,
in spite of being bound to God's will and by the natural and revealed
orders, is finally able to determine and formulate his behaviour,
in its content, as the word addressed to the Father.

We have pointed out in a different context [16] that St Paul's
notion of the liberty of the children of God means anything but a
freedom from the natural law, however relative and limited we
conceive this freedom to be. On the contrary! For him this freedom
is the freedom to accept God's appeal. It is gained by us in the
power of God's love and includes God's will as expressed in the
natural law. If St Paul says that the law 'came afterwards,' [17] it must
be remembered that he is dealing here with the Law of the Old
Covenant, positively presented in history. The demands of the
natural law are not ' the Law ' in this sense.[18] It is moreover
possible to qualify this phrase 'came afterwards' as the characteristic of 'exterior coercion' which man, marked by original sin,

---

Ehe. Eine Anthropologie der Geschlechtsgemeinschaft, Stuttgart 1948; *Gläubige Existenz*,
Heidelberg 1952. E. Brunner prefers the term 'subject to God alone' (*Reichsunmittelbarkeit*), in which state we come to know the divine will not by means of a
law, but directly from God, in the freedom of the Christian and in faith; cf. *Das Gebot
und die Ordnungen*, 122 ff., 'We shall have to resist with all our strength " to say at
last, what the law is," even though we run the risk of disappointing those who expect
from us what it is legitimate and in good taste only for a Catholic ethic to say, namely
the anticipation of our own decision, the deliverance from our direct ties to God and
to our neighbour. Protestant ethics must consider it their primary and most important
task to safeguard this direct dependency (*Reichsunmittelbarkeit*) of the children of God
on their master alone . . .' On the conception of the law as something in between
and therefore hindering the immediateness of the relation between God and man cf.
K. Barth, *Die kirchliche Dogmatik*, III 4, 13; E. Brunner, *Das Gebot und die Ordnungen*,
122; E. Michel, *Gläubige Existenz*, 37.
[16] Cf. Chapter II.
[17] *Rom.* 5: 20; cf. *Gal.* 3: 19.
[18] In this precise sense also E. Brunner, *Dogmatik*, II, 267.

resents so plainly in every law including the natural law. It is superadded in so far as love, graciously given in the state of paradise, did not allow man to experience such a coercion. The case is exactly similar with the power of love that has been given us by Christ in grace. All of this is in full agreement with the Pauline cast of thought. The comparison is made, however, between the state in paradise and the state after original sin; not between the latter and the 'nature' of man.

It will not be sufficient to consider every law, including the natural law, as something *separating and hindering* a direct relationship between God and man. This *medium* between God and man must be considered as something *interceding* between God and me. It must be thought of as God's word addressed to me in which he makes his will known to me. Certainly, a law is something permanent and to that extent rigid. It fails *to express* the intimacy of the contact between God and me in the sense of an immediate and direct relationship which does not result from the essential reality of the situation. If, on the contrary, one does not adhere to a concept of 'pure act' but conceives man's likeness to God in an existential and substantial sense, this creates no difficulty but the true position becomes all the more evident. Man's subjection to God alone, his partnership with God, must not cause us to overlook or undermine the equally real relationship of the creature to his Creator. This exists in the state of nature as well as the state of sin and Redemption. It is contrary to the reality of his status as a creature that the will of man should be determined by God alone in direct action but without a permanent legal order. This is true at least for the ultimate and actual injunction, as is confirmed by many a Protestant theologian. It is, moreover, ultimately contradictory that man, as Michel points out, should bargain with God instead of obeying him, in order to fashion for himself a finally valid answer. Man has only one duty: to try to understand the total reality of a given situation in order to hear clearly God's word of demand expressed in it— and then fulfil this demand. God himself determines the factual answer which man is to give in the ontological reality of the situation; he himself, not man, is ultimately the moulder of moral reality. Every other attempt overlooks the existential and substantial reality of creation as God's image.[19]

For this reason it cannot be truly human nor *a fortiori* truly Christian to violate the order of the natural law in certain exceptional cases, as it were, from within. It is not permissible, in short, to take its directives into account yet omit to follow them as a true moral demand in the end.[20]

The validity of the natural law and Christian love

A one-sided understanding of the ' Christian ' virtue of love often involves the danger of considering all norms (including those of the natural law) as general yet, as we have said, *in the end* not absolutely binding directives. God is necessarily and always concerned with the total and unselfish self-surrender of man. This is to say that he is ultimately concerned with love. He cannot be content with this or that act nor with the fulfilment of this or that demand of the natural law. It may be asked: is not every natural law being rendered relative, indifferent, ultimately unimportant and therefore without any absolute and *demanding* character? If the only thing that matters is love, understood in the sense of unselfishness and a contradiction of all self-justification, then a further question seems to be justified. Are absolutely binding natural laws not impossible in so far as they expect a precise fulfilment through one's own act? Do they not produce, consequently, a self-justifica-

---

[19] Because of this objective and existential determination of the situation, a casuistry, rightly understood, is certainly justified. The 'case,' in opposition to the situation, has no unique character. Its solution constitutes a general moral principle that can be valid fundamentally in many similar cases (that is, in situations in which the facts envisaged by the 'case' are realized, though in a unique manner). The solution of the case is therefore only by degrees different from other general norms, in so far as it takes a greater part of reality into its consideration. Thus K. Barth is perfectly consistent from his point of view, when he considers *all* material ethics claiming true obligations as belonging to the category of casuistry (*Die kirchliche Dogmatik*, III 4, § 52, 1: Das Problem der speziellen Ethik). The objective and existential determination of the situation occasions likewise the legitimacy of the question of the so called moral systems. Wherever subjective knowledge is unable to grasp the framing of certain facts by objective moral norms, the morality of the practical activity must be decided upon on a different level, because in its ultimate basis the latter is a realisation of a personal being. [20] E. Michel wants to substitute the *potentia obedientialis* as 'ability to obey' by the 'ability to be a partner' (*Partnerfähigkeit*) (*Gläubige Existenz*, 62, n. 1) and adds, 'Already in the Old Testament Abraham, for example, does not only *obey* God but *he goes into consultation* with Him' (*ibid.*).

tion instead of an unselfish love and a self-surrender, which leaves all justification to God? Are ethics, grounded on the absolute demands of the natural law, not really based upon man's self-interest instead of unselfish love; is this not so precisely because their task is to *find out* and teach *what it is* that objectively constitutes moral rectitude for man?

These questions, largely brought forward by Protestant moralists, are justified [21] in so far as God demands the act of love and claims the whole man and not only particular acts. It is also true that God cannot accept the man who lacks this love of God even though he has faithfully observed the whole natural law and has fulfilled all its commandments. An act, be it as good as it possibly can be but which is not somehow sustained by love, *simply cannot* persist before God; it lacks that vital completion through loving surrender without which man has no true relationship with God.

We know from theology that the supernatural communion with God which marks the beginning of everlasting life in this world is impossible without *caritas*. A fulfilment of the natural law that is not to some extent animated by *caritas* does not lead to God and remains, as such, sterile for life everlasting. It is in this sense that 1 *Cor.* 13 is to be understood.

This does not imply however that love must always and in every moment be a *reflexively conscious act*. A fulfilment of the demands of the natural law which intends to be nothing but fulfilment of these demands in the unreflexive conscience, is not necessarily a mere interested legalism and a self-justification. It is quite possible that there is present even here an ultimate fulfilment by means of

---

[21] E. Brunner distinguishes clearly and rightly between love as motive and love as material demand (*Dogmatik*, II, 266 ff.; *Gerechtigkeit*, 19 ff.). However, according to him the material element in itself has no theological significance. The object of our actions is merely technique, *adiaphoron* (*Das Gebot und die Ordnungen*, 117 and 581, n. 9 and 10). It is not good in itself but has its goodness *only* through love (*ibid.*, 106, 129). Consequently, the order as such is but the framework (*ibid.*, 212), indication and instrument (*ibid.*, 254) of love. Taken as *absolute* demand, the material law could place itself at the disposal of uncharitableness (*ibid.*, 180). Love cannot deduce, or know in advance but has to seek and find what is unique in every circumstance (*ibid.*, 117 ff.) and constitutes, therefore, the terminus of the law (that is, not of the 'orders' but solely of the legal conception of these orders) (*Dogmatik*, II, 268). Cf. also Thielicke (*Theologische Ethik, loc. cit.*, I, nn. 1229–49). Thielicke emphasizes that God is interested primarily not in the conservation of the universe but in the salvation which is to be worked out. Thielicke thus indicates a relativism of the material commandments.

love. If a man abides in love, his fulfilment of the demands of the natural law should also, at all times, be an actual expression of his love and should be sustained by love. This remains even though it takes place only in the sphere of mediate and unreflexive consciousness.[22]

A certain measure of self-interest or ego-centric regard does not exclude an ultimate love that surrenders itself, a love of God that is above every love of self. Not every love of oneself is egotism but only that kind of love that loves itself, not in its objective reality or in its openness to God and our fellows, but in a love that claims for itself a more or less absolute value. A genuine love for oneself is indeed reconcilable with the essence of man's likeness to God, that is, in the man who recognizes the image of his God in himself and acknowledges this image. The true and highest love of God is conformable to man's created nature and is therefore always the highest form of self-love, precisely because God and man who is his image are not contradictory concepts. It is therefore necessary that man's love for himself as the image of God does accompany, somehow, every moral decision and act of man. It does this, if not as a motivating factor, at least as a conditioning one. Even 'the most unselfish' love of God derived from God's grace in man is possible in no other way than this. Above all, the man who places himself, in love, into God's self is bound to see and embrace himself also with the eyes and love of God.

Hence the absolute validity of the natural law does not prejudice the possibility of the benignity and even the necessity of love. On the other hand, the necessity of love does not call in question the absolute character of the natural law. True, the danger that man may place the motive of self-interest in the foreground and that love should lose more of its motivating power cannot be overlooked. When does man take any good into his hands without the danger of misusing it?

It is furthermore necessary to see clearly the connection between the demands of love and the demands of fidelity to the natural law.

---

[22] Cf. G. Gilleman, s.j., *Le primat de la charité en théologie morale*, 2 ed., Louvain 1954. (E. tr. *The Primacy of Charity in Moral Theology*, London 1959).

Indeed, love (not yet understood here as *caritas christiana*), as well as the material commandments, constitute fundamentally a demand of the natural moral order.[23] The natural law does not only know of fidelity in the sexual order or in the order of private property etc. It knows also the love that renders this fidelity to God *in the manner in which it is due*. It is necessary to distinguish between the formal and the material demands of the natural law. The material commandments are as irrevocable and absolute as the formal command that our lives must be based upon love and that without love they lack the necessary form of their ultimate realization. With the necessity of love, the necessity of true material requirements is not denied. Man, certainly, is not moral in the full sense without being supported by the motive of love. Yet the required motive of love has no other way of being realized than through material commandments. It is part of the nature of these that their work be sustained by love *so done* as to be apt expressions of love. The directive of the natural law in its content is a determined and limited demand of love.[24] The absolute character of both the necessity of love and the absolute commandments, results in the fact that the two cannot contradict one another. Love cannot demand something that contradicts the imperatives of the natural law. Moreover, whatsoever infringes the material order of the natural law is evil in itself and is consequently and necessarily in contradiction to love. It would be wrong to say that only love causes everything to be good. The fulfilment of the law and the will to fulfil it are likewise good. Love gives the fundamentally necessary and demanded perfection. The fulfilment of the law is not all that is required but it is part of it.

The work which love is bound to accomplish from the standpoint of the natural order has not, therefore, a mere technique and is by no means basically 'indifferent,' an *adiaphoron*. It has a value in itself. Our meditations on man's likeness to God have shown this already. The violation of the natural moral order affects God himself in his image, even independently of the absence of love.

---

[23] For further details cf. pp. 164 ff.
[24] Cf. also the position taken by the Church against Fénelon: *Denz.* 1327–49.

God truly wills the observance of the natural order. He is concerned with man's esteem for his creation. We must not [25] bring salvation and creation into opposition so that we can say that God wills our salvation but does not really will his creation. He claims his creation, the image of his glory, from us. He wants our salvation and this is decisive. It is not as if we were to care about our salvation and consequently about love, *instead* of caring about the creation and consequently about the natural order. It is never a question of love without being, *with the same necessity*, a question of the natural order. God desires both his creation and our salvation. Without safeguarding the creation our salvation is impossible. Moreover this safeguarding of the creation leads to our salvation, but of course only if sustained by *caritas*. One is the necessary matter, the other the necessary form. These two may not be played off one against the other. Love will express itself in an observation of the commandments of the natural order. It is evident that these commands cannot be considered in an abstract and atomistic manner. They must be seen in unison, that is, in their universality. As we have pointed out before, what God wants is not 'sexual activation according to sexuality as such' but 'sexual activation, indeed according to its particular nature, yet above all sexual activation of the whole human being,' according to its nature as a *person*.

Consequently, the natural law is not a directive that fails to bind man ultimately and absolutely and that, perhaps, may or must be ignored in view of the call of love. In its absoluteness, the natural law must never—indeed *cannot*—be employed for uncharitable purposes. It is precisely the unselfishness and readiness of this love to surrender itself which tries to recognize and fulfil the will of God expressed in the natural law. The fact that love always intends what is unique and concrete does not prove anything to the contrary. What is unique is not removed from nature but *is* the unique reality of nature. It is dominated by the law of nature as far as this law can be formulated as being of a general nature.[26] Naturally, love in the actual situation does not demand a 'general' fulfilment of the

---

[25] Cf. for example H. Thielicke, *Theologische Ethik*, I, n. 1240.
[26] On the question of terminology ('deduce,' 'estimate'), cf. above pp. 112 ff.

law. Such a 'general' fulfilment does not exist. Love demands a response to the particular situation which, indeed, is dominated by the general law. If love knows the negative commandment of the natural law: 'Thou shalt not kill,' it conforms itself in this particular situation to the concrete (here and now unique) appeal of God by respecting the life of another. If love knows the commandment of charity, it tries to find out, in the particular situation, what this demand signifies under the given circumstances. Love looks *always* for a unique response but it does so according to the spirit and will of the general law and never contrary to the law. It depends on what the law requires in the actual situation. Love does not diminish the absolutness of the natural law but bows to it and embraces it as the holy word of the absolute God. For this reason love is able to recognize or 'deduce' from the law (formulated in a general way for every situation as 'Thou shalt not kill') the will of God in *this* situation: 'I must not kill.' That is why it takes the words 'Be merciful' very seriously. It cannot be dissuaded from finding out what this demand means objectively and actually in the particular situation, so that love may be truly merciful here and now.[27] True love, far from exempting man from the obligations of the natural law, renders its true exigencies more radiant in the contingencies of each unique and unrepeatable situation.

[27] In the same way as *love*—when it is genuine—does not proclaim a unique demand over and above all norms and laws, likewise the *conscience*. It is true that the conscience is the final arbiter for every moral decision; it is also true that man's morality—which is indeed within him—depends on the fidelity of this moral decision to the response of the conscience. Yet the conscience is by no means a court of unique demands outside the domain of moral norms and unbothered by the general moral norms, a court which voices completely impenetrable and unexpected appeals in a mysterious or mystical way or even in a way that is directed by the Holy Spirit. On the contrary, it is the task of the conscience to throw light on the total reality in the moral sense (to which reality may well belong a special call of God *clearly* recognizable as such). Hence it should do so in the light of norms taken from this same reality and not independent of or in contradiction to them. It must be admitted that a moral decision made according to an inculpable erroneous conscience makes man morally good. But the error to which the conscience has submitted in its judgment and the embodiment of this error in the moral decision and in the realisation of one's life, constitute something 'that should not be.' These constitute something that brings a disharmony into the reality of this world. Moreover, an erroneous conscience is not seldom the reflection of one's own wishes, though frequently arising from vital need.

CHAPTER SEVEN

THE PERCEPTIBILITY OF
THE NATURAL LAW

A conception of the natural law that would truly merit the name must contain the objective element of human *nature*, together with the moral order implied by it. It must also include the subjective element of *rational knowledge*. We proceed now to study the implications of the revealed 'weakening' of man's reason by original sin and on the other hand we shall examine the effects of those things that God has made known to man, through Revelation, about himself and the moral order.

The question at once suggests itself: to what extent is our knowledge of the natural law deficient and how much of our actual knowledge would be more properly described as faith than understanding? The problem is emphasized by those Protestant theologians who take almost the same position as ours on the objective element (for example, Brunner), as well as by those who call any objective element into doubt in a radical manner. For this reason the latter dislike the use of the words 'natural law' and prefer to speak of the 'law of *creation*'; a concept of existence which we know, in fact, only through Revelation. It is evidently their intention to demonstrate this in their deliberate use of the word 'creation'; it expresses a fact revealed to us, unlike the word 'nature' which expresses a reality directly and naturally given to us.[1]

---

[1] Thus for example, E. Brunner, *Das Gebot und die Ordnungen, loc. cit.*, 607.

The notion of nature and a natural knowledge of morality

We have already established the fact [2] that the 'weakening' of human reason as revealed to us must be related to the original state of man as a point at which comparison becomes intelligible. By this (unlike the Protestant theologians) we understand, not the loss of the natural power of man's intellectual knowledge, but the loss of the preternatural abilities of man in paradise. 'Weakness' in this sense does not carry any right to contest the expression 'natural law' or to doubt the ability of human reason to acquire a natural knowledge of morality. Neither is a destructive right of criticism secured by trying to bring this 'weakness' into relation with the state of a possible '*natura pura.*' Similarly, nothing is gained by trying to understand it in the sense that in the present state we are lacking certain supports to intellection which were given to the man of the '*natura pura*,' as demanded by his nature.

Reason remains one of man's faculties and truly belongs to his nature, even though this nature is fallen. In accordance with its inner structure, reason is directed towards the knowledge of reality. No special grounds can be adduced for excluding knowledge of the natural law from the capabilities of the human intellect. Knowledge of the natural law basically signifies knowledge of the concrete human being and its given relationship to God, our fellow-men and the world. This is merely to assert a true knowledge of being. It means, moreover, knowledge of the inherent human demand to unfold the concrete being of man by activating one's own life and thus live it out true to reality (that is, to live the truth). Particular moral problems are often difficult enough but it is hard to see why the power of reason should be arbitrarily limited on such grounds. It is quite a different question whether the correct use to be made of the power of moral understanding is extrinsically and even massively endangered by forces outside his intellectual powers. This, without doubt, must be affirmed. There are habits, inclinations and dispositions in every man that hinder him from acquiring an insight into reality. These have the same effect as

[2] See Chapter III.

blinkers; they obscure the field of vision without necessarily injuring ones eyes or destroying one's sight.

The fundamental human ability to acquire a natural knowledge of morality, of which man was not deprived even by sin, is ours precisely because we are men. It must therefore be considered as genuine *intellectual* knowledge. By this is meant a knowledge that results from a true insight into the intelligible object. It does not mean a blind feeling of a moral order; neither is it a blind decision of good will. Natural knowledge is not lived out in the dark sphere of the irrational. One may, without reflection or without a deep analysis of the procedure, look at man's common moral knowledge and be inclined to take this for an emotional intuition or, more or less, as a decision of the will. A deeper investigation will recognize moral 'valuation' as an extremely complex act, the deepest root of which is genuine rational knowledge. The 'reasons' of knowledge are, of course, not always brought to light in the reflex consciousness *but they are in fact understood*. Knowledge of the truth is brought about *in* its reasons.[3] We might justifiably call such moral knowledge an intuition, as opposed to that knowledge which is brought about in our reflex grasp of the foundation of truth: this would, indeed, be a question of a more or less well chosen terminology.

It is evidently not our intention, in emphasizing its rational character, to underestimate the significance of other factors in the acquisition of moral knowledge. This holds good above all for the emotional disposition to acquire it and the often strongly felt effort of the will in overcoming inner resistance to the truth. St Thomas Aquinas teaches that rationality is the heart of moral knowledge, yet he also speaks of a 'conatural' sensitivity to moral truths.[4]

From this it follows naturally that knowledge of the natural law is fundamentally possible for *scientific* ethics also. They are nothing but a method of bringing largely imperfect processes of everyday moral knowledge into the light of fully reflex scrutiny. Scientific ethics imply, therefore, genuine and secure knowledge of the truth

[3] Similar to the 'syllogistic' knowledge of the angels in the doctrine of St Thomas: 'in causis vident, et in effectibus causas' (*S. Theol.*, I, 58, 3 ad 2).
[4] II-II, 1, 4 ad 3 and 45, 4 c.

and they are not (as some theories of relativity and modernism would have it) limited to the possibility of proving the vitality of the moral ideal of Revelation.

If the sinner has remained truly a man and is consequently basically capable of acquiring pre-scientific as well as scientific moral knowledge, this must lead to more than 'idealistic phantasms,' [5] understood as a subjectively imagined domain situated between the supermundane God and our mundane reality. If sin has not destroyed man, his knowledge of the moral order and of moral norms must be possible as a genuine intellectual perception of reality. General moral principles gained in this way may not be legitimately questioned in their moral 'truthfulness' or validity, on the grounds that they are rational abstractions from reality.

The power of human reason

It is frequently overlooked that the First Vatican Council (1869–70) was already concerned with the question of natural moral knowledge. True, at the time it was not so much the question of *moral* knowledge that the Council was directly concerned with; it was rather the problem of the knowledge of God. Yet the knowledge of God includes knowledge of morality. Speaking of this knowledge of God, the Council states in the second chapter of the third session, [6] that Holy Mother Church holds to the truth and teaches that *God, as the origin and end* of all things, can be known from creation by the natural light of human reason. For evidence of the truth of this doctrine the Council appeals to the first chapter of the Epistle to the Romans. According to the relevant Canon (1) the *anathema* falls upon whoever says that the one and true God, *our Creator and Lord,* cannot with certainty be known from nature by the natural light of human reason. [7] The documents of the Council

---

[5] Cf. the misunderstanding of natural law in G. Wünsch, TLZ, 77 (1952), 243.
[6] 'Eadem sancta Mater Ecclesia tenet et docet, Deum, rerum omnium principium et finem, naturali humanae rationis lumine e rebus creatis certo cognosci posse . . .' (*Denz.* 1785).
[7] 'Si quis dixerit, Deum unum et verum, creatorem et Dominum nostrum, per ea, quae facta sunt, naturali rationis humanae lumine certo cognosci non posse: anathema sit' (*Denz.* 1806).

show clearly that for the Fathers of the Council the basic knowledge of God thus described is not only a theoretical but also a practical knowledge of God. It includes the knowledge of at least the fundamental principles of morality.[8]

To be in a position to weigh the significance of the statements of Vatican I on natural moral knowledge, it is necessary to take into consideration the notion of nature as expressed in these texts. We have already said that the Council dealt with nature 'in general' (*in genere*),[9] that is, without taking into account its particular historical realization. This is the reason for its use of the abstract expression 'the natural light of *human reason*.' Hence we ought to assert that human reason is able *per se* and intrinsically (wherever and whenever it is found) to recognize fundamental moral truth. This holds true, therefore, for man in his present state also.

In the paragraph [10] which follows, the Council turned to the nature of man in the state of *original sin* and spoke of the multiplicity of obstacles outside reason which thwart the exercise here and now of his rational powers. It spoke of man's *actual* intellectual knowledge in this present state. In this connection the Council defined the object of our knowledge in a way that is quite different from the previous paragraph. In place of a knowledge of God 'as origin and end' it said here: knowledge of 'things divine which are *per se* not inaccessible to human reason.' This expression is more general and does not restrict the assertion to fundamental truth, as does the previous paragraph and its definition. If we are to understand 'things divine,' not in the sense of theoretical but practical knowledge of God, this paragraph speaks of the entire sphere of the natural law and its knowledge. This is stated to be *per se* accessible to human reason, even in the present state. The negative formulation 'which are *per se* not inaccessible to human reason' has been chosen only to avoid a definite decision on the question whether there are also natural 'things divine' which are

---

[8] *Acta et decreta Sacrorum Conciliorum recentiorum. Collectio Lacensis*, VII, *loc. cit.*, 133.
[9] *Ibid.*
[10] 'Huic divinae revelationi tribuendum quidem est, ut ea, quae in rebus divinis humanae rationi impervia non sunt, in praesenti quoque generis humanae conditione ab omnibus expedite, firma certitudine et nullo admixto errore cognosci possint. Non tamen hac de causa revelatio absolute necessaria dicenda est . . .' (*Denz.* 1786).

simpliciter inaccessible to the human intellect. The Council taught, therefore, *the natural ability to know the natural law in its complete extension*. It remained undecided whether certain truths are altogether inaccessible to the human intellect in every state. This doctrine refers to human reason *as such*, that is, human reason in the state of original sin.

While Vatican I spoke of natural moral knowledge only under the title of the knowledge of God, the Encyclical *Humani generis* of Pope Pius XII (following Pius' XI Encyclical *Casti connubii* [11]) distinguished expressly between the knowledge of God and knowledge of the natural law. This was done in order to assert all the statements of Vatican I on the knowledge of God as applying *explicitly* also to our knowledge of morality.[12] The Encyclical neither departed from Vatican I nor did it go beyond it. It indicated merely that the question of a natural knowledge of the natural law is much more acute today that it was in the last century.

Vatican I came to the same conclusion on the relationship of reason and Revelation as it did in reviewing the doctrine of the knowledge of God. An absolute necessity for divine Revelation exists only for knowledge of the mysteries of the faith in the strict sense. No such necessity obtains for our knowledge of otherwise supersensible realities.[13] The truths of the natural law are indeed part of these 'divine' supersensible realities, yet nobody would think of placing them among the mysteries. Human reason, according to Vatican I, has adequate access to natural moral knowledge. The Council furthermore refused to admit a contradiction between Revelation and intellectual knowledge.[14] It was obvious to the Fathers of the Council that there does exist a valid intellectual knowledge in questions of morality. They were of the opinion that this knowledge is consonant with the data of Revelation. According to the words of Pope Pius XII already quoted, the principles of natural law and of Revelation are 'two parallel currents both of which have their source in God.' [15] To this context belongs a second

[11] AAS, 22 (1930), 579 ff.   [12] AAS, 42 (1950), 561 ff.
[13] *Denz.* 1786, 1795 ff., 1816.
[14] *Denz.* 1797.
[15] Allocution, 1 May 1941, AAS, 33 (1941), 197.

11

line of thought taken from the doctrine of the Council on the
motiva credabilitatis which has been touched upon already. Revelation necessarily requires man as a personal partner of the personal
God and a responsible subject capable of the act of acceptance.
It is possible to come to an acceptance of Revelation (and therefore
to an acceptance of its statements on the moral order) only if the
possibility of a natural knowledge of God is fundamentally certain.
This is necessarily a knowledge of God not merely *theoretical*
but also *practical*; this implies that it is a knowledge of moral
principles and the reason for this necessary implication is that in
the moment *and in the act* of accepting Revelation (but not necessarily before) the question of its liceity must be decided. Un-
grounded faith has no moral significance. Likewise, the faithful
acceptance of Revelation implies a *moral* verdict on the *obligation*
to believe. Both these decisions must necessarily be formed by
means of natural moral knowledge without the help of Revelation.
Our conception is therefore diametrically *opposed to the conception
of the dialectical theology*. Faith fundamentally presupposes the
possibility of a natural knowledge of God and of morality. Anyone
who wishes to understand the norms of morality through Revelation
must accept the possibility of a natural moral knowledge. Consequently, no grounds remain for limiting this possibility to these
two decisions. They are absolutely necessary decisions indicated
particularly because they are already precise determinations of more
universal judgments of the natural law. When applied to the
concrete man, our statement must be considered in the light of the
doctrine of the supernatural, the Fall and Redemption.

The weakness of human reason

The Encyclical *Humani generis* repeated almost word for word
the doctrine of Vatican I on the natural knowledge of God. It
emphasized our *moral* knowledge when it stated (following, once
more, *Casti connubii*)[16] that 'a divine Revelation is morally necessary
to enable *all* men to come to know those religious and moral truths

---

[16] AAS, 22 (1930), 579 ff.

which are *per se* not inaccessible to reason, and to know them more easily, securely and without error *in the present situation* of mankind.' [17] Consequently there exist, in the present situation of mankind, difficulties that impede such an easy, secure and unerring knowledge of the natural law. In order to overcome these difficulties, divine Revelation is morally necessary. Yet Vatican I seems to indicate that these difficulties do not prevail in knowledge of the *fundamental* truths of the natural law; these fundamental principles are not only in themselves intelligible to human reason as such but are also easily discernible, in his present state, by each and every man. We find this suggested in the distinction made between *the area of fundamental* truths and the remaining domains of the natural law. We find it also in the distinction made between nature 'in general' and the *natura lapsa*.[18] This supposition does not call in question the fact that divine Revelation is also of prime importance for the fundamental principles of natural ethics. The distinction made by Vatican I would confirm the *philosophical* reflection that the natural law, at least in its fundamental principles, must be readily accessible and therefore known to all men in every state of salvation. A further confirmation of this theory is to be found, it appears, in a phrase of Pope Pius XII in his Encyclical *Summi pontificatus.* He states that the voice of nature teaches 'even the uneducated and what is more, those who do not yet enjoy the cultural values of mankind, what is just and unjust, permitted and forbidden.' [19] To understand this, at least the main principles of the natural law must be known easily by all whereas we notice that the more difficult and detailed moral norms are in fact often unknown. There is, consequently, a domain of the natural law that is easily and correctly known to everyone, even in the state of original sin. Nonetheless, the exercise of the intellectual faculty is impeded in other ways to a greater or lesser extent.

It is significant that the Church shows her awareness of the difficulty, following original sin, of coming to know what she calls

---

[17] AAS, 42 (1950), 562. For the corresponding passage of the First Vatican Council, cf. *Denz.* 1786 (see above, footnote 10).
[18] *Denz.* 1785 as compared to *Denz.* 1786 (see above, footnotes 6 and 10).
[19] AAS, 31 (1939), 423. Cf. similar expression used by Pius XI in the Encyclical *Divini Redemptoris*, AAS, 29 (1937), 76.

natural law. She speaks quite openly about it. She even believes Revelation to be a moral, though not an absolute, necessity in overcoming it. How indeed could she overlook this difficulty? Catholic no less than Protestant theologians know well that moral views are changing with time and place. In fact the encyclical begins its explanations with a statement of this fact. It goes on to say that this is not surprising because of the many difficulties that prevent the application of this knowledge which is *per se* accessible to human reason. The Pope was thinking there, above all, of the various subjective constraints on fallen man.

The acceptance of suprasensible truths of the natural law has decisive consequences. This was of less importance to man in the original state since a supernatural power to love God was given him as a help in harmonizing the natural tensions between body and spirit. Once man is deprived of this special power or even (as a certain opinion in Catholic theology would put it) once man has lost the possibilities he would have enjoyed in the state of the *natura pura*, it becomes conceivable that he should seek, voluntarily or involuntarily, plausible objections to the certainty of moral truth. He finds such objections easily enough, especially in those difficult questions which render true moral knowledge *subjectively* doubtful. The mighty power of the senses, of imagination, concupiscence and the prejudices formed through education and habit, together with the corresponding negative dispositions of will and intellect, are all realities. They prevent only too easily a correct activation of our real native ability to come to a true moral knowledge.[20] Already these subjective sources of error have been used to a great extent to explain the subjective insufficiency of moral knowledge in men. This can be attested by experience. They have also been used to argue against the value of man's natural rational faculties in morals. It remains true, notwithstanding, that only *the fact* of certain deficiencies is incontestable.

There are, of course, objective facts that also make natural moral knowledge very difficult, though not basically impossible. Following Vatican I we shall omit here the question whether certain

[20] Cf. the Encyclical *Humani generis*, AAS, 42 (1950), 561 ff. and 571 ff.

particular truths of the natural law are absolutely (that is *in every state*) inaccessible to human reason. Many moral questions are, in themselves and objectively, more than merely complicated. Their solution may have been easy for man in the original state by means of special aids. We lack these aids and the human intellect, even in the case of experts, often fails in its attempt to acquire this knowledge. We have in mind certain questions of the right to dispose of one's body, or particular border-line cases of the sexual order, or the exact determination of right and justice (of the *suum cuique* in a singular situation). It cannot be denied either, as we have mentioned in a different context, that the sinfulness of man in his present state adds considerably to the objective difficulties. The unjust and sinful social *organization* of the lives of men very often creates situations in which clarification in the light of the principles of the natural moral law is extremely difficult. What has been said above in connection with the explanation of the secondary natural law is evidence of this. In summary, this is the great problem of applying the absolute natural law to concrete and complicated particular situations, above all in a sinful world. It is the problem which Protestantism erroneously sees as the paradox of transforming the absolute natural law (in the sense of 'original' law) to the sinful situation of man [21] in his present condition.

Difficulties against a natural knowledge of the natural law arise also from the *reality of the supernatural*. Here we find absolute limits which cannot be overcome with the help of reason. This is especially the case in assessing the significance of the natural law in the supernatural state. In particular, reason is incapable of delimiting the extent to which fulfilment of the demands of natural law signifies justification in the theological sense and, consequently, the sense in which it constitutes a means of reaching our supernatural end. It is simply not true that reason *necessarily* misinterprets the natural law as a means of justification when unguided by

---

[21] We do not understand the above to be said, consequently, in the sense that the universe does no longer harbour any kind of order. The latter interpretation is expressed, for example, by Thielicke: 'In the fallen world, it is in fact not only impossible to *do* good but also to *know* what is good. And the fact that the good does not present

faith.[22] No doubt, reason can fall into the *danger* of attributing a justifying value to the fulfilment of the demands of the natural law. If reason proceeds correctly (as it is capable of doing in itself) it will arrive at the quite valid judgment that the observation of the natural law is a good and a duty. This is all; but this observation of the law is necessary in order to reach our final goal. As the natural law is based upon the *natura absoluta* of man and because man always has the obligation to reach his destiny, so the observation of the natural law in any state is an absolute necessity. Notwithstanding, to say that this 'natural' conception of the natural law, as an absolute and vital law, is a misinterpretation from which only faith can save us,[23] it itself a misunderstanding of Revelation and is, bluntly, an erroneous belief. There remains a genuine difficulty [24] for reason, even enlightened by faith. This lies in the difficulty of clearly distinguishing *in everything* between the pure natural law and the application of absolute natural norms to supernatural realities or to the realities that are conditioned by the history of salvation. Reason is able to establish in *many* cases that we are dealing here with the absolute natural law. In others, it is unable to come to a decision. Here again, it would be wrong to hold that reason must presume in these cases *an error* in its natural moral decisions on the realities of experience. This would be mistaken whether they be considered as supernatural or conditioned by the history of salvation as absolute natural law. We have admitted that reason is exposed to the *danger* of such an erroneous judgment.

---

itself to our understanding is by no means caused only by a diminution of our rational functions but above all by the fact that this good cannot be found objectively 'in this *aion*,' that this *aion*, because of its inadequacy to fulfil the will of God, is unable to bring forth what is good' (*Theologische Ethik*, I, n. 2130). 'Here, nothing less than the world *post lapsum* becomes manifest, the world whose injustice *cannot* be made clearly apparent, because it does not have any definite zones of justice with which the injustice might be contrasted' (*ibid.*, n. 2072). 'It would thus be wrong to explain the insecurity of applications of the natural law exclusively by the subjective imperfection of our acts of knowledge, resulting from the intersecting spheres of deduction and experience. No, this insecurity must be seen as being based on the objective structure of the universe. It is precisely this structure that is penetrated by guilt and does not admit any " pure " cases of the kind which the Thomist conception of *ordo* and *natura* is bound to envisage' (*ibid.*, n. 2073).
[22] Cf. for example, E. Brunner, *Das Gebot und die Ordnungen*, 58 ff., 205 etc.
[23] Cf. *ibid.*, 205, 207 etc.
[24] As has been pointed out above, pp. 56 ff.

It is not bound to succumb to this danger. It is able to reach a correct and valid moral decision in a concrete situation from the standpoint of the norms of the natural law *without being able to determine in every case* the purely natural character of the given reality and consequently of the moral judgment. Reason merely knows that, from the viewpoint of the natural law, its judgment is truly possible and that its judgment is formed in this knowledge.

The conquest of this weakness

Two theological facts are consequently established: the ability of human reason to come to a knowledge of the natural law, and the inhibition of the individual, in the state of original sin, from actualizing this knowledge. It is therefore necessary to overcome these obstacles, as far as possible, in order to secure the development of all those human possibilities that are basically present. We shall omit here consideration of biological and physiological conditions, however necessary in certain cases. We presuppose man as being biologically and physiologically mature and as being more or less normally developed and sane. But beyond this, it is possible and necessary, in the natural sphere, to establish favourable conditions for a concrete and easily accessible knowledge of the natural law. This is just as true in natural morals as it is for any other knowledge. It is even more certainly true in the present connection. The perceptions of natural morality must *in the first instance* be exercised repeatedly by one's own efforts and with the help of appropriate and, where necessary, 'technical' guidance. *Scientific* moral knowledge presupposes moreover a training in sound philosophy. A man growing up in surroundings in which moral beliefs are distorted or someone trained in a false philosophy, will only acquire with difficulty a sufficient knowledge of the natural law. One who thinks little in moral categories must not assume that he will be able to find the proper solution to difficult moral questions with any real facility. Because of the subjective sources of error it is important that the individual be genuinely concerned about good-will and the elimination of disordered inclinations. Only a truly moral man is able to acquire a true and unclouded knowledge of the natural law. Whoever believes in the fruitfulness of dialogue with those who do not share his convictions on the basis of the natural law, must always keep this truth in mind.

In the case of man in the state of original sin, God comes to his assistance in a *supernatural* way in order that he may fulfil the conditions necessary to live well. God acts in the heart of man through his grace and how often unnoticed! He is able to come to the aid of our reason in its struggle for knowledge, so that reason may find what ought to be done. He gives man's reason the light of supernatural grace all the more generously when it is a question of our discovering the way to our supernatural end. The end, too, is proclaimed in different (and at least general) statements, by Revelation and the authorities of the Church. God has the power to strengthen man's will with his grace so that he may embrace what he knows to be true and good. He fortifies us similarly against all contrary inclinations so that they ultimately lose their influence. The helping grace of the Redeemer assists the individual on his way to his supernatural end by enlightening and guiding him. *But even though grace enlightens and strengthens man*, it is the natural *reason* that remains the light of knowledge of the natural law. It is impossible to say when, where and whether God's grace is at work in genuine moral knowledge. It has been said that for St Paul the Holy Ghost acts in every Christian. He gives the Christian the insight and the strength to do that which is good, including the 'works of the law.' It follows that, in preference to any other law compelling man to accomplish the good, the Holy Ghost is our law. He in fact communicates himself to our spirit, that is, to our conscience and will (cf. *Rom.* 8: 16). Many theologians think that God draws man in a supernatural way to himself continually. They believe that he does this even by means of the natural knowledge which man has of God and of the natural law. Some go even further and admit that in the natural knowledge of God and of the natural law—as in the whole spiritual life—man *knows* himself to stand face to face with the 'Holy Trinity, the source of eternal salvation,' although not in a reflex manner. In this view the Holy

Trinity is continually drawing him nearer, guiding and enlightening him. So is the natural law, as it derives from the God of our salvation who is not known only through the influx of divine grace. This knowledge is already supernatural life *with and in* the presence of God acting in a supernatural way.[25] *It would be wrong to say that through grace the 'weakened' reason of man has once more habitually been set into 'working order,' as if reason has been redeemed from a state of utter inability to come to any certain knowledge.*

The First Vatican Council in the second chapter of the third session referred to the help which is brought to man in his sinful state through Revelation. The Council does not imply that the reason of man after the Fall is set into 'working order' [26] by means of this help. Reason is not immediately and in itself strengthened in any way through Revelation. Yet the Council (and *Humani generis* as the Council's interpretation) holds the *Revelation of the natural law to be of such importance that it calls it morally necessary in the state after original sin.* It is not necessary in the sense that man's reason may, in general, be able to come to knowledge. It *is* necessary in the sense that all men, intellectually mature and 'open,' may be able to come to a knowledge of the natural law easily, securely and free of error. God himself must therefore provide a practical knowledge of the natural order for man. Otherwise many will never come *de facto* to a sufficiently comprehensive knowledge of the natural law, and certain spheres of this law will in fact never be known at all. Today we see the truth of this theological assertion certified in a world almost void of faith.

The Revelation of the natural law, like any other Revelation, must be found in Holy Scripture and in oral tradition, as its two sources. Holy Scripture contains many statements on the natural law, yet it contains no complete system of natural ethics. Precisely how many genuine, revealed elements of the natural law are contained in tradition can hardly be established exactly. Even the doctrinal statements of the Church as such do not necessarily

---

[25] Cf. K. Rahner, s.j., 'Natur und Gnade,' in J. Feiner, J. Trütsch and F. Böckle (ed.), *Fragen zur Theologie heute*, Einsiedeln 1957, 223.
[26] Thus Thielicke, (*Theologische Ethik*, I, n. 1461 ff., 1891) seems to misinterpret the teaching of Vatican I (*Denz.* 1786).

contain formal elements of Revelation. It is the duty of the ecclesiastical magisterium to protect those natural, but *not formally
revealed*, truths that are intrinsically connected with Revelation.
It can be said that at least the fundamental principles (and beyond
these, also, certain more concrete details of the natural law) have
been revealed to us. Moreover, every concrete proposition of the
natural law contains general statements that are either formally
revealed or proposed by the Church. It has been indicated already
that it is not only a formal divine Revelation that is important for the
knowledge of the natural law in the state after the fall of man.
So, too, is its doctrinal *proposition to us* by the Church. It is from
her *as the authentic interpreter* that we must receive the divine
Revelation and the natural law, in so far as it has not been formally
revealed. The complex of the natural law is set into relationship
with the totality of revealed truths. These are *the* way to the supernatural end of which we are told through Revelation, especially
in our present state. The Church, as our guide on this way, has the
obligation of proclaiming and protecting the entire moral law,
including the natural law, even in as far as it has not been formally
revealed and even down to its concrete applications. It is by virtue
of her office that she must guide us to this end; it is for this that
the assistance of the Holy Spirit was promised to the Church.
The Holy Ghost helps her to fulfil faithfully her task of giving
testimony and teaching 'all that I have commanded you.' [27]

Everything that we accept in *faith* concerning the natural law
as Revelation and as infallible doctrine of the Church, is meant
to be a help in coming to an easy and unerring knowledge. True,
not every doctrinal proposition of the Church regarding moral
questions is infallible. Many statements contained either in the
ordinary teaching or even in papal encyclicals and allocutions and
in the decrees of the Roman Congregations do not have that character of infallibility that gives ultimate security. Consequently they
cannot be the object to our irrevocable faith. They are, *all the same*,
the work of that teaching office to which the assistance of the

---

[27] *Matt.* 28: 20. On the question of the teaching authority of the Church in regard
to moral questions, cf. also the definition of Vatican I: *Denz.* 1831 and 1839.

Holy Ghost was promised, although that does not mean that the Holy Ghost will supplement or effectively make up every human deficiency when no ultimate issue is at stake. Where the silence of the Holy Ghost is not evident, the presumption is first of all in favour of the word of the Church and against a personal conviction standing in opposition to this word. Thus the Christian can see in word of the Church a real aid to the knowledge of the truth in matters bearing upon his moral behaviour, and he ought to accept it as such with joy.[28]

Abstracting from the question of the Church's infallibility, to what extent is divine Revelation and the doctrine of the Church of importance in facilitating our knowledge of the natural law? Because Revelation is extrinsic to reason, it is first of all evident that reason is not modified in itself or, as we have said above, that reason is not set once more into 'working order.' Nevertheless it is true that Revelation gives reason a most powerful assistance. It secures above all a knowledge of the natural norms that we would probably not have otherwise or which would have been at least doubtful for the individual because of the obstacles set up by the state of sin. This is especially so where the teaching of the Church is concerned with very detailed and difficult questions in the various domains of the moral and juridical orders. In numerous problems arising out of the fifth, sixth and seventh commandments, in the moral questions of marriage, economics and politics, the *Christian* comes *in fact* in this way to a knowledge of the true order. This is a facility lacking to non-Christians. The result is very often not merely simple consent to the teaching of a higher authority. A willing acceptance by intellectually able men initiates a personal human reflection upon these truths which often leads to a genuine intellectual *insight* into their inner content and causes. Once reason

---

[28] Cf. the Encyclical *Humani generis*, AAS, 42 (1950), 567 ff.; CIC can. 1324. Concerning this whole question, cf. also the text of the Encyclical *Casti connubii*: In 'order, therefore, that not an imagined or corrupt Law of God but its true and correct knowledge illuminate the mind of man and determine his act, filial and humble obedience towards the Church must be added to the submission to God and the sincere desire to serve him. For she, the Church, has been appointed by Christ, the Lord, himself, as the teacher of the truth, and likewise to govern and guide all men in their moral life, although many things are in themselves inaccessible to human reason (AAS, 22 (1930), 580).

is alerted, once the way to knowledge is pointed out through acceptance of the proposed doctrine, once personal obstacles are removed, this insight is considerably clarified from the viewpoint of the object. A large part of a genuine doctrine of political science, for example, would hardly be known at all if inner tendencies and inclinations pointed in a direction opposed to our actual social instincts. Yet as soon as such a doctrine is accepted from authority and is incorporated in the attitude of the believer, analysis of the doctrine causes few further difficulties. Take another example: how difficult it is even for the specialist versed in ethical thinking to understand correctly the moral structure of certain actions, in themselves immoral, but employed to kill unborn life in situations which bear so agonizingly upon the mother! This is difficult even for the trained moralist, not only because it is difficult to come into possession of the correct knowledge but because the feelings of mercy and compassion prevent the mind from maintaining its calm and necessary detachment. If someone has accepted in his heart the word of the Church on this question and on her knowledge of its significance, then *his own thinking* will lead him more readily and accurately to the fully objective truth.

The word of God and the word of the Church offer, moreover, an even greater security in those cases where personal and fully developed knowledge does exist. It is possible that certain difficulties and apparently contrary reasons (probably largely emotional) still remain, barring the way to full acceptance of one's personal thinking and knowledge. Such security delivers us from fear of error even if it were only the commonest of all human fears: 'you might be wrong, and still, so much depends on your consideration'! Both the word of Revelation and the teaching authority of the Church constituting a higher authority than personal consideration, if accepted in the true attitude of the Christian, will silence these contradictions and exclude the general suspicion of considerations purely personal. Thus a life based upon the truth of the natural law will become easier, happier and more intense.

Most of the problems of our lives, private or public, must be solved in the light of the natural law. Will the Catholic moralist, economist, politician not be able to go to work with a strong consciousness of his mission, if he relies on an authority far higher than any merely human authority? May it not be that some may then seek influential positions of power and trust because of such a consciousness of their mission and not for egoistical reasons? Such men know well that the world can recover and live only by means of that truth which is indeed an image of reality. They know the truth without being hindered by the hesitations of the Hamlet-thinking which is at the heart of man. They know, because all truth comes from God, that in this way they can bring his kingdom into this world in all its domains, even into the profane. More! The faithful Christian, conscious of his mission and relying on the word of God and his Church, can truly engage in dialogue only when he is based upon the natural law. He will be able to do this with all the greater confidence and audacity when he realizes that he has no need of an isolated reliance on his personal thinking about this law. Even with all this, he will not expect too much.

It is naturally very difficult or perhaps even impossible to say to what extent we actually draw our *knowledge* of the natural law from Revelation. How can we determine the extent that our own *cognition* of this law was in fact (either directly or by way of communication through others) brought about or even made possible by acceptance of the word of God or the Church? The teaching of the Church on the possibility of natural moral knowledge does not seem directly opposed to the theory that probably all our knowledge of the natural law goes back to a divine Revelation of the Old or the New Testaments or to primitive Revelation. This is a possible case if we eliminate at least the general principles or by postulating a final concrete and singular knowledge from Revelation. The knowledge of fundamental principles, according to which it is morally permissible and even obligatory to believe in Christian Revelation and which themselves stem from the natural law, can exist principally under a certain subjective influence of Revelation which is, however, only known as exercised and not yet acknowledged. Such knowledge must, by its very nature, in some way precede the acceptance of Revelation even though this priority is not one of time. But such possibilities can not easily be proved actual.

It should be plain that the significance of Revelation for the moral knowledge of man in his present condition must not be underestimated.[29] On the other hand two facts remain: human reason can attain a natural knowledge of the natural law independently of Revelation and our knowledge of the fundamental moral principles can justly be described as easy of acquisition. After acknowledging the role of Revelation and the teaching of the Church in natural law, it still remains imperative that we recognize a personal knowledge, based upon intrinsic objective reasons, as possible and as constituting an easier way actually operative in daily life. We have the right to speak of this as *natural* knowledge and thus the right to use the term '*natural* law' as an absolutely correct description. We are *not* obliged in the interest of accuracy or convenience to confine our description to a 'law of creation,' known only by means of Revelation.

We may validly believe in the existence of a properly philosophical and not merely a theological ethic. In this event philosophy is to be understood as a knowledge based upon intrinsic objective reasons, no matter whether this knowledge could have been acquired without previous recognition or acknowledgment of Revelation. Here the question can intelligibly be raised: is there a philosophy that is intrinsically independent of Revelation? Indeed, it must not be overlooked that nearly all true insight by man into human affairs is gained only after other men have laid their results and proofs before the public gaze. There is only one difference between this fact and the influence of Revelation, namely, that Revelation comes from God while this 'traditio' is simply that of men whose thinking is part of nature. If ethics based upon Revelation are called a middle term between philosophy and theology and if this expression is meant to indicate that on the way to acquiring these ethics, in themselves purely philosophical, Revelation is to be found, then we may not reasonably object to this formulation.

[29] Cf. J. C. Wu, 'Christianity, the natural Law and the common Law,' *American Benedictine Review*, 6 (1955), 137–47.

CHAPTER EIGHT

SOTERIOLOGICAL SIGNIFICANCE
OF THE NATURAL LAW

We have seen that 'nature' is an abstraction from the full reality which is man. The *natural law* corresponding to this nature participates logically in the abstraction. There exists, without the immutability of the absolute natural law being infringed, an accidental mutability of the natural law together with that accidental mutability of nature of which St Thomas speaks. We have studied ways of realizing this law in the particular states of the history of salvation and in the history of each individual. Because man is never nature merely, the natural law can be only *part* of the whole moral order of human being. Similarly, an absolute statement of the natural intelligibility of this law is also an abstraction. Our ability to carry this knowledge into action changes with the salvation-situation and the personal character of each individual.

When we turn now to the soteriological significance of the natural law we must remember that every consideration of it, too, is bound to be abstract to a certain extent. The actual and concrete significance of the law can only be evaluated in the light of the totality of the concrete human reality. In our present salvific order, the natural law is concerned not only with the conformity of human activity to the essence of the *Creator of nature* without which man cannot reach his true final destiny. The historical man, as he exists in God's eternal counsel, is more than nature. According to God's design, nature is not the decisive element in the creation of man. This is the reason why the natural law implies much more than its own essence, in the 'abstract' and 'in itself,' allows us to assume.

We shall, however, first raise a preliminary question that has arisen already in another context. Is *love*, emphatically presented again and again as the Christian virtue par excellence, also part of the natural law which we have been studying in the Christian salvific order? Alternatively, is love to be taken as the completion and the elevation of the natural law, so that it must be excluded from any question of the soteriological significance of the natural law?

Some preliminary questions on law and love

The preliminary question appears largely as an opposition of law to love. The question is whether or no the law is to be attributed to the natural human order and love to the Christian moral order. It would exceed the proper limits of our study were we to examine more closely the *Protestant* conception of the relationship between law and love. Besides, opinions are widely diverse. The Protestant conception can shortly be formulated without going into precise differentiations, in the following way: love is the truly Christian element. Love is the principle effectively operative in the sphere of Christian life, in the religious sphere and in all personal relations. In the domains of command, of duties, of this world, of community life, of the State, it is not love that reigns but the law, including the natural law as far as it is recognized. This does not mean that all Protestant theologians set these two spheres side by side without admitting any relationship between them. Most emphatically this is not to suggest that they all refuse to allow for a significant love for the 'world.' On the contrary, some of them emphasize the fact that love must not only watch over of the ordinances of the law, but they also stand for the firm establishment of these lawful decrees and satisfactory social rights. They believe that although a law is something profane in itself, God will give judgment according to the efforts of love in the sphere of law and order.[1]

---

[1] A solution relatively close to ours is offered by H. M. Müller, 'Das christliche Liebes-gebot und die *lex naturae*,' *Zeitschrift für Theologie und Kirche*, NF, 9 (1928), 161–83. Müller distinguishes between the *commandment* of love and the *act* of love, the first belonging to the natural law and the second being a Christian element.

No doubt in Catholic minds also the idea is prevalent that love is the new and Christian element and this is thought of in opposition to the natural law. In what sense, then, can love be called the Christian element, as opposed to the natural law, *especially to rights in the strict sense*? Is the co-ordination of *law and love* adequately accomplished if one says that the natural order, that is the order of the natural law, is insufficient for our lives precisely because it is a *juridical* order which has to be completed by the order of Redemption or love? If Suarez allots the borderline case of the plank of Carneades to the *ordo caritatis* and not to the *ordo justitiae*, does he thus appeal from the natural order, which seems unable to solve the problem, to the supernatural redemptive order? Do both the *ordo caritatis* and the *ordo justitiae* exist in the same domain, for example, in the domain of the supernatural redemptive order? Is it possible, without being inexact, to distinguish between 'the natural order based upon justice and the order of Redemption springing from love' and to say that God 'called the order of the world into being by creation and based it on law and justice that he might repair it through Redemption and complete it through love'? Have authority and love the same relationship to one another as 'nature and grace'? Does the order of creation demand and seek 'the idea of authority' while 'God the Redeemer reveals his essence in the word of love.' Is it so that 'whoever wants to deduce guiding principles of the natural law from the order of creation' must be prepared to devise, in the use of this material, rigid and legal formulae'? Having done this, is he only to call afterwards for a complementary reactionary force 'which Christianity provides' in its gospel of love but *the new love* in the sense of the agape of the New Testament'? Are natural law and Christian love (as a biblical-supernatural idea) opposing one another in the sense that the natural law is demanded of non-Christians, 'but of Christians . . . even more, . . . this immense yet wonderful tension . . . that he be filled with love in his justice'? If we think not only of rights but of the entire natural moral law, must the non-Christian conscience model itself with the help of prudence, yet must the Christian conscience do so with the help of prudence

12

and love, so that for the Christian, and only for him, 'the moral
conscience becomes a personal religious conscience' as well? Is it
of interest only to the Christian, instructed by Revelation? Is it
vital for every man who is moulded by the natural law in his heart,
'whether his conduct truly corresponds to the God-created,
obligatory order of reality *and* whether he acts in the way that God's
love expects of him in every moment?' These questions are to be
understood in this way: is the difference between the non-Christian
and the Christian merely a matter of fact or is love, in opposition
to prudence, outside the sphere of the natural law? Is it true that
the Christian element begins only with love, with the Sermon on
the Mount, whereas the Ten Commandments, in opposition to
the law of the Christians, bind all man? If we select from the Sermon on the Mount the commandment to love our enemies, does
this love also already belong to 'natural ethics and morals?' Does
it belong to the natural law or is it only something about which
Christians should be concerned 'because they *can* as Christians be
no longer adversaries and enemies; they are united " in the Lord "
and members of one eucharistic communion of love in which the
same Lord and Redeemer has become a reality in all his members?'
This results in the fact that all natural enmity is not only avoided
and suppressed but is penetrated by the rays of this fraternity that
has become real.

This comprehensive compilation of questions drawn from
statements by modern Catholic writers is intended to draw special
attention to the formulations we chose in our desire to emphasize
the distinctively Christian element in moral doctrine. It has as its
purpose the further inevitable question whether such formulations
are objectively justified.

Even Pope Pius XI, in his Encyclical *Quadragesimo anno* [2] set
love as the spirit of the Gospel in opposition to the work of justice.
Here justice is *not reserved* to the natural law alone nor is love
reserved to Christianity. Justice as well as love are seen as the
teaching of the *Gospel* and as a power enabling us to lead a Christian
life. They are not confronted with one another in the same way

[2] AAS, 23 (1931), 222 ff.

as the principles of nature and Christianity in the allocutions of Pius XII [3] or as the order of creation (nature) and Redemption in the publications of Pius XI himself.[4]

In order to understand this question correctly, a clear distinction must be made between the soteriological and the metaphysical viewpoints. The importance of this distinction results from the fact that in the Catholic theology of the natural law we use the term 'nature' in the metaphysical and not in the soteriological sense at all. In other words, because there is a danger of ambiguity if law and love are compared with one another in the same way as nature and the supernatural or the natural and the redemptive order, it is possible that the soteriological novelty of love is being opposed to the natural order understood in the metaphysical sense. The novelty of love as a Christian demand must indeed be seen fundamentally, not from the standpoint of metaphysics, but from the viewpoint of the history of salvation. It is not as if Christians only (and they only through Revelation) are bound to charity and to the love of God. The novelty consists rather in the fact that because of Revelation and the gift of grace, love is not only demanded but is also *expected* of the Christian, whereas the Jew and the heathen do not in fact render the love that is demanded by the natural law. Astonishingly enough that which was unknown in history but was always demanded from the standpoint of the natural law, is now at last to be fulfilled in the Christian and becomes visible as a mark of distinction: 'A new commandment I give to you.' [5] 'By this all men will know that you are my disciples, if you have love for one another.' This new love is opposed to nature not in a metaphysical sense but soteriologically. It is opposed to the nature of fallen man and, according to St Paul, so far as it is carnal and not spiritual it is subject to God's scorn. Justice and love have not the same relationship to one another as nature and the supernatural or the natural and the redemptive orders, if nature is taken in the metaphysical sense. Even the love for one's enemy does not stand outside the

---

[3] Allocution, 23 December 1949, AAS, 42 (1950), 127; allocution, 7 September 1953, AAS, 45 (1953), 607.
[4] *Casti connubii*, AAS, 22 (1930), 541.
[5] *John* 13: 35 and 34.

sphere of the natural law, not even if seen in the light of Christ's teaching (*Luke* 6: 32 ff; *Matt.* 5: 43-48). This does not mean that the love demanded and rendered possible by Christ is absolutely identical with the love demanded by the natural law.[6] It is in fact love as a new God-given power that gives *itself* by following the example of God's love revealed in Christ. It sees the love of God and of fellow-men in a new light. Both justice and love are equally part of the natural and redemptive order; they are both of the natural law and of the Christian moral law. The qualitative uniqueness of the order of Redemption applies equally to both. The latter is already given with the fact that the intrinsic meaning of justice is love and that therefore justice intrinsically participates in love in order to be an expression of love. Within the natural order of creation justice participates in the *amor* of the natural order and, within the supernatural order of Redemption, it has part in the *caritas* of the Revelation. It is said that the order of justice is completed by the order of love as social justice is by social love; so natural justice is thus not brought into connection with *supernatural* love but Christian justice with Christian love. If the measure of justice is determined according to the natural law, it should be remembered that the order of supernatural love is likewise determinded by supernatural principles, both of them according to the self-evident consideration that the supernatural and grace do not contradict nature but make it part of themselves.

It has recently been strongly argued again that all that is good, all virtues, participate in the Christian *caritas*. All this has been said of what is good in the Christian sense and of all Christian virtues. It is significant that at the same time the idea has been canvassed repeatedly that in the natural order, too, good and virtuous acts are a participation and mediation of the natural *amor*, in analogy to *caritas*. If, in the present order, *caritas* is the form of all the virtues, this *amor* should be the form of all natural virtues. The qualitative difference between such an *amor* and *caritas* is

---

[6] Cf. Leo XIII, *Sapientiae christianae*, AAS, 22 (1889-90). 402: 'And the divine Legislator called this commandment a *new* commandment not because mutual love was not yet prescribed by law and by nature itself but because the manner of love was completely new and unheard of from time immemorial. The same love with which Jesus Christ, etc.'

already evident here in the fact that it is by virtue of *caritas* that the results of a morally good life do not constitute just any kind of a communion with God but *intimate communion with the Holy Trinity*, a reality that *amor* is unable to bring about. In spite of this difference no virtue would be realized, even in the natural order, without this *amor* conceived as love of God and our fellowmen. Virtue would have to be considered as being analogous to the *ordo amoris*, and the famous words of St Augustine could be modified accordingly: *Virtus est amor, quo id quod diligendum est diligitur.*[7]

The proof of this conception is established in the fact that *love*, not only the love of God but also the love of our fellows, can be proved to be a demand of the *natural law*, whereas the New Testament affirms *justice* to be a demand of the Christian moral order.

Love as a demand of the natural law evidently presupposes a knowledge of God and of the relationship between man and God. But is the natural law not part of the same order of being to which we attribute a natural knowledge of God? Christian political and social representatives should never forget this fact if erroneous statements are not to become practically unavoidable. In the case where a man defends a natural knowledge of the moral order and at the same time pretends a knowledge of God to be absolutely impossible except through Revelation, it could be concluded that certain essential principles of the moral order can be acquired only through their Revelation in Christ. Presupposing the existence of a personal God as Creator, there clearly exists a demand *of the natural* law to love God and our fellow man and this is demanded *as a theological virtue*, even though it is qualitatively different from *caritas*, as has been pointed out already. This difference is to be explained by the consideration that there is in fact a communion with God upon which love is based in the natural order. Certainly this communion is not based in the same way as our communion

---

[7] The text in St Augustine reads *caritas qua* for *amor quo*, see *Epist.* 167, 4, 15; PL, 33, 139. On our present problem cf. the excellent work of G. Gilleman, s.j., *The Primacy of Charity in Moral Theology*, quoted above. Love in the sense of right is likewise the subject of the work of G. Küchenhoff, *Naturrecht und Christentum*, Düsseldorf 1948.

with God in the supernatural order. This is a gift of grace. It is not only the unity of man's nature that urges and obliges us in a natural way to love. It is also man's natural likeness to God and his natural ordination to the final union with God in joy that moves him. Because of our proximity to God and because of God's love of man, our love of God is bound to turn to our fellow-man. Our love of God would not be genuine if it did not embrace also God's love for our fellows and if we did not participate in its realization.[8] The *natural* social principle of greatest natural importance is therefore the commandment, 'Thou shalt love thy neighbour as thyself.' [9]

Justice, on the other hand appears in the New Testament simply. It does so without expressly mentioning the motive of love as a Christian demand. 'But you yourselves wrong and defraud . . . Do you not know that the unrighteous will not inherit the kingdom of God? . . . Neither thieves nor the greedy . . . nor robbers will inherit the kingdom of God,' [10] says the Apostle. It has already been pointed out that for St Paul all demands of the natural law are at the same time Christian demands. Christ himself refers the rich youth to the *legal* prescription also expressed in the decalogue.[11] He acknowledges the rights of the public authority and demands from the judge the administration of justice.[13]

Law and authority ('secondary' natural law), most of the precepts of the decalogue, and all moral knowledge of prudence are part of the natural law and are included in the Christian moral law.

---

[8] Cf. J. Messner, *Das Naturrecht, Handbuch der Gesellschaftsethik, Staatsethik und Wirtschaftsethik*, 3 ed., Innsbruck-Wien 1958, 396 ff.; J. Lotz, s.j., J. de Vries, s.j., *Die Welt des Menschen. Eine Vorschule zur Glaubenslehre*, 2 ed., Regensburg 1951, 382; E. Elter, s.j., *Compendium philosophiae moralis*, 3 ed., Rome 1950, 135; E. Bach, *Die Feindesliebe nach dem natürlichen und übernatürlichen Sittengesetz*, Kempten-München 1914, 13-16. In his writings earlier than the *Summa Theologica* St Thomas believed that the commandment of the love of our neighbour in the Old Testament did not aim at supernatural charity but at natural love. In regard to other moral precepts, he understood them only as applications of the love prescribed by the natural law. (Thus T. A. Deman, in the German edition of the *Summa Theol.*, XIV, Heidelberg 1955, 302).
[9] J. Messner, *op. cit.*, 396.   [10] I *Cor.* 6: 8; cf. I *Thess*' 4: 6.
[11] *Mark* 10: 19.   [12] *Luke* 20: 25, 22: 66 ff.
[13] *Luke* 18: 1-7. On Christ's attitude to justice cf. F. Tillmann. 'Die Verwirklichung der Nachfolge Christi. Die Pflichten gegen sich selbst und gegen den Nächsten,' *Handbuch der katholischen Sittenlehre*, IV/2, 4 ed., Dusseldorf 1950, 324 ff.

Love presents itself to these as their perfection, that is to say, in the natural domain it is a natural but truly religious *amor*; in the supernatural sphere it is *caritas*. Love, including the love of one's enemies, belongs therefore to the natural as well as the supernatural order of Redemption. It is so that every other virtue may be formed and perfected in its own sphere.

The significance of the natural law for the Christian order of salvation

Having clarified the preliminary question of the 'position' of love, we proceed now to determine the full meaning of the natural law in the actual order of salvation. Man in his historical existence is *called* upon by God to share in the full companionship of the Holy Trinity, in the vision of God. This destiny surpasses the intrinsic possibility of what we have called his nature. But man as he exists is not nature only. Nature is a certain abstraction, the *substratum* of a greater reality—the supernatural. The law of nature cannot therefore in itself be a guide to this actual destiny, the eternal vision of God. Nature does not itself deny a vocation to such a destiny; so that natural law does not resist being chosen by God as the way to this destiny. In fact, man has been created *as such* according to God's plan precisely in view of this supernatural vocation. If it is *man*, characterized by his 'nature,' who has been called by God then the natural law becomes the necessary means to the vision of God; this is precisely because it is *man* who has been called to this destiny. Further, man's vocation to the beatific vision represents at the same time a different kind of vocation, namely, that of fidelity to the natural law and the realization of all that human *being* which is not yet given with nature. Because he is *man*,—with a self-knowledge of his nature, accepting it and consequently realizing the moral law of this nature as a radical openness to God's call—he shall enter into communion with the Holy Trinity. Only *the life of a man*, in which the reality of God radiates as in its image is vividly reflected or at least not contradicted, only a life following the directives of the natural law, can be called upon to participate in the inner reality of God, disclosing itself in free supernatural love. The significance of the natural law, testifying to the appearance in man's life of the light of this supernatural destiny, is immediately superior to what his actions mean in themselves, taken in abstraction. This superiority is of course not merely external and juridical. God, who ordains his creation to the beatific vision positively 'fulfils' the natural law accordingly. This 'fulfilment' consists in the fact that man must accept and strive for his supernatural *destiny* and must therefore likewise attend to the co-natural beginnings of eternal life by living a life of grace and supernatural love (*caritas*) in this world. All this is 'fulfilment,' not only as an addition from outside but as intrinsically affecting the natural law. Every demand of the natural law is consequently an intrinsic participation and 'mediation' in regard to every obliga- tion. The realization of this 'pleromic' obligation will express itself in faithfulness to the natural law. Such is, objectively, the full significance of the natural law according to God's plan; its so- called 'proper' meaning is only an abstraction.

The call to share in God's fellowship by participating in the life of the Holy Trinity has been addressed to man since his creation. It will continue as long as this world exists. The absolute natural law is, as we have seen, only an abstraction. It never had an intrinsic 'natural' meaning. Man has always possessed more than this 'nature.' The natural law in this sense is always more superabund- antly 'fulfilled' than its constituitive notes would themselves indicate. *The meaning and the 'fulfilment,' which are given with the creation in Christ and our destiny to the beatific vision of God, change with the various states of the history of salvation.*

Consider, first, man in paradise, that is, man not only *called* by God to that blessed companionship for life, but as already *participating* through grace in God's life. He has already received that Love which is God and he himself embraces his God in this Love. He is the man who enjoys, at the same time, the fulfilment of his supernatural vocation in his freedom from death and con- cupiscence. The nature law depicts man in this state as God's son in the fullness of his vocation. In doing so it expresses its special significance. Of course, to repeat this, advisedly, once again: in itself this law is merely an abstraction and its special, restricted meaning exists only in an incohate way, open to being 'fulfilled' and in fact being 'fulfilled' in the sense explained.

All this changes with *original sin*. It is not changed as if the destiny of man to a supernatural end instituted by God has been lost. Again, it is not as if there were now no man living in the grace of the sons of God. Rather this divine filiation is something that is not given to man at his birth, something to which man must open himself in the course of his intellectual development. After the Fall, man has need of positive justification in order to create a distance between himself and hereditary and personal sin. The natural law is the way which allows him to disclose himself. Here its meaning is to guide man so that he may put no obstacle in the way of his just and justifying God. Yet, once more, this law has this significance not merely in itself. Justification in the sense of the remission of guilt as well as in the sense of granting participation in the intrinsic life of God by means of the grace of divine filiation, can indeed come only from God. From him, too, comes the special 'fulfilment' of the pure natural law. It consists in this: that God promises his salvific justification and this postulates confidence in his promise and a longing for its fulfilment. The call to justification signifies for man *at the same time* the demand for a moral life according to the natural law. This is so because it is *man* who shall be justified. Such is moral life, a life of hope and longing for the justifying God, so that the obligatory acceptance of the natural law during man's life becomes an expression and a 'mediation' of this hope and this longing. *It is never merely a behaviour in harmony with the natural law.* Consequently the natural law, as a guide to justification, has found not only its *exterior* but also its intrinsic 'fulfilment' in corresponding to the salvation-situation.

Our justification comes, moreover, through the Redeemer, promised in the proto-gospel. The coming *Christ* was the source of the justification of all the just that lived before the Christ. The hope and the longing, supported by love for him, represents in a way that corresponds to the knowledge of this promise, a special form of the hope and the longing for justification common to all men. This applies already to the time, which in some documents of the Church is called the time of the natural law,[14] that is, the time before God's positive Covenant with men. This is the period before the Old Covenant and, for those non-Israelite peoples that were not included in the Old Covenant, it was in fact, the entire period before the coming of Christ. Within these restrictions neither the law of the New Covenant nor that of the Old Covenant was valid. From the time of original sin down to the coming of Christ, the natural law had the task of offering to man in his need for Redemption, a quasi 'body' for his hope, so that this hope might have a means of expression. The same is true for the Old Covenant, with the one difference that the positive law of the Old Testament gave a new explication of the natural law and completed it by giving new, purely positive, precepts. These became, themselves and in a special way as purely positive law, a 'body' of hope. Yet this hope was not itself an expression of the special communion with the God of the Old Covenant. With the coming of Christ and the work of his Redemption this situation is changed but only in so far as its centrepoint—the fulfilment of the natural law—is no longer hope and longing for the coming of Christ. It is now a hopeful faith and trust in Christ manifested as the Son of God, as he is actively completing the work of his Redemption, through his death, the Church and the sacraments.

In the *justified*, the natural law indicates the way of life in accordance with justification, that is, the way of life as a son of God, however inadequately. This way is simi!ar to what we have said about the state of paradise, with the difference that it is now a real union with Christ as the Son of God and Redeemer. We have said that the natural law is only an inadequate image of the life of justification. It has not only been partly modified to a 'relative' natural law, as we have seen. It has also been completed by the positive divine law (for example, in reference to the sacramental life, the life of faith etc.). All this is part of the life in justification.

---

[14] Thus, as we have already indicated, at the Synod of Arles in 475 (?); cf. *Denz.* 160 a and b; see p. 178, n. 20. For the time of the Old Testament cf. J. Pinsk, 'Der christliche Sinn der zehn Gebote'; *Leb. Zeugnis*, February 1954, 3–39.

But if the life in justification is a life of *love*,[15] the natural law represents an obligatory way in which love expresses itself. Not only the *specific* acts of love of the justified are love but so, implicitly, are all his good actions and omissions. The natural law is (however inadequately) the subject in which love manifests itself and acts. It is the mosaic in whose colourful variety love tries to find its expression. The love of the justified walks only the paths of God whom it loves. The meaning of the natural law is love.

Nevertheless this love is not any human love of God (*amor*) but the love that God himself 'infuses'[16] into the heart of man, and through which man is now able to love God (*caritas*). It is the same love that burns in the Holy Trinity, in which the Father and the Son breathe the Holy Spirit. The love of the justified therefore participates in the internal love of the Holy Trinity. A life in accordance with the natural law signifies, then, not only a representation of the Glory of the Father resplendent in the *Logos*. It signifies a continuation of this love of the Father and the Son in the Holy Ghost. The natural law indicates to the justified the inadequate human way of true and gracious imitation of the intimate life of the Holy Trinity.

Christ himself lives in the justified through his Holy Spirit. The mystical union of Christ and the justified—itself an essential fact—is being *unfolded* in the life of the Christian. It would be very one-sided to think here only of those accomplishments in life which are not yet indicated by the natural law. On the contrary, the acceptance of this law is part of Christ's life in man, justified through his Holy Spirit. For Christ must always be seen as true man and the Holy Ghost must be seen as he who takes possession

---

[15] Of course, the life of grace is not only a life of love but likewise a life of *faith*, and the faith finds—like love—its expression in the fulfilment of the demands of the natural law by the justified Christian. But faith has entered love already as practiced faith (fides formata) and is—consequently—already presupposed when we speak of love and does not need explicit mention. The same must be said about hope, because love without hope (spes formata) seems to contradict man's nature itself as well as the nature of love (cf. to this T. Deman, O.P., 'Eudémonisme et charité en théologie morale,' *Ephemerides Theologiae Lovaniensis*, 29 (1953), 41–57; also G. Gilleman, S.J., *Le primat de la charité*, loc. cit., 114–39). Besides, in the unjustified man (if he does not altogether lose sight of his salvation) hope itself, instead of love, will break through and find its expression in the fulfilment of the demands of the natural law, and with it also faith.
[16] *Rom.* 5: 5.

of the *man* Jesus Christ. The natural law indicates inadequately how *a life in Christ and dominated by Christ* will appear and how the unfolding of Christ in every justified man will be brought about.

Because the union with Christ signifies neither man as absorbed in Christ nor Christ absorbed in man, that is to say because Christ and man face each other as persons, the unfolding of Christ in our own lives is at the same time true *personal imitation of Christ*.[17] The Christian is called to continue, not only the love of the *Logos* and of the Father immanent in the Holy Trinity by actively accepting the natural law, but also the incarnation of this love in the *historical* Christ. Where the natural law is not emphasized in the teaching on the imitation of Christ, the soteriologically important truth of the Incarnation of the Son of God will not be brought to light adequately.

The communion of life with Christ has, however, different forms, indicated and brought about by the different sacraments. All of them are causes of communion with Christ, though each in a different way. This is especially evident in the three sacraments that impress upon man a special character-baptism, confirmation and holy orders. The other sacraments have something similar (called *res et sacramentum* in theology) signifying a special, real, though mysterious, relationship to Christ. In marriage and the anointing of the sick, each of these special relationships to Christ, which exist even for the *sinner* who has received the sacrament, implies always a particular command that the recipient should lead a Christ-like life according to this relationship; especially in the sacrament of the anointing of the sick the meaning of this obligation is evident. These obligations give a new meaning to the natural law not only extrinsically but intrinsically. Man *called upon* by these obligations is bound to fulfil that law of his life which is given with his human nature, as demanded by his actual situation. This is the natural law. Here as well, the natural law is the (inadequate) way in which the sacramental but real and mystical union with Christ is to be unfolded and its obligations carried out. If therefore

---

[17] The relation between the unfolding of being and 'imitation' is well explained in N. Krautwig, O.F.M., 'Entfaltung der Herrlichkeit Christi,' WW, 7 (1940), 73–99.

the soteriological significance of the natural law exceeds by far its 'natural' meaning for the individual, it must not be overlooked that through the Revelation in Christ this natural law has received a new significance extending also to the *community*. The redeemed individual is redeemed only as a member of the redeemed community, which is the mystical body of Christ. This community has its own life, its own rhythm of life and its own order of life. This order is not abstractly supernatural. On the contrary! To it belongs the natural law, though 'fulfilled' and completed, because we are dealing with a community of men. Moreover, in so far as Christ is not only head of the body—the Church— but head and king of all mankind, the natural law is (again, inadequately) the law of the whole universe under Christ. Thus the orders of the natural law [18] among men, for example, marriage, the family and the State have received a new and deeper meaning. They certainly retain their natural meaning; but beyond this its purpose now is to serve the new life in view of Christ. Because this new meaning has become an essential part of these orders, many who do not even know Christ realize this meaning *objectively*—as *good* husbands and wives, parents and rulers. They are in the service of Redemption. Christ continues his Redemption in his Church and it is consequently true that, since the Redemption of the universe, these orders are ordained to the Church. Of course, this ordination can be realized to its full extent only by the man who knows this ordination and accepts it. We are not dealing here with a mere difference of interpretation; part of the natural order is being enriched in its content in a definite way. The orientation of marriage, of the family and the State to the Church issues in an attitude which is not merely the result of the natural significance of these orders alone.[19]

---

[18] Cf. on this subject C. Weier, o.s.b., *Die natürlichen Ordnungen, loc. cit.*, E. Berbuir, o.f.m., *Natura humana*, München 1950, 167 ff. Berbuir's formulation 'that natural law conceived without being bound to Christ is deprived of its meaning and does not lead to salvation' (49) errs by excess in its first part, because the natural law has its meaning even when considered in its abstraction as the law of the *natura absoluta et metaphysica*, a meaning which cannot be lost in any situation of the history of salvation.

[19] See above p. 121 ff.; cf. especially C. Weier, *op. cit.*

The salutary power of the natural law

The salutary power of the natural law was not the same at all times. Directly and in itself in as far as it abstracts from the natural-supernatural reality, the natural law possesses absolutely no power regarding supernatural salvation. If we ask for the meaning of the natural law in the fictional and merely hypothetical state of the *natura pura*, the only answer to be expected is that it has no salutary power of its own. It has only a 'possibility' of guiding man to a merely 'possible' natural end. In creation, *as it exists*, it possesses a genuine power to guide man to the supernatural destiny of the vision of God. 'If you would enter life, keep the commandments' (*Matt.* 19: 17). Nevertheless as we have said when considering the true and full meaning of the natural law, it must always be added that it has this power not merely in itself. In itself the natural law can never be a power by which we are able to gain the super-natural. Even after the Fall, the natural law has maintained its salutary power. This is expressly stated by the Synod of Arles for the so-called period of the natural law in the time before the Old Covenant. Moreover, the *lex naturae* 'which God has written into all hearts' received the distinguished title of 'primary grace' (*prima gratia*). Yet the Synod does not forget to add that even at that time the natural law was in possession of this power only in view of the Redemption in Christ and of the mediation of his holy blood.[20] The natural law did not lose its power even after the Redemption had become a historical fact. It is, however, not always easy to see the particular way in which the natural law has been formed and fulfilled in the various phases of salvation.

It is possible to determine the salutary power of the natural law more precisely. Evidently the first justification is always and without exception the free work of God; otherwise grace would

---

[20] *Denz.* 160 a: '. . . damno vobiscum sensum illum . . . , qui dicit ab Adam usque ad Christum nullos ex gentibus per primam Dei gratiam, id est per legem naturae, in adventum Christi fuisse salvatos . . .' *Denz.* 160 b: 'Assero etiam per rationem et ordinem saeculorum alios lege gratiae, alios lege Moysi, alios lege naturae, quam Deus in omnium cordibus scripsit, in spe adventus Christi fuisse salvatos; tamen ab initio mundi, ab originali nexu nisi intercessione sacri sanguinis non absolutos.'

not be grace.[21] The accomplishment of the natural law can be disposed to grace only if it is done in a purely negative manner. The accomplishment of the demands of the natural law by the justified has, on the other hand, truly the power to *merit* an increase of God-given sanctity, achieve the beatific union with God in heaven and an increase of our eternal participation in God's glory.[22]

Nevertheless, it must be noticed how insufficient and inadequate this power is. A life in accordance with the natural law can in no way bring about our salvation (not even as a disposition to our justification) if it is not supported at least by the working of God's actual grace. The genuine power to *merit* supernatural life [23] presupposes that man be justified and that the dignity and the holiness of his participation in God's nature become resplendent in him. It presupposes, moreover, that man thus sanctified in himself but in community with God (who works in him through his grace), fulfils the law of nature. From this it follows—not only as a demand but as actual result—that in his faithfulness to the natural law the justified brings forth much more than this fidelity. In so doing he loves his God with a divine love. The natural law becomes the mouthpiece of his love.

There remains one more question. Is the justified man, living in accordance with the natural law, really *conscious* of this fact alone or is he also aware of the supernatural fullness that accompanies it? The conception of Christian love contained in all good deeds reveals that there is good reason to accept the second opinion. We have no *reflex* conscience of the supernatural reality in the realization of naturally good works; yet an immediate, direct and unreflex consciousness is indeed possible and is, in fact, more than probable. We believe that the Christian never wishes to live *only* by the law of nature. He goes, in fact, beyond this. He wishes to

[21] Council of Trent, sess. 6, ch. 8 (*Denz.* 801): '. . . nihil eorum, quae iustificationem praecedunt, sive fides, sive opera, ipsam iustificationis gratiam promeretur; si enim gratia est, iam non est ex operibus; alioquin (ut idem Apostolus inquit) 'gratia iam non est gratia' (*Rom.* 11: 6).'
[22] *Ibid.*, can. 32 (*Denz.* 842): 'Si quis dixerit . . . ipsum iustificatum bonis operibus, quae ab eo per Dei gratiam et Jesu Christi meritum (cuius vivum membrum est) fiunt, non vere mereri augmentum gratiae, vitam aeternam et ipsius vitae aeternae (si tamen in gratia decesserit) consecutionem, atque etiam gloriae augmentum: A.S.'
[23] as *meritum de condigno.*

realize his own being. All this, including the natural law, possesses the power of salvation.

Although God's grace is therefore co-operating in every salutary fulfilment of the law of nature, this does not imply that man is not able to live such a life by means of a purely natural power. On the other hand, it is certain that he would fail to do so because of his actual weakness. Moreover all men, even the justified, do fail in small matters—and this is defined doctrine [24]—if a special grace does not come to their aid. This was the case with the Blessed Virgin. There is in fact a very probable opinion according to which fallen man cannot sufficiently ordain his life to God without grace guided by the natural order. This is so even though the disposition is a demand of the natural law itself. He is unable to express his love for God *super omnia* by acting according to the natural law alone, although this again is exactly what the natural law demands of him. What we are saying in effect is this, the weakness connected with the natural law and the difficulty of attaining to our salvation resulting from this weakness, are permanent signs of the obstacle in the way of salvation: the fact of original sin. We know of this connection only through Revelation and faith. On the other hand, the permanent and faithful fulfilment of the natural law allows the faithful to see God's benevolent grace at work in the accomplishment of what is naturally good *in view of our salvation*. Here again it must be seen that, even without faith, we experience the effects of this divine activity many times and in particular cases in our faithfulness to the natural law, yet without being able to recognise their true nature.[25] All this shows the way in which natural law, in connection with the various supernatural realities, receives a salutary significance and is thus raised above itself.

[24] Council of Trent, sess. 6, ch. 23 (*Denz.* 833).
[25] Cf. also K. Rahner, s.j., 'Persönliche und sakramentale Frömmigkeit,' *Geist und Leben*, 25 (1952), 421: 'For this reason the actual moral fulfilment of the law of nature is already an intervention of the gracious will of God in Christ, especially if this fulfilment is moulded by supernatural, divinizing grace and, through this new form, is being modified in its *per se* natural structure.' (*Schriften zur Theologie*, II Köln 1955, 115–41).

CHAPTER NINE

THE PROBLEM OF A
CHRISTIAN SOCIOLOGY[1]

The professor in any newly established chair of Christian sociology is compelled to ask himself the question: what is the object of this discipline? Nikolaus Monsel thought it fitting to devote his inaugural address at Munich in 1956 to this theme.[2] Others, like Gustav Ermecke, Werner Schöllgen, and Adolf Geck dealt with the same subject from their own points of view. Is there a 'Christian' sociology as opposed to a science presented to us outside theology? Is it a theological discipline, and, if so, in what sense? How does Christian sociology differ from other sociologies, and—a very important question—to what extent is it in agreement with them?

The problem is of much wider import than merely justifying the existence of professorial chairs. The sociology and especially the social ethics which we, theologians and faithful engaged in public life, consider as 'Christian,' must in the last analysis provide guidance for the organization of social life. A 'naturalistic' concept of society which would consider it more or less as a self-contained entity closed to outside influences and properly speaking 'profane,' constitutes an obstacle to the 'Christian' organization of the world.

[1] This chapter was published under the title 'Christliche Gesellschaftslehre?' in *Stimmen der Zeit*, 164 (1959), 161–70.
[2] Nikolaus Monzel, *Was ist christliche Gesellschaftslehre?* (*Münchener Universitätsreden*, NF, 14), München 1956; Gustav Ermecke, 'Die Sozialtheologie als christliche Gesellschaftslehre und ihre Beziehung zu verwandten Wissenschaften,' *Theologie und Glaube*, 1958, 1–18; Werner Schöllgen, *Christliche Soziologie als theologische Disziplin, Aktuelle Moralprobleme*, Düsseldorf 1955, 27–43 (E. tr. *Actual Moral Problems*, New York 1964); A. Geck, 'Die Bedeutung der Sozialwissenschaft für die Moraltheologie,' *Trier. Theologische Zeitschrift*, 1958, 162–80.

However, at the other extreme, a 'supernatural' vision of society that pays too little attention to the given natural facts because they are a '*profanum*,' is in grave danger of going a long way towards halting this Christian organization. Nature and the supernatural, taken in isolation, are only abstractions from the various elements that belong to one reality. The Christian reality is a combination of both. By 'Christian reality' we mean human society as it actually exists which can be known in its totality only by using Christian faith and knowledge. In this essay we shall above all try, though only under certain aspects, not to lose sight of the whole of Christian sociology. In as far as it is Christian, it cannot accept one-sided concepts, be they concepts of a 'natural' doctrine or of a supernatural pseudo-theological doctrine.

The Christian concept of human society

If Christian sociology had no more to teach about society than any other sociology, it would not matter in this respect whether those organizing society be Christians or non-Christians. Society might therefore be looked upon as the work and the property of its Creator and be organized with that in mind. It might as easily be considered and organized as a mere '*profanum*' of its very nature. The point above all others that *Christian* sociology must emphasize is that human society is more than a *profanum* or a purely natural structure. As yet there are all two few signs that Christians recognize the sacred vocation of their social existence. There is little evidence that they look for more than a structure of natural law or that they see in such a structure any extension of the Incarnation of the Eternal Word into the created sphere of humanity.

A sociology which recognizes God as the principle or the model and end of society is not therefore a fully Christian sociology. Such a God is indeed the God of Christian doctrine, but he could just as well be the God of philosophy. It seems to us that the Christian doctrine of human society must go beyond this and take into account the relationship between the social being and the intimate life of the triune God. Although one may find a more perfect *imago Trinitatis* in the activity of the created spirit, it is nonetheless undeniable that the uncreated unity of identity in the triune God has its reflection (*vestigium*) in the created unity of the social order. But it must be the first task of Christian sociology to make *the faithful* conscious of the fact that human society has been created in the eternal and incarnate Word, in Christ, and through him and for him. What Holy Scripture says so clearly about the existence of all things in Christ (*Col.* 1: 15) should be used to achieve a better understanding of what human society really is. There is no such thing as a human society that lives out a purely human and profane history. On the contrary, its role is to continue without interruption the Incarnation of the Son of God in history so that all may be taken up into his reality. A 'pure' sociology is a mere abstraction. It neglects an essential part of that reality constituted by society which, in fact, has been created by God.

Even that sociology which considers the source of society to be God is not acceptable. It is necessary in accordance with the teaching of the Apostle, that we acknowledge both the bond linking society to God and the solidarity which bases the structure of society intimately in God, to be primarily a union with Christ and a solidarity in Christ. Thus, in the Holy Spirit of Christ we have a union with the Father and a solidarity in him. All of this is in harmony with the hierarchy described by St Paul: 'you are Christ's, and Christ is God's' (1 *Cor.* 3, 22 ff.). All this is ignored by a merely 'natural sociology' of human society. It is not sufficient to underline God's sovereignty over humanity and its social institutions. One must never lose sight of the sovereignty of the God-man, Jesus Christ. This awareness will lead to the conviction that human society (and our own lives) must be organized, not haphazardly but in accordance with the mind of Christ. One must be careful, then, not to confuse our personal views with the mind of Christ. Rather must we fix our attention on the mind of Christ, especially in its active manifestation in the world. Consequently, we must be concerned with the interior grace obtained through prayer and from the duly constituted Church in which he 'continues to live.' Only in this way is justice done to the fuller reality of human society as belonging to Christ: only in this way too is society as Christ's possession made subject to him in the development of the life of man (cf. *Phil.* 3, 21). Only thus is human authority understood, exercised, and accepted by both rulers and subject as coming to human society from the kingship of Christ. It is in society as the authority that not only pursues the profane good but puts itself at the disposal of the reign of Christ and of the Father.

It is the destiny of human society *with all its elements* to be the mystical body of Christ. Social life, which in its many details is subordinated to pursuing very diverse intermediate ends, should be the life of the body of the Lord. This is the singular means by which it is able to achieve fully the true destiny assigned to it in the plan of the Creator. An organization of society which cannot be directed to the building up of the body of Christ is fundamentally wrong and is based upon error. The nature of marriage is such that, when incorporated into the body of Christ by baptism, it becomes the life of that body. When marriage has not been taken into this mystical community it is but an image of the life within the body of the Lord although at the same time, it is the basis on which the life of this body can be built. The same can be said of the other forms of human society. From this it follows that every valid organization of human society serves in a mediate way *and even in its profane status* to render the mystical body of the Lord possible, even when this is subjectively not intended. The mystical body of Christ is the visible Church capable and responsible for leading human society, by means of its 'own profane existence,' to its true destiny as the body of Christ. Human society and thus sociology, in so far as it is human, is open to a Christian fulfilment. Social life is only understood in its full sense if the true meaning of the service it is supposed to render for the working of Christ and of his Church in human life has been recognized.

Consequently, Christian sociology must make it clear that the continuation of the Incarnation of Christ in human society is brought about in the conflict portrayed in the history of salvation. Only in this way can the full import of the struggle for the accomplishment of the different structures of society be really understood.

It requires, therefore, a knowledge of the submission of the good angels to Christ and the rejection by Christ of the bad angels, a knowledge of the perpetual opposition and battle between Christ and anti-christ and, finally, a knowledge of Christ's victory that has already been gained but must be gained over and over again. This is essential because the life of society must be seen as the continuation and realization of all this. It is important not to overlook the forces that are at work in this conflict and in the life of human society: angels and demons; Christ still active with his Holy Spirit; grace working in man and the Church of the Lord working through its sacraments, magisterium and government as the life-giving principle of all human society.

It is therefore necessary that Christian sociology be on its guard in these matters against all one-sided supernaturalism. If it does not overlook that element which (beyond or in the 'profanum' or the 'nature' of human society) constitutes the reality of that society, it can never underestimate nature to such an extent as to regard it as non-Christian. In fact neither the one element nor the other, taken in isolation, is Christian; only the two together have an actuality for us. Many statements about Christian sociology and notably about Christian social ethics (Christian social morals in general) would be much more accurate if attention were paid to these facts. If 'natural' sociology in all its aspects were to be eliminated from 'Christian' sociology, the most profound and most singular basis of such a sociology would be ignored. It would be just as much a simple abstraction from the total reality as would a purely 'natural' sociology or one based upon natural law alone, to which the epithet 'Christian' would be arbitrarily added.

A Christian sociology which does not deny its natural basis must never lose sight of the fact that 'natural' sociology, though linked to 'Christian' sociology, is in and for itself only a precision and an abstraction of the total reality known to Christian doctrine.

On the other hand, even in all that is accessible to our experience and natural knowledge, it is not 'pure nature' that lives. Even natural sociology has as its object a society in which opposing forces are at work in the great conflict of the history of salvation but these forces are not part of 'nature.' Man or the philosopher is not by himself capable of analysing the action of grace or sin by means of the mere reality which he experiences in human society. No doubt many true and intelligible things can be said about human society as such but a 'natural' sociology, more or less all-embracing, could be taught as such from any chair of sociology. It will in fact deal with many themes which presuppose the reality of grace and sin and these are realities that are part of the history of salvation. We shall come back to this point. Christian sociology must know and emphasize the different elements, even though it does not always—and rightly—distinguish them.

Christian sociology and natural law

Supporters of an uncompromisingly 'Christian' sociology see their science primarily in contradistinction to a sociology and above all to a social ethic exclusively based on 'natural law.' Christian sociology cannot restrict itself to being a doctrine of nature or the natural moral law. We recall in this connection the controversy between *Monzel* and *Johannes Messner*, for whom the content of natural law is that which can in itself be known to man without the help of Revelation. The point of the controversy was the fact that Christian Revelation adds new and essential notions to the content of Christian social ethics. This statement is not without foundation. For example, in the question of the relationship between Church and State, it cannot be denied that Revelation is our only teacher on this important point and there could be no other. This one example suffices to demonstrate that an essential part of the Christian teaching about the State is laid down by Revelation. Further examples can be had in the domain of religious worship or of marriage in the context of human society; the coming of Christ, the divine institution of the Church, the raising of Christian marriage to the dignity of a sacrament. All these brought into the very core of human society rulings and laws about religious cult and Christian marriage which, without Revelation, could not have been known. The importance of these notions for our society, even outside the limited circle of Christians—in civil legislation, for example—is apparent every day in the discussions of political philosophy of a pluralistic society. The same is true of the sacramental reality which we know only through Revelation. Do we not find ourselves here face to face with resources and duties—for example, in the establishment of marriage and family—which would otherwise be unknown to us? Are not holy days a specifically Christian question raised in order to allow the participation of all men in sacramental worship? To take another example that has already been mentioned: is not the claim which is properly made for the Church, that she is the vital principle of every human society, an essential element of the Christian doctrine of society? Yet it is a fact that cannot be discovered unless one goes beyond natural law. On the other hand, it is important to make clear that a link exists between such elements of Christian sociology as do not belong to the natural law, and the natural law itself. This in turn and in its entirety is part of Christian social ethics. Here a cardinal point presents itself, namely, that the truths which are new in their content (that is, which go beyond natural law) presuppose realities in human society (like the Church and the sacraments) which do not spring from man's nature but are derived from a supernatural disposition established by God. They cannot be known except by means of Revelation. Once these 'new' truths have been revealed in their essence and their full meaning as intended by God, we discover in human nature *in natural law* the consequences which are required by these divine dispositions for the establishment of objective moral ethics. In this sense one could be tempted to say that Christian Revelation does not offer any social teaching which goes beyond that of the natural law but that it is sufficient to apply the principles of natural law to the revealed truths. It remains true, all the same, that these consequences, which are henceforth part of Christian social ethics, would have been unknown without Revelation, and that they go beyond natural law in the sense defined above. They truly add something 'new' and exclusively 'Christian' to social ethics based upon natural law.

From this point of view other elements of Christian social ethics are understood as something 'new.' In contrast to the 'new' elements we have just been discussing they are new, not in material content, but rather as being formal changes of the principles of natural law, brought about by Christianity. By way of example, consider the father of a family who has the obligation, imposed by natural law, not to neglect his other duties such as the care of other people and other communities. Quite frequently the father of a Christian family has to face the problem of how much of his free time, which he would otherwise devote to his family, he should give to an important apostolate in society. Or take the question whether he should give up his career, with all the possible consequences for his family, to become involved in public life so. that through him this may be shaped according to the spirit of Christ and in harmony with the nature of society existing *in Christo*.

Another example: that upright frame of mind rooted in the natural law and springing from a genuine and all-pervading altruism in human society, which brings with it a code of conduct motivated in part by a sense of duty and by the interior promptings of generosity, surely this altruism quickened by a new life-force, will be lifted on to a different plane by a knowledge of Christ and of that common bond with Christ which links my inmost being to that of my fellow men. Moreover, is it not true that social moral behaviour attains its due perfection only when it is supported by supernatural love? Yet this kind of obligation is alien to natural law, since the latter knows nothing of supernatural love. In connection with these different formulations of the natural law, we could say once more that such formulations are intended by this law because of the realities resulting from a divine supernatural disposition which itself is known to us only by Revelation. They cannot then be looked on as part of the law; they must be considered rather as something 'new' for natural law.

There is consequently a difference between Christian social ethics and ethics based only on natural law. Though this difference must be stressed, it is also necessary to be cautious in deciding what exactly the difference is. We are quite justified in considering, for example, Christian love of one's neighbour as a reality which does not come within the scope of natural law. Unless one is to be driven to denying the existence in the natural moral code of a law of true brotherly love, one must with great care clarify what exactly it is in this love of one's neighbour (for example, its supernatural character, the example of Christ) that surpasses natural morality. The same can be said of love of one's enemies. Otherwise, would it not be morally permissible for a non-Christian to treat his 'enemy' with indifference or even hate? The same is likewise true for the devoted care given to a mortally sick man. Has such loving compassion an objective moral worth only within Christianity? Besides, there are two problems which should not be confused: There is the first problem of the general and objective validity of the precept of love for one's neighbour even outside Christianity where, as we saw, it has its own form. It is thus a precept of the natural law. The second problem is the extent to which man, after original sin, can know or live the precept of love of neighbour without Revelation and the grace of Christ. It is therefore necessary to distinguish carefully between the substance of a moral precept (say the Christian form under which it presents itself) and the fact that historically it has been known and accepted by fallen man even in the Old Testament.

Whenever there was question in Christian social ethics of the difference between that which was known only by Revelation and that which is based on natural law, natural law has been envisaged from the point of view of its natural intelligibility and not from the standpoint of its object. This comment is important. Man and even human society, understood and judged according to natural law and therefore according to natural knowledge, does not exist as 'pure nature.' Consequently not only nature but also a large part of what results from the supernatural Christian mode of man's being, is included in this natural knowledge and becomes the object of moral evaluation. We are dealing here with valid concepts of natural law, yet with concepts which have as their object not merely the 'natural' man but the supernaturally transformed man *as such*,

as well as the society of which he is part. The directives evolved
for actually existing human society according to which the civil
authority has, under certain conditions, the right to inflict capital
punishment or to resist an aggressor by declaring war, presupposes
a man deprived by original sin of the state in which grace had
originally placed him. Social ethics, it seems to us, must underline
this aspect of certain principles of natural law if it is to be in
harmony with its Christian character. True, it is no longer disputed
that these rights of authority in the State are based upon man's
nature as such, but, because they are said to be applicable to
concrete society, they presuppose a certain situation of the history
of salvation which is not required by human nature as such.

In Christian social ethics we emphasise that which is 'new.' We
equally insist on the fact that social ethics based upon natural law
fully and entirely constitute a part of Christian social ethics;
without them our social ethics would not be truly Christian. It is,
on the other hand, necessary to make quite clear that the natural
law itself has, within Christian social ethics, a profound Christian
significance unknown to itself.

If Christ is the personal and universal norm of Christian morality
and thus also of Christian social ethics then the social ethics based
upon the natural law represent at least part of *the development of
what Christ signifies* and a norm for human society. If, according
to a long Christian tradition (cf. St Thomas Aquinas, *Summa Theol.*
1a 11ae, 106–8), the fundamental element of the new law of Christ
is constituted not by the 'commandments' but by the grace which
has been given to us and by the Holy Ghost urging us from within,
then it follows that the social ethics based upon natural law express
what the dynamism of grace and the urgings of the Holy Ghost
demand with an exigence which cannot be ignored. Given that
grace and the Holy Ghost awake in us primarily the fundamental
power of charity, the social ethics based on natural law explain,
within their scope, the relationship existing between Christian
charity and the social life of men. Given also that the different
steps in the sacramental life of a Christian each represent a different
form of union with Christ and of participation in his grace, that

element of Christian sociology which is rooted in natural law explains in particular the concrete form under which the ethos proper to each of the sacraments must be expressed.

Finally, in accordance with what has been said above about the significance and the purpose of the concrete human society, we must admit that even the social ethics based on natural law have, in the Christian order of salvation, a more profound role to play. This role is directed, through the organization of society, to work towards the redemption of mankind. It is instrumental in achieving the final realization of Christ's kingdom, placing itself at the service of the mystical body of the Lord; in a word, it is its function to work towards the ultimate perfection of man in Christ.

Revelation and social ethics based on natural law

The intimate union in Christian social ethics of the elements belonging to natural law and those not belonging to it allows us, from the very beginning, to suppose that Revelation is concerned also with the elements of the natural law. Revelation is not charged with the sole task of making known unfathomable mysteries but, in a wider sense, it has also the task of making available to fallen man the knowledge of all that he requires in order to achieve his salvation. Admittedly, Catholic theology teaches—and rightly teaches—that human reason is in itself capable of coming to the knowledge of natural law. The Protestant social ethic frequently opposes this statement of the case. However, are Protestant social moralists not inclined to forget that the Catholic teaching is fully aware of the limitations of the individual man as a consequence of original sin? The Church makes a more clear-cut distinction than many natural law specialists would do between the faculty which is proper to human intelligence and the exercise of that faculty by the individual. The Church speaks in this connection (at least in as far as there is no question of the most general fundamental norms) of a moral necessity for the revelation of the natural law. She does this at least to obviate the necessity of a vast majority

being left with a totally insufficient knowledge of it through ignorance, inaccuracy, error and uncertainty. The basis of this necessity
for Revelation is not found in man as man. Its basis is not, namely,
a social creature composed of body and soul but, in the inherited
fallen state of his whole being, his consequential loss of the preternatural resources and harmony found in paradise.

It is sometimes remarked that natural law comes up against the
difficulty that we are in no position to establish precisely what in
fact constitutes the basic, unchangeable nature of man, what is
traditionally called his essence. This remark is justified in certain
particular cases, but otherwise our knowledge of human nature
permits us without such precisions to make a correct judgment
in a concrete social situation. This is true whether there be question
of an essential element of human essence in such a situation or no.
Even those realities resulting from man's supernatural state of
which we do have experience may be judged by us from a moral
and juridical point of view, as we have pointed out.

Given that Revelation and its true guardian and interpreter, the
Church, work in collaboration to guarantee that the knowledge
of natural law will be taught, it must be explicitly stated that it is
not merely our own knowledge which enables us to grasp the natural
law of social ethics in all its details. Our knowledge of the natural
law in such cases may derive from formal statements in Revelation
or from the Church. It may include, for example, statements
concerning society, the State, marriage or the family or this knowledge may include applications or conclusions of these principles
formulated by Revelation or by the Church. Nevertheless one must
maintain that these notions of natural law which are part of Christian
sociology, can in themselves be known by man and therefore by
natural reason and are *in fact* known to a large extent, though not
to a great number of people and often only after the directives of
Revelation and the Church have pointed out the path to the truth.
The Christian, attentive to Revelation and to Christ, will thus
more easily than another, succeed in exercising his native faculty
of knowing the elements of natural law concerning social ethics.
There we will also find a fundamental explanation for the fact

that a discussion on the natural law with this 'other' does not necessarily result in changing the latter's conviction. Furthermore, it must not be forgotten that the inner working of supernatural grace accompanies the knowledge of social ethics based upon natural law, for the good reason that both man and society exist only within the order of grace.

The special characteristic proper to Christian sociology consists, therefore, in the fact that its object is society in its entirety, in all its dimensions. A 'profane' sociology or a sociology based purely on natural law does not attain the total reality of human society because it does not take Revelation into account. This is precisely the reason why a Christian sociology must pay particular attention to the elements borrowed from Revelation. It must expressly point out the link binding all sociology with Revelation. We have tried to demonstrate this by using various examples. Christian sociology must, on the other hand, take care not to see its own essence as consisting in the difference between itself and a purely natural sociology. This would unduly lead to the exclusion of all 'natural' elements or, at least, of the natural foundation of such elements, from Christian sociology,—a tendency we encounter far too often. Moreover, in this way, the fact is overlooked that Revelation, far from excluding nature, actually gives it a new foundation and postulates it. If, therefore, a sociology based on natural law is a truly Christian sociology, though seen in itself it is so only as an abstraction, such a sociology has nevertheless its place in sociology as a theological discipline, embraced by Revelation and the supernatural. It presents itself, in a way different from the isolation of abstraction. Neither 'nature' nor the Christian 'difference' constitutes the Christian man. The God-Man, Christ, is the ideal and the norm of man and of human society.